MW01196371

ALSO BY AUGUSTINE SEDGEWICK

*Coffeeland: One Man's Dark Empire and
the Making of Our Favorite Drug*

Fatherhood

A History of
Love and Power

Augustine Sedgewick

SCRIBNER

New York Amsterdam/Antwerp London
Toronto Sydney/Melbourne New Delhi

Scribner

An Imprint of Simon & Schuster, LLC

1230 Avenue of the Americas

New York, NY 10020

For more than 100 years, Simon & Schuster has championed authors and the stories they create. By respecting the copyright of an author's intellectual property, you enable Simon & Schuster and the author to continue publishing exceptional books for years to come. We thank you for supporting the author's copyright by purchasing an authorized edition of this book.

No amount of this book may be reproduced or stored in any format, nor may it be uploaded to any website, database, language-learning model, or other repository, retrieval, or artificial intelligence system without express permission. All rights reserved. Inquiries may be directed to Simon & Schuster, 1230 Avenue of the Americas, New York, NY 10020 or permissions@simonandschuster.com.

Copyright © 2025 by Augustine Sedgewick

All rights reserved, including the right to reproduce this book or portions thereof in any form whatsoever. For information, address Scribner Subsidiary Rights Department, 1230 Avenue of the Americas, New York, NY 10020.

First Scribner hardcover edition May 2025

SCRIBNER and design are trademarks of Simon & Schuster, LLC

Simon & Schuster strongly believes in freedom of expression and stands against censorship in all its forms. For more information, visit BooksBelong.com.

For information about special discounts for bulk purchases, please contact Simon & Schuster Special Sales at 1-866-506-1949 or business@simonandschuster.com.

The Simon & Schuster Speakers Bureau can bring authors to your live event. For more information, or to book an event, contact the Simon & Schuster Speakers Bureau at 1-866-248-3049 or visit our website at www.simonspeakers.com.

Interior design by Kyle Kabel

Manufactured in the United States of America

1   3   5   7   9   10   8   6   4   2

Library of Congress Cataloging-in-Publication Data has been applied for.

ISBN 978-1-6680-4629-6
ISBN 978-1-6680-4631-9 (ebook)

For my parents, and for my son

I am no god. Why would you think such things?
I am your father, that same man you mourn.
It is because of me these brutal men
are hurting you so badly.

—Homer, *The Odyssey*,
translated by Emily Wilson[1]

Contents

Fatherhood

MEN BEFORE FATHERHOOD

In the late 1950s, painter Norman Rockwell and at least two of his three sons were in treatment with renowned psychologist Erik Erikson at the Austen Riggs psychiatric hospital in Stockbridge, Massachusetts, and they had plenty to talk about. Rockwell was then one of the most famous artists in the world. His covers for the *Saturday Evening Post*, the most popular magazine in the United States at the time, had made his name synonymous with a sentimental ideal of home and community. Erikson meanwhile was well on his way to becoming "an intellectual hero," as the *New York Times* described him in 1975, who reasonably hoped to win a Nobel Prize.[1] Soon he would write celebrated biographies of Martin Luther and Gandhi, formulate enduring theories of childhood and human development, and coin the terms "life cycle" and "identity crisis," among others. But as a father, neither Rockwell nor Erikson was quite who he appeared to be in the public eye.

Erikson had grown up in turn-of-the century Frankfurt as Erik Homburger, the strikingly blond son of two dark-haired European

Jews, Karla Abrahamsen and Theodor Homburger. Theodor was a pediatrician who had originally been Erik's doctor, not his father. When Karla and Theodor married in 1905, they assumed that Erik, then three, was still too young to know precisely who was whom. He learned the truth at age eight, and though he begged his mother to reveal the identity of his "biological father," she never did. After high school, Erik drifted around Europe, in and out of art classes, before landing in Vienna. There, in 1927, he was hired to teach at an experimental school founded by Tiffany heiress Dorothy Burlingham and her partner, Anna Freud, who encouraged Erik to train in child psychoanalysis under her father, Sigmund.

In 1933, having begun a practice and a family of his own, Erik, with his wife, Joan, and their sons, fled rising anti-Semitism in Vienna for Copenhagen and then Boston. Erik taught at Harvard and Yale before heading west to study Oglala Sioux parenting on the Pine Ridge Indian Reservation in South Dakota and later take a job at Berkeley. Working among the Sioux, Erik was especially struck by the fluid concepts of self and group that united their community across generations, and he began to question Freud's emphasis on Oedipal conflict. On September 26, 1939, Erik became a U.S. citizen—Freud had died just three days before—and turned his naturalization into a name-giving ceremony for himself: Erik Erik's son. He named himself his own father, though he often said that his eldest son had come up with the name, which the rest of the family also, of course, adopted.

In 1942, Erikson published an article arguing that Adolf Hitler had tapped into a strain of adolescent rage latent in German culture. Erikson proposed countering Nazism by promoting stable paternal authority, and his idea informed the Allied approach to psychological warfare and made him an increasingly public figure.

Two years later, Joan Erikson, under heavy sedation, delivered their fourth child, a boy named Neil who was severely disabled with Down syndrome. While Joan was still unconscious, the doctors told Erikson that his newborn son would live two years at most and should be institutionalized immediately rather than integrated into the family.

Normally Joan took charge of family decisions. Without her, Erikson called his close friend Margaret Mead, famous for her study of the comparatively conflict-free patterns of family life in Samoa. Mead agreed with the doctors. Erik told his children that the baby had died, hoping to protect them. Joan was haunted by the decision made on her behalf but accepted it, recognizing that Neil's disability would have complicated her husband's image as the head of a thriving family.

Seeing patients in California after World War II, Erik Erikson began to feel an unexpected kinship with veterans suffering from post-traumatic stress. He started to think that he shared with them a common experience: the loss of one sense of self and the search for another, what he would later call an identity crisis. In 1950, Erikson resigned from the University of California after refusing to take a Cold War loyalty oath. He accepted a job at the Austen Riggs hospital in Stockbridge, Massachusetts, and moved his family across the country, leaving behind Neil, who lived to be twenty-one.[2]

Norman Rockwell and his family arrived in Stockbridge at the end of 1953, when Norman was in the middle of an identity crisis of his own. Rockwell thought of himself as a kind of twentieth-century Charles Dickens, his hero.[3] Like Dickens, Rockwell worked on newsprint. Between 1916 and 1963, he created more than three hundred *Saturday Evening Post* covers, included some that featured his sons as models. His paintings arrived in millions of homes by mail, postcards from a quainter neighborhood in a slightly better town, where Sunday mornings, sick days, diving boards, ice cream, haircuts, and bedtime were all just slightly more poignant. As an artist, Rockwell's trick was to saturate the mundane with color and meaning, finding enchantment in even the quietest corners of everyday experience, but he struggled to do the same in real life, with his real family, just like everyone else.

The Rockwells—Norman, his second wife, Mary, and their three college-age sons—had moved to Stockbridge to be closer to the doctors at Austen Riggs. Mary was already getting treatment at Riggs for alcoholism and depression, and she would live there for a time as an inpatient, as would their middle son, Tom, who dropped out of Princeton with overwhelming anxiety. Intrigued, Norman entered analysis, too, with Erikson, who had recently published his first book. Rockwell thought that a fellow artist might be especially sympathetic to his problems.

Though he occasionally used his sons as models, Rockwell's family life wasn't anything like the domestic scenes he painted. He and Erikson started meeting twice a week, and the agenda was often the same: Norman complaining that Mary was drunk and overcritical and dragging him down. Rockwell's first wife, Irene, had killed herself after divorcing him in 1930 for "mental cruelty"—she claimed that he hardly looked at her during their marriage, preferring the company of his male friends and models. Now Norman feared that he would never be free of Mary and she would never get better. To pay for her intensive treatment, he had started taking jobs that he felt were beneath him, painting cherubic faces to sell cornflakes. By the summer of 1954, family stress had pushed Rockwell to the brink of a breakdown.

Miserable at home, Norman was thrilled when his son Tom's prospective father-in-law, the owner of an advertising business, invited him on a late-summer trip to Europe. Norman very much wanted to go—alone. Yet Mary also thought a few weeks in Europe would be just the thing. Rockwell complained to Erikson, who intervened with Mary's doctor on Norman's behalf, to stop her from traveling.

"Norman Rockwell is now rather depressed," Erikson wrote to Mary's doctor, "to the point of suicidal ideas. . . . He desperately needs a vacation *without Mary*." The timing wasn't ideal, Erikson conceded, anticipating the objections of Mary's doctor. By the start of the trip, the three Rockwell boys would be back at school, and Mary would be left alone. "Yet this period will be a trying one for Norman, too," explained Erikson, "and I am now definitely worried about him."[4]

For all his tender attention to life's sweet and vulnerable moments, Norman Rockwell didn't really paint families, at least not families in the "Norman Rockwell" sense. At most, nine of his three-hundred-plus *Saturday Evening Post* covers depict father, mother, and children together. It would have been one more, but Rockwell altered the picture he was working on during that tense summer of European-itinerary hostilities: *Breaking Home Ties*.

The painting took the title of a famous one from 1890, showing a son bidding goodbye to his family and their hardscrabble farm, presumably on his way to the city or points west, where the money would be better. In Rockwell's update, a father and son sit on the running board of a dusty truck, waiting for a train. The son, upright and alert in a bright suit and tie, peers expectantly out of the frame to the viewer's left, toward college, a suitcase and a companionable dog at his feet, saying goodbye. The father—"probably the most sad-looking man to appear" in Rockwell's work, according to Deborah Solomon—slumps in the opposite direction, shoulders hunched inside a faded denim work shirt, cigarette dangling from his closed mouth, eyes down, hat in hands, impatient but going nowhere.[5] The diverging futures of father and son pull the painting into tension that will never be resolved. Originally Rockwell had included a third figure, too, a woman, a wife and mother. But that summer, as he was trying to leave Mary and Stockbridge behind, he painted her out, and filled the space with a large red flag, meaning stop the train, so we can get on.[6]

In the end, neither Norman nor Mary went to Europe. Both stayed home and suffered their own ailments under the care of their own doctors. *Breaking Home Ties* was published on the cover of the *Saturday Evening Post* at the end of September, which was to have been the month of the trip. The father in the painting isn't glum because he's losing his son to a world he doesn't understand or appreciate or belong to. Instead, he's jealous. He wants to break home ties, too, and go away with his son—or, more specifically, with his son's father-in-law-to-be.

Erik Erikson believed that people tried to resolve their identity crises in the simplest possible way. Norman Rockwell once told his son Tom that he'd kill himself if not for them, his boys—and that he was mad at Erikson for taking his gun away and refusing to give it back. The father responsible for some of the most iconic modern images of domestic life was looking for a way out of his own. For help, he turned to the father whose secret family crises would lead him to become a world-famous authority on identity. "You know," Erik Erikson wrote to Norman Rockwell, "I think your family has logged more hours of psychiatric care than any other family in America."[7]

*   *   *

The history of fatherhood is a succession of identity crises spanning thousands of years. Across the centuries, in times of historic transformation, upheaval, and revolution, our foundational stories about men, love, and power have collapsed, leaving us searching for new stories to take their place and quiet the forces that shook the old ones.

I use the word "story" in a specific sense. By any measure, fatherhood is one of the most meaningful concepts in human culture, which anthropologist Clifford Geertz defined as the stories we tell ourselves to understand ourselves.[8] Fatherhood is a story of the kind Geertz had in mind: a story of who we are and where we come from, who we're related to and different from, what we're capable of and limited by, what we have and what we lack—a story about inheritance and legacy in all its forms. And everyone has at least one fatherhood story of their own.

Yet through the middle of this common human experience of fathers runs a curious divide. Our private, individual stories about fathers tend to be full of complication and conflict, sometimes even more than we realize. In contrast, our public, shared stories tend to be fantasies, melodramas, and parodies populated by heroes, villains, clowns, and ghosts. This "Rockwell paradox" has a cost: distorted, misleading, unattainable ideas of what it means to be a man, a father, a family.

Norman Rockwell and Erik Erikson hid their private conflicts behind public images of fatherhood and family that they could never live up to. Today Rockwell's work in particular is often seen as simplistic, unrealistic, and unrepresentative, even as it continues to shape the sentimental architecture of domestic life. Yet from another angle, a Norman Rockwell father is also something else, something more like the father in *Breaking Home Ties,* like Rockwell himself, and like Erikson too: a conflicted figure whose real nature has seldom been fully visible. And in that way, he is a fitting image of the history of fatherhood after all. We need better shared stories about fatherhood—about what it means and why it matters—even when better means worse. Not because fatherhood must be salvaged or redeemed or restored one more time, but because without a deeper and more humane understanding of the role of men in the world we will continue to struggle to see and know ourselves, one another, and the richest parts of our lives. The goal of this book is to find just that.

The trouble, intriguingly, is that though fatherhood is often used as a metaphor for origins and history, it has none of its own.

Most every living thing has parents, but only a small minority of animals exhibit any degree of paternal care. Almost none approach the amount of male investment in children that characterizes human societies, and some of our closest primate relatives appear to be especially unlike us in this regard.

Precisely where and when this aspect of human uniqueness took shape will probably never be known. Men writing about men have dominated the field of history from its beginnings thousands of years ago all the way to the present. A 2016 study found that more than 75 percent of popular history books were written by men, while more than 70 percent of historical biographies were written about men.[9] Nevertheless, or more likely for that reason, the history of men as men—exploring the origins and transformation of the very ideas of men, and manhood, and masculinity—has hardly been written. Feminist theorists and historians pointed in that direction in the second half of the twentieth century, particularly after Simone de Beauvoir's 1949 book, *The Second Sex*, which traced the "man-made" inventions of womanhood and motherhood. Yet even as extraordinary books about motherhood have multiplied, fatherhood has been comparatively overlooked.[10] We remain a mystery to ourselves, without even realizing it.

Recently a team of scholars proposed that around 5 million years ago, the drying of the African savanna caused food scarcities that prompted male hominins to begin contributing to the care of children in exchange for the benefits that came with group membership, including access to mates.[11] As plausible as this story sounds, there is no concrete evidence to support it. The conclusion was based on computer simulations of game theory that presumed male hominins had acted rationally, and of course no team of scholars is needed to find abundant evidence of men acting irrationally.

For much of the history of our species, there was likely no idea of conception that could have supported what we now think of as "biological fatherhood"—the idea that a single act of sex could lead to a pregnancy that only became unmistakably evident months later. In fact, only in the 1980s, with the development of gene-based testing, did it become possible to establish paternity with absolute certainty.

Formal definitions are not much help in tracing fatherhood's historical lineage. Dictionaries say that fatherhood is "the state of being a father." Etymologies agree that "father" and its close cousins, common in languages across Eurasia, derive from a "nursery word," such as "fa," "pa," and "da." Theories of infant language hold that hard consonant sounds are generally easier to form than "ma," and tend to become attached to the first thing the infant recognizes outside of itself, which is not how babies are thought to see their mothers. Evolutionary biologists have suggested that parents care for children in part because children ask them to, activating by their murmurs and cries parts of the parent brain that may have first evolved in male fish.[12] But it was men who made this infantile sound into a metaphor for history itself, who made it mean founder, inventor, creator, God. The questions are why, how, and at what cost.

This book tells the story of the transformation of fatherhood, from its earliest traceable beginnings in the Bronze Age to what has been alternately hailed and decried as its end today. I focus on Western culture because, in that time, the West has been the world's dominant patriarchal tradition, and I focus more specifically on the chief beneficiaries of that tradition: men who, as a result of the histories of power and care they helped to shape, could now be described—though not simply or without ambivalence—as white dads.

The fathers in this book are well known, but less so as fathers. Their names are already familiar: Aristotle, Saint Augustine, Henry VIII, Thomas Jefferson, Ralph Waldo Emerson, Charles Darwin, Sigmund Freud, and Bob Dylan. To use a similarly fraught and fragile image, these men make up a kind of Mount Rushmore of two thousand years of Western culture. It would be hard to overstate the importance of their ideas of how the world works, how it should be governed, what it means to live a good life, and what it means to be a man. Yet these ideas, often presented as simply ideas, were in fact deeply connected to intimate experiences of and anxious questions about manhood and fatherhood. By tracing out these less familiar connections, I show how, in moments of historical crisis and transformation that unsettled the existing grounds of masculine power, authority, and identity, the men in this book developed new ideas and models of fatherhood that helped to sustain "the power of the fathers," as Adrienne Rich defined patriarchy, across generations.[13]

Fatherhood's successive crises of identity have been sparked in two ways: by larger upheavals in the wider world, and by focused challenges to the existing terms and models of masculine power and authority. The corruption of Athenian democracy. The fall of Rome and the rise of Christianity. The Protestant Reformation and the European encounter with "the new world." The overthrow of monarchy and the invention of the nation-state. The Industrial Revolution and the spread of capitalism. The discovery of natural selection. Decades of world war. The social revolutions of the 1960s. Across profound historical transformations, men have held on to disproportionate power and authority in part by developing new ideas of fatherhood.

Fatherhood has proven vulnerable to recurrent crises for at least two reasons.

First, fatherhood has historically been conceived as a form of "power over others," as Adrienne Rich put it, thereby inviting dissent, challenge, and outright revolt.[14] In the Western tradition, male power and authority has taken shape not only around shifting concepts of sex, gender, and class difference, as might be expected, but also and especially around race and slavery. As two forms of blood logic—paternity and race—were spliced together, racism and patriarchy fused into a single system of social power through which true fatherhood was cast as white, and white fathers claimed a trinity of privileges: race, gender, and class, all at once. These were the terms on which white fathers claimed and exercised power and authority over others, by which they defined and enforced their social standing. Yet this power has never gone unchallenged, and it has always been more tenuous than advertised.

The second reason that fatherhood has proven so vulnerable to crisis is that its claims to hierarchal power and authority are rooted in extraordinary, even impossible promises—and this is one place that love enters the picture. As biologist Sarah Baffler Hrdy points out, there is more variation within practices of human fatherhood than there is among the more than three hundred other primate species combined.[15] Yet these variations are anchored in an underlying set of expectations widely shared across societies and cultures: protecting and providing, now for status as much as for survival.

Fathers have often likened themselves to gods, begetting, bestowing, smiting, and saving at will. But for mortals, such expectations can only end in failure and frustration. Protection will fall short. Provision will run out. At some point someone is going to die, and there's nothing any man can do about it. A key theme across the history of fatherhood is that men have defined their own obligations and responsibilities in terms that cannot be sustained—perhaps in order to secure extraordinary privileges by elevating themselves above women, whose power to create and sustain life was vividly clear.[16]

The story of fatherhood is not just about when, where, and why men started to treat children as their own—how fathers embodied arguably the greatest human value, caring for those who could not survive without. But nor is it merely the story of patriarchy— arguably the oldest and most widespread form of social hierarchy.

Instead, it is the story of how these strands of history, care and dominance, love and power, became so entangled that they are often indistinguishable.

Most accounts of the origins of human fatherhood begin with the obvious: walking. Our last tree-dwelling ancestor came down to the ground roughly 5 million years ago. Over the next several million years, the human body changed to favor life on the earth, narrowing the pelvis, and stacking the ankles, knees, hips, spine, and head directly above the feet, which became arched, with fixed rather than opposable toes. These changes put an upper limit on fetal development: babies could only get so big if they and their mothers were to survive birth. At least since *Homo erectus*, who emerged roughly 2 million years ago, human infants have been born into a uniquely long period of helplessness—one only extended by the significantly larger brain sizes of *Homo sapiens*, who emerged roughly three hundred thousand years ago and became the sole surviving human species within the last fifty thousand years.

The disproportionate size of human brains and pelvises has posed two critical challenges to human survival and flourishing. First, extraordinary physical danger for mothers. Even today, giving birth remains statistically the most acutely deadly thing that any human adult will ever do. No species risks so much in labor.[17] Second, and relatedly, human infants, born comparatively young and small, require extraordinary amounts of care, often well beyond what their mothers are immediately capable of providing alone.

There is no obvious reason why this necessary care should have been provided by men—especially by just one "father." Particularly in

13

the absence of a nuanced understanding of reproduction, other men and women, especially older women past childbearing age, might have stepped in to provide "alloparental care," and in many cases they surely did.[18] This is sometimes called the grandmother hypothesis, which describes menopause as an evolutionary adaptation allowing older women to make crucial contributions to the care of children.[19]

One notable pressure point for nomadic early humans would have been "infant carrying." *Homo erectus* roamed long distances, hunted with tools, made and maintained fires. Yet their upright posture, added to the loss of body hair and gripping toes, made it more difficult for children to help out by hanging on as their parents moved about. Some scholars have proposed that infant carrying, which among humans would have been necessary for up to five years, may have helped to recruit men for paternal care, as has been observed in other species of primates especially.[20]

The fossil record can fill in some of the picture. It seems likely that the relatively shorter length of human forearms compared to those of other great apes, the elbow dividing the arm effectively in half, is an adaptation to the problem of infant carrying. This proportion is generally equal in male and female bodies, though women's elbows tend to fall nearer to the upper ridge of their hip bones, leverage at the point where it is most convenient to carry and feed a baby.

Another piece of evidence, the Laetoli footprints, dates from nearly 4 million years ago, perhaps 1 million years before the use of stone tools. Discovered in present-day Tanzania in 1976, the prints show a group of three early humans, walking upright, equipped with chimpanzee-sized brains, moving through fresh volcanic ash. Interpretations of the tracks have suggested that one of the three members of this party, the smallest of the group, was carrying a weight on the left side of the body.

The symbolic record, much shorter than the fossil record, seems to confirm the importance of prehistoric mothers. All known evidence of human meaning making is less than one hundred thousand years old, and interpretations of this evidence are necessarily speculative. Even so, among the most suggestive prehistoric artifacts are carvings known collectively as "Venus figurines." Found across Eurasia, these include perhaps the earliest likenesses of human form: relatively small statues, generally under six inches tall and rendered from stone, ivory, wood, and ceramics, whose round breasts and bellies seem to represent female reproductive power.

One or two of the figurines may be hundreds of thousands of years old—as old as *Homo sapiens* herself—but the oldest verified findings cluster in a later period, between fifty and ten thousand years ago. Many of the sculptures are headless, faceless, and lack defined feet, characteristics that have led some scholars to speculate that they were made by women looking down at their own bodies. Possibly their features signify pregnancy and fertility— possibly they signify worship. The Venus figurines are perhaps the most important material evidence in support of claims for prehistoric matriarchies—the contention that early societies worshiped female creator gods and venerated women, whose role in group survival was unmistakable.

Compared to such "maternal" artifacts, imagery that could be described as paternal is strikingly rare. The cave paintings at Lascaux, dating from around 17,000 BCE, include an ithyphallic figure, to use the technical term, combing a bird's head, a human body, and a large, unbirdlike erection. But this is something of an outlier. Other phallic images date from around twelve thousand years ago, and were found at Göbekli Tepe, one of the oldest known temple sites, in present-day Turkey. One historian has claimed that the "cult of the phallus" didn't take shape until around 8000 BCE, possibly marking a new understanding of paternity.[21] Then again, it's not obvious what a visual representation of fatherhood would look like, or what its absence might signify. Freud, for one, proposed that the apparent lack of understanding of paternity in prehistoric cultures may have been the result of self-interest rather than simple ignorance, allowing men to claim that children were put into women by ancestral spirits, thereby extending the line of the clan back into the imagined past, where it could become heroic.[22]

Then there is a shift. As soon as there is writing, there is father-hood. Many of the oldest known written texts, dating from roughly five to six thousand years ago, dedicate themselves to specifying in painstaking detail the privileges and obligations of fathers.

This is the aim of a text known as *The Instructions of Shuruppag*, cuneiform inscriptions on clay tablets made nearly five thousand years ago in Sumer. The instructions themselves are prefaced by an origin story that dates them to a much earlier time ("those far remote days . . . those far remote years" before a great flood swept almost everything away) and presents them as advice from a father to his son.[23] The father, the instructor, is Shuruppag. Identified as the son of Ubara-Tutu, Shuruppag has no clear historical counterpart. The known Shuruppag was a place rather than a person: a large city-state on the Euphrates, at the southern edge of present-day Iraq. Shuruppag's son, the instructed, is Ziusudra, meaning "the one who survives"—thanks, by implication, to the instructions of his father. Ziusudra shows up in *Gilgamesh* as the wise boatbuilding prince Utnapishtim, and as Noah in the Old Testament version of the same story.

The text belongs to a genre that scholars of the ancient world call "wisdom literature"—not law, exactly, but exerting a similar pressure. Father and son stand in for ruler and ruled, but anxiously. From the outset, Shuruppag knows he is swimming upstream. "My son," he begins, "let me give you instructions: you should pay attention! Ziusudra, let me speak a word to you: you should pay attention! Do not neglect my instructions! Do not transgress the words I speak! The instructions of an old man are precious: you should comply with them!"

His subjects are the eternal ones: where to live, who to marry, how to maintain a household, what to do about work, sex, drinking, friends, and family. But property comes first: "You should not locate a field on a road.... You should not make a well in your field: people will cause damage on it for you. You should not place your house next to a public square: there is always a crowd there." Personal conduct goes hand in hand with the management of resources. "My son, you should not commit robbery . . . you should not sit alone in a chamber with a married woman . . . you should not have sex with your slave girl . . . you should not curse strongly . . . you should not use violence."

Twice more Shuruppag pleads for his son's attention and obedience, before turning to his final set of instructions: how to manage a happy household. "The elder brother is indeed like a father; the elder sister is indeed like a mother. . . . The mother, like Utu, gives birth to the man; the father, like a god, makes him bright. The father is like a god: his words are reliable. The instructions of the father should be complied with," Shuruppag insists one more time. The books that make up the Old Testament, said to have been first recorded between one and two thousand years later, resolve all of Shuruppag's anxiety with a single phrase: "Noah did everything just as God commanded him."

Between *The Instructions of Shuruppag* and the Ten Commandments sit the oldest surviving bodies of law. The Code of Hammurabi is a set of 282 dictates—crimes paired with punishments, written in four thousand impossibly minute lines of Old Akkadian cuneiform—that were carved into a strikingly phallic seven-foot-tall pillar of black basalt in Sumer around 1750 BCE.

The intricacy of the text, laid out in a format already antiquated when it was carved, possibly to suggest continuity with the past, helps to create its meaning. Hammurabi was a Babylonian king, sixth in his line, who greatly expanded his realm through ambitious conquests along the Tigris and Euphrates. By the time of his reign, there was probably a basic Babylonian legal tradition already in place. What his code recorded were the parts of it that he wanted to emphasize, perhaps especially in the newly conquered areas.[24]

Hammurabi claimed to have transmitted his laws to his subjects directly from the Babylonian god of justice. The substance of the code, like its form, was made for travel. First, the text explains its intent and authority. Hammurabi describes himself as "a father to his people" who aims to "enlighten the land, to further the well-being of mankind," and especially to bring about "the well-being of the oppressed."[25] Here fatherhood means law, it means justice, it means welfare, it means care.

Second, the code is formulaic and standardized, making no allowance for local conditions or customs. It focuses not on compensation for victims but on prescribed punishments for offenders, apportioned on the Hammurabic principle—later a biblical one—of "an eye for an eye." The code's promises of justice and welfare

are backed up by the severest threats, up to and including public impaling. In this way, Hammurabi's code differs from Shuruppag's *Instructions*, to which no punishments or penalties were attached except those that were likely to follow in the course of events, and would be amply deserved by, for instance, whoever would be so foolish as to build a well near a public road. Otherwise the priorities of the two texts, both claiming the sanction of fatherly concern, are much the same: property, business, conduct, sex, and especially the household.

Fully a third of the Hammurabi's 282 dictates cover domestic relations. Together they outline fatherhood as a wide-reaching set of privileges: to divorce and take concubines, to adopt or beget children outside of marriage, to direct children's lives, even to make them stand for a father's own debts or crimes. In some cases, a father's word is literally law. If for example a man had illegitimate sons whom he addressed as "my sons," then for all intents and purposes they were. But if he did not call them his sons, then in effect they were not.

Yet a father's privileges were not unlimited. Divorce required financial support for the ex-wife, who maintained custody of her children. If a man wished to put his son out of his house, he had to make his case before a judge. If the judge decided the son could stay, he could. If the son was found guilty of some significant offense, the father was to give him one chance at redemption. Kinship was presumed to be meaningful. A builder's son could be sentenced to death if his father built a house that collapsed and killed the inhabitant's son. The loss of a son was a serious consequence for a serious infraction.

Historians have often suggested that these laws were not enforced to their letter, and perhaps were never meant to be—that their real purpose was to create a set of highly visible deterrents meant to stabilize the related realms of property and family. Within that framework of stability there was some flexibility, even a measure of protection for women and children. But to challenge a father's authority was to risk the greatest pain. If an adopted son disavowed his father, his tongue might be cut out. If a son were to strike his father, his hands could be cut off. If the wife of one man conspired with another man to have their spouses killed, presumably to get together themselves, then both would be publicly impaled—the most gruesome punishment contemplated.

The spectacular severity of these punishments can be read as a distorted echo of Shuruppag's plaintive requests to be heard. Hammurabi made no pleas. Instead, he made promises and threats. Should is implied. For this reason, scholars have said that the Code of Hammurabi, with its promises of well-being backed up by threats of grievous injury, stands as a monument to an epochal historical transformation: the invention of fatherhood itself, the earliest institutionalization of patriarchy, set in monumentally phallic stone.

For over a thousand years after Hammurabi's death, his code circulated as part of a scribal "curriculum"—a route or course—in Mesopotamia and beyond. Copied and distributed widely across an expanding network of empire and trade, the code became a foundation of legal traditions across the ancient world, including in Greece.

Where that route leads is clear enough. In the years after World War II, at the beginning of the "American Century," a relief portrait of Hammurabi was installed in the House Chamber of the United States Capitol. In 1977, the government of Iraq donated a replica of the original pillar to the United Nations—albeit one that had been rendered in pale concrete. But how exactly did fatherhood wind its way from Babylon? Where did the idea of fatherhood come from in the first place?

The conventional explanation goes something like this: The domestication of plants encouraged humans to settle in one place and draft animals into their service. In these settlements, men's secondary role in child-rearing freed them for the strictly timed seasonal labor that crops and herds required, as well as for travel, trade, and war, increasingly common occurrences—and sources of wealth and status—in the late Neolithic and Bronze Ages, roughly nine thousand to four thousand years ago. Men who gained control of resources beyond their immediate needs could secure their surpluses over time only to the extent that they could also control the reproductive capacities of women. Women were treated as another resource to be managed—gains from children's labor balanced against the costs of supporting them. The management of women was justified as they were cast as troublesome characters in origin myths and prejudicial codes of law. Writing, private property, states, religion, and the patriarchal family seem to have emerged almost simultaneously, complementary systems for keeping track of what belonged to whom: masculinity's anxious foundations.

In *The Second Sex*, Simone de Beauvoir described the biological capabilities of women's bodies being turned into constraints, women bound by their capacity to give birth. Her depiction of motherhood as a patriarchal invention, a form of control over women that helped men identify their children and define their privileges and responsibilities, was a key starting point for second-wave feminism and feminist histories alike. As Adrienne Rich put it in *Of Woman Born*, her 1976 book on motherhood that extended

Beauvoir's analysis, "the woman's body is the terrain on which patriarchy is erected."[26] The pioneering historian of patriarchy Gerda Lerner particularly emphasized the role of violence in this process. Lerner's 1986 book *The Creation of Patriarchy* proposed that slavery, "the first institutionalized form of hierarchical dominance in human history," arose in early states out of the wartime capture, imprisonment, and rape of women for the purposes of population growth.[27]

If motherhood was invented for subjugation, was fatherhood designed for ascendance? Was it a strategy for overthrowing a social system that had formerly been to some degree matriarchal, and had thereby disadvantaged men? Was it an attempt to claim some of the power women may have possessed by virtue of their obvious importance in the creation of new life?

These questions highlight the initial weakness of fatherhood as an idea and institution. Though fatherhood was clearly a priority of early states and law codes, it had to be explicitly announced as such, and enforced at the price of extraordinary pain. The obvious anxieties of early patriarchal regimes in turn underscore the importance of the process by which such prescriptive laws and extreme punishments became unnecessary—by which fatherhood and the forms of male power and authority attached to it were internalized as a kind of common sense—as well the occasions when that illusion broke down, or threatened to.

How, in other words, did fatherhood become natural? There is evidence that Simone de Beauvoir's argument that women had been subjugated through their identification with motherhood might apply to men and fatherhood, too, though in reverse. In some early states, the social power and status of men was directly linked with their reproductive capacity, their actual or potential identities as fathers. Certainly the implications of this identification were different for men than they were for women. If women were bound through motherhood, men, or certain men, were lifted by ideas of fatherhood that proclaimed their life-giving power.

By around 3000 BCE, there is evidence of a cult of masculine fertility in the ancient Egyptian City of the Sun: an understanding of fertility as a masculine attribute in which "the life-giving fluids of the penis, rather than what goes on in the womb, ultimately create new life." Heliopolitan creation myths, inscribed on the walls of pyramids, give accounts of the primordial god Atum (who had created himself) ejaculating children. Similar Sumerian myths dating to around 2000 BCE—within range of Hammurabi's Code and the recording of the Old Testament—tell the story of the creator god "father Enki" who "stood up full of lust like a rampant bull, lifted his penis, ejaculated and filled the Euphrates with flowing water . . . the Tigris rejoiced in its heart like a great wild bull when it was born. . . . It brought water. . . . It brought barley." By the second millennium BCE, the father was seen as begetter and the mother as bearer: "the credit for creativity—for new life—rested with the male. . . . Ideologically speaking, it was the penis that gave rise to all that was, and all that was good."[28]

Where could this cult of fatherhood have originated? The story of the lustful, bull-like Enki may hold a clue. In her underappreciated 1975 book *Women's Creation*, Elizabeth Fisher proposed that the rise of patriarchy followed from the domestication of animals, which is likely to have been work done by men. Learning to manipulate animal reproduction might have shown men how human reproduction worked. Men began to assert control over women as they had over animals, including by forced mating: rape. In Fisher's analysis, a newfound awareness of the male reproductive role, violently demonstrated in the breeding of nonhuman animals, underpinned the rise of the power of the father.[29]

Bulls specifically may have additional significance. Bull cults were common across Eurasia in the Stone and Bronze Ages. For instance, the cave paintings at Lascaux are dominated by four black bulls, the largest of which measures more than seventeen feet long. Yet the line from bull cults to patriarchy, if it exists, is not direct.

Two contrasting examples show how it might have worked. The first is from Çatalhüyük, the site of a large Neolithic settlement in what is now southern Turkey, about one hundred miles from the shore of the Mediterranean, that was inhabited from roughly 7500 BCE to 6400 BCE. As one of the most extensive and elaborate archaeological excavations ever undertaken, Çatalhüyük has become a touchstone in narratives of human prehistory, and is seen as a uniquely clear window on the transition from nomadism to settled agriculture. The site encompasses the remains of a residential community of perhaps eight thousand people.

The interiors of houses at Çatalhüyük were vividly decorated, and the dominant motif is the bull. Many homes feature large-horned cattle skulls built into the walls and furniture, testifying to the role of cattle as an important source of food, and also, relatedly, as a focus of community ritual and collective meaning.

Yet despite the prominence of its bull cult, Çatalhüyük was "an aggressively egalitarian community," in the words of Stanford archaeologist Ian Hodder. Male and female remains show soot on the ribs, indicating that men and women spent about the same amount of time indoors. Markings on bones indicate that everyone was involved in similar repetitive tasks. Burial sites suggest that children were not necessarily brought up with their biological parents but by the community at large. In Çatalhüyük, the veneration of bulls does not seem to have precluded gender equality, nor to have translated into a possessive or hierarchical concept of fatherhood.[30]

But there is another factor to consider. Though there were domesticated plants and animals at Çatalhüyük, the bulls worshiped there were wild. In this regard, the people of Çatalhüyük differed from other bull worshipers, and particularly from raiding bands of herders who came down from the Eurasian steppe on horseback roughly six thousand years ago, wielding broadaxes and capturing women. According to one archaeologist, these raiders carried with them a worldview that centered on "their cattle and their sons." Their arrival in the heart of present-day Europe coincides with the earliest genetic evidence for the patrilineal family—kinship traced through fathers.[31]

The story need not be as simple as violent outsiders imposing patriarchy on societies that had been comparatively egalitarian. Yet the apparently simultaneous ascendance of cattle herders and the patrilineal family highlights a potentially powerful connection between animal husbandry and fatherhood. Hunting wild bulls would have brought one form of awareness of masculine power, breeding and herding them another. Cattle and sons were related issues.

Bulls were not the first animal to be domesticated, trailing sheep and goats by perhaps two thousand years. Yet from a human perspective, cattle were fundamentally different from sheep and goats. Breeding enormous adult bulls weighing more than a thousand pounds and predisposed to aggression is an intensely violent and dangerous enterprise. Any society that bred cattle, as Egyptians did, as the Sumerians did, as the Babylonians did, owed a significant part of its survival to the mastery of a fearsome performance of male procreative power.

And if cattle breeding was a source of "the discovery of fatherhood" as has been suggested, it would have also been vivid evidence that it was not necessary to have one man for every woman—that not every man needed, or merited, a mate.[32] The patriarchs of the Old Testament, whose lineages were recorded around this time, were said to have been rich in herds and slaves, and to have practiced polygamy and concubinage, some with hundreds of wives, to better fill the earth with the stock of the chosen.

It's probably not possible to establish a direct causal relationship between cattle breeding and the invention of fatherhood. Yet this hypothesis helps to highlight the fact that men in general didn't dominate early states—fathers did. Men who were not fathers were in some cases explicitly excluded from participation in public affairs. And when there was a crisis of state or society, a period of instability or uncertainty, fatherhood was mobilized as a solution: a tool for reinforcing or reforming public and private order that would be used so often, and in so many ways, that it came to became identified with order itself. When the ground under patriarchy shifted, new stories about fatherhood helped men work out and put in place new terms and conditions of rule. Having invented fatherhood, men shaped and reshaped it to fit their needs, fantasies, and fears, sometimes in collaboration with women, but more often at their expense.

That was exactly the situation 2,500 years ago in Athens, the site of what may be the first recorded debate about what it meant to be a father, where the city's intellectual leaders were bitterly divided over whether fatherhood was to be the salvation of their troubled civilization, or its ruin.

CHAPTER ONE

NATURE: Plato and Aristotle

The authors of the most popular creation myths in ancient Greece were so determined to honor fathers that they endowed male gods, especially but not exclusively Zeus, with the power of mothers: the ability to grow children inside themselves and bring them into the world.

According to these myths, there had been a time before fathers, when the world was chaotic and incomplete. The female Gaia, Earth, had emerged from the void. Alone, she conceived and gave birth to Uranus, her son and husband, the embodiment of the heavens. Together they had six sons and six daughters, the Titans. Jealous and wary of his powerful children, Uranus imprisoned them. Furious, Gaia urged the Titans to rise against their father, but only the youngest, Kronos, dared to try. Wielding a sickle his mother had forged, Kronos castrated his father, Uranus, whose penis fell into the sea, causing the water to foam. From this foam, or *aphros*, Aphrodite, goddess of love, was born, and Kronos became the leader of the Titans.

With his sister Rhea, Kronos fathered six children, the Olympians. Fearing that one of these children would supplant him, as he had supplanted his father, Kronos ate five of them as they were born. The sixth, Zeus, escaped only because his mother hurried him away to Crete, where he was raised in secrecy. When Zeus was grown, he convinced Metis, a nymph, to help him poison his father. Kronos drank what Metis prepared and vomited up Zeus's brothers and sisters. Together, the reunited Olympians banished Kronos from the upper skies, and Zeus became their leader—"father of gods and men" as Homer described him in the *Iliad*.

Yet Zeus was just as anxious about securing his power as his father and grandfather had been. When he heard a prophecy that Metis, then pregnant, would soon give birth to an heir who would unseat him, he ate her whole. Afterward Zeus was stricken by a fierce headache and cried out in pain. The Olympians showed up to help. They split open Zeus's head and Athena emerged, fully formed, clad in armor, the goddess of wisdom, patron of the city of Athens, where fathers were considered the "true parent" of any child, the proper heads of household and state—at least until, in the midst of a troubling political crisis, Plato and others began to worry that powerful patriarchs were leading Athens not to glory, but to its demise.[1]

Plato, who had no children of his own, publicly questioned the role of fathers after the trial and execution of the man he considered his intellectual father, his teacher, Socrates.[2]

The surviving accounts say that Socrates was tried in 399 BCE for three reasons: the first was failing to honor Athens's gods, the second was introducing new gods, and the third was corrupting young men. At the time Athens was reeling in defeat after decades of war with Sparta that had been compounded by years of plague. The population had cratered, and Spartan oligarchs had dismantled the city's political institutions, replacing democracy with "ancestral laws."[3] Even after the oligarchs had been run off and democracy restored, Athenians looked distrustfully on dissent, and dissent happened to be Socrates's specialty. There may also have been more personal issues in play.

The charges against Socrates came from three accusers. The leader of the three was Anytus, who dishonored himself as a general in the Peloponnesian War but nevertheless returned to Athens to run a prosperous tannery he had inherited from his father. Socrates had been the teacher of Anytus's son, and he had apparently been fond of the boy, lamenting the "servile occupation that his father has provided for him,"—namely, tanning—and his lack of a "worthy adviser."[4] According to Plato, Anytus had been offended by these comments, and claimed that if Socrates were acquitted and allowed to continue teaching, eventually all the sons in Athens would be "utterly ruined."[5] This was a dire forecast: Athens was only as good as its best sons, because no one else was eligible to rule.

The trial of Socrates took less than a day. It would have been longer, but Socrates declined to call his sons to testify on his behalf as most defendants did, believing such manipulative "spectacles" to be beneath him, Athens, and justice itself. Instead, he insisted on confronting the law as it actually existed: in the form of a jury of five hundred Athenian men, who sentenced him to die by drinking hemlock. It was hard to resist the conclusion that Socrates was performing his martyrdom on a public stage to raise a larger question: How could this have happened under the watch of Athena, goddess of wisdom? What had really corrupted the sons of Athens, once the foremost Greek city-state, now so faded and weakened?

Most importantly, what could be done to restore justice and virtue and Athens itself?

Plato put these questions at the center of *The Republic*, which never mentions the trial directly. He is thought to have written the book perhaps twenty-five years after Socrates's death, around 375 BCE, but he chose to set it fifty years earlier, around 425 BCE: in the midst of the war against Sparta and just after two devastating plagues killed perhaps 20 percent of Athenians.

The Republic is a provocation disguised as a proposal. It's clever, cutting, and even funny, and intended more as critical food for thought than an actual blueprint for state-building. *The Republic*'s dialogue opens during a festival for Bendis, a fertility goddess of unique significance, for her cult was foreign, native not to Athens but to the region of Thrace. Despite its foreign origins, the cult of Bendis had been welcomed in Athens, even granted land for the building of a shrine, possibly to solidify or reflect a strategic military alliance with the Thracians. Perhaps Socrates had "introduced new divinities"—but so had the city's politicians and diplomats, and then they lost the war anyway.

Socrates is the speaker in *The Republic*, as he is in virtually all of Plato's writing, yet the book is usually grouped with the "later dialogues," thought to express Plato's own ideas rather than his understanding of Socrates's teachings. The dialogue explores how justice gets corrupted, how the common good goes bad, and what can be done about it, given the obvious tendency of men to favor their own money and their own families. Plato's answer centers on getting rid of the private patriarchal household—a plan Plato has Socrates boldly present in the home of a rich man before an audience made up of this patriarch's sons and expectant heirs, as well as Plato's own brothers.

As Socrates lays out his notion of an ideal society—Plato's republic—the audience of sons challenges and pushes him for clarity and detail, especially on his surprising ideas of sex, marriage, and the household. Socrates tries to evade the questions, but the sons pin him down. "I must stand my trial, then," Plato makes Socrates say, twenty-five years before he did. "I can assure you it won't be easy to explain." In the Western tradition, unconventional ideas about sex and marriage rarely have been.

In the Athens of Plato and Aristotle, there was no word for family as it has come to be defined, by kinship and affection. Instead, there was "the household," encompassing both people and property, including the enslaved. The patriarch was head of the household, charged with its survival and flourishing: generating and sustaining heirs by using the resources, both people and things, he controlled, including the heirs themselves, and their mother, and the enslaved. The patriarch held the house and everything and everyone in it. As the fundamental unit of Athenian society, the household was often taken to be a fitting model for the state itself, and the patriarch for government.

In the Athenian household, as in the state, women were not eligible to govern. Instead, they were born to be mothers, and many of them also died that way. Marriage followed closely on, and sometimes even preceded, the start of menstruation—fourteen was typical. During the ceremony, it was customary for the father of the bride to announce to the groom: "I give you my daughter for the plowing of legitimate children," reflecting a commonplace view that women were essentially soil in which men planted seed and cultivated produce. After marriage, sex was obligatory, and it was not unusual for a woman to experience more than six pregnancies in her lifetime. Each was perilous, especially after the third. The inherent risks were heightened in many cases by malnutrition, a chronic condition among women, whose hunger was not prioritized within the household. The archaeological record shows that perhaps 20 percent of pregnancies in classical Greece ended in the mother's death. As Euripides has Medea say, "I would rather stand three times in the front of battle than bear one child."[6]

Births took place in the home, attended by midwives as well as female neighbors, friends, and family of the woman in labor. A doctor might be called for complications, but the most urgent conditions, such as hemorrhage, were usually not treatable. Even when doctors were present for the entire birth, they were not necessarily much help. Religious taboos prohibited Hippocratic physicians, all men, from performing dissections. Lacking direct knowledge of the female reproductive system, they tended to view a woman's role in childbirth as passive.[7] In many cases, the principal role of the doctor attending a birth was to serve as a representative of the interests of the expectant father, to ensure that the pregnancy was genuine and the baby he was presented with was in fact his. Midwives, who were actively involved in births, were often suspected of helping to terminate or fake a pregnancy, or otherwise subverting what were considered women's responsibilities to their husbands and households.[8]

Under these circumstances, women turned to the gods for help even when there were doctors in the family. The favor of those gods who oversaw fertility, pregnancy, and childbirth, especially Artemis, Apollo's twin, and Ilithiya, was highly sought by women of all social classes, who participated in tributes and rituals that together formed virtually the only opportunity for Athenian women to meet in public. Yet even in the best cases—when the gods responded when summoned ("Come, come," women in labor and those at their bedside would cry), and when no other gods sent their wrath, and when the midwives worked effectively and successfully at every step, and mother and newborn came through in good health and at minimal risk—even then, childbirth in Athens did not result in the birth of a child. Instead, what came out of the mother and into the world was still called by the name that had applied before its birth: *brephos*, meaning both fetus and newborn. Philosophically, legally, and socially, the *brephos* was a nonbeing even after it had been born. Pregnancy and childbirth may have been a matter for women and the gods, but neither could create a child. Only a man, the head of a household, could pick up a newborn fetus and say, This shall be a child, and this child shall be mine.

That was the point of the ceremony known as the *amphidromia*. The word means "circling around." Five or seven days after a birth, the patriarch would carry the newborn around the hearth of the household, a circle that could end in one of two radically different places. While turning around the hearth, the father would raise the child up for inspection, examining it "from every angle," as Plato put it in another context, "to make sure we are not taken in by a lifeless phantom not worth the rearing."[9] The question was real enough, though in practice it almost certainly would have been answered well in advance of the ritual performance of the father's power.

If the patriarch found some cause for concern, then it was entirely within his right to refuse to accept the *brephos* into the household. Visible birth defects or deformities would have likely led this way. Being born a girl was also risky, as was being born to an enslaved mother. Other disqualifying conditions were detectable only by a subjective evaluation of the small body's liveliness, balanced against the patriarch's resources and priorities. If a determination was made that the *brephos* was not viable, physically or economically, then it was "exposed"—meaning to the elements, outside the house, away from the hearth, on the assumption that it would die from starvation, or be eaten by an animal, or freeze.

On the other hand, if the *brephos* was judged to be viable, the newborn was formally welcomed into the household and became legally a person, a *pais,* which was the word for a child of either gender, subject to the rule of the father who had created it.

In *The Republic,* Plato laid out a proposal, a thought experiment toward a just and virtuous society, that departed from these familiar Athenian household conventions in provocative ways. His proposal is a critique rather than a direct guide to practical action. If the possessive concepts of property and sex that defined the patriarchal household were corrupting Athenian men, politics, and justice, what might be possible if those conventions were overturned?

In Plato's experimental ideal, there was to be no private household of property and kin formed under one patriarch. Instead, men and women would be chosen by fitness and merit for a ruling class of "guardians." Guardians would reproduce with each other not as a husband and wife, father and mother, but instead in public festivals of polygamous sex. The most meritorious men, including those most decorated in war, would enjoy the most access to women—an expedient way to ensure that as many children as possible would acquire such meritorious qualities.

At the end of whatever pregnancies resulted from these festivals—paternity remaining a mystery—babies would be taken from their mothers by specially appointed officers. The officers would assume the power of Athenian fathers to determine which infants would survive. Defective and inferior children would be "quietly and secretly" disposed of; sound children would be raised by nurses. Intriguingly, Plato's proposed method of selecting viable infants by public officials was much closer to the practice of Sparta, whose warriors had defeated Athens only five years before the trial of Socrates.

This would have been a profound change for fathers in Athens. They stood to lose not only the power to determine the size and shape of their households that they exercised through the *amphidromia*, but also the very ideas of "their children" and "their household": the core principles of Athenian patriarchy and masculine identity. In Plato's Republic, no parents in the guardian class would know their own children, and no children their parents.[10]

Yet this was not the same as getting rid of fatherhood altogether. The name "father" would still be used, but with different meanings and intents. A man would call all children born in a seven- to ten-month window "after he has been a bridegroom" his sons and daughters. In turn, these children would call him—along with all other "bridegrooms" of the same period—Father. Family names became markers, boundaries to prevent those men and women who might theoretically be closely related to each other from reproducing in the future. At the same time, names were also ranks, for bearers of these titles would be by law "required to behave accordingly, to show their fathers all the customary honor and love, and to obey their parents."

The laws and norms governing sex and family life in the Republic aimed especially to transform the social roles of men—to transform fatherhood. Plato refers to his concept of the public household as a "community of women and children." Men are holders of this common stock. As a holder of women and children in common, a man will come to view anyone he meets "as related to him, as brother or sister, father or mother, son or daughter, grandparent or grandchild." In turn, his "private joys and sorrows" will be replaced by "common feelings of pain and pleasure." The point was that the household had become too small, dedicated to itself and its members at the expense of the community. *The Republic* imagined a radical way to bind the community together into a single household the size of the state.

By the time Socrates has finished making his case for Plato's Republic, even his skeptical audience agrees that the proposal makes a lot of sense. Still, there is no moment when they seem particularly likely, let alone eager, to act on it. Plato was a teacher, not a politician. And as influential as Plato's teachings were, they were likely meant to be imaginative exercises rather than policies to be enacted. Yet if the more far-fetched aspects of Plato's ideal household-state were exaggerated for rhetorical effect, the humor was entirely lost on his sharpest student, who loved a risky joke himself. Aristotle's most enduring works directly refute his teacher Plato's critique of fatherhood, and defend the power of fathers to rule at home and beyond.

Aristotle had been born in 384 BCE in Stagira, a rustic corner of Macedonia, to an elite family. His father, Nicomachus, had served as a court physician to the Macedonian King Amyntas but died before he could pass his knowledge and trade to his son, as was customary. Aristotle's mother, Phaestis, came from a landowning family on the large island of Euboea, near Athens. When she, too, died, Aristotle was adopted by an uncle, Proxenus, who saw to his education and sent him to Athens.

One purpose of Plato's dialogues was to advertise his school to students beyond Athens. By 367 BCE, when Aristotle arrived as a seventeen-year-old orphan from Macedonia, *The Republic*, published eight years earlier, had attained hallowed status. Aristotle would spend twenty years at Plato's Academy, eventually rising to teach himself. "In Plato," one historian writes, Aristotle "sought and found a man to lead him in a new life."[11]

Just as Plato thought of Socrates as his "intellectual father," his own students were the next generation.[12] In ancient Greece, pregnancy was a common metaphor for education. The work of teachers was to fill students with knowledge and then draw out ideas from them. This was a model for all relations between older and younger men in Athens, including sex, which was also understood to be a process of learning and developing toward manhood. In school and in sex, young boys received lessons from older men. When boys reached intellectual and sexual maturity, they were generally expected to take the active role for which, Aristotle later said, they had been fitted by nature.

Aristotle had arrived in Athens carrying the outsider status that barred him from owning property in, and participating directly in the celebrated political life of, the city with which he is most associated. Ancient sources suggest that he was as eager to fit in as he was incapable of doing so. He adopted the fashionable lisp of the Athenian elite, wore fussy clothes, memorable rings, and an unusual hairstyle that did little to soften the sharp edges he presented to the world, often in the form of cutting insults. He was also known to hold himself apart from the other students at the all-male Academy, even as he tried to make himself superficially more like them. In light of this tendency, Plato is said to have joked that the Academy consisted of two parts: the student body and Aristotle's brain. The ancient historian of philosophy Diogenes Laërtius suggested that this was a case of Aristotle learning to do what Plato did, rather than what Plato said, and this made Aristotle, Diogenes thought, "Plato's most genuine disciple."[13]

But Aristotle would not be Plato's heir. After Plato died in 347, leadership of the Academy passed to his nephew, Speusippus. One possible explanation is that Plato or his designees simply favored his nephew. Another is that because Aristotle, a foreigner, could not legally own property in Athens, Plato maneuvered to ensure the real estate would remain under control of the school and his own family line, though he had rather famously critiqued the idea of private property, and for that matter a family line, of one's own.[14]

Aristotle left Athens around that time. His departure was not necessarily the result of having been passed over. King Philip II of Macedon—the son of King Amyntas, to whose court Aristotle's father had tended—had a conquest of Athens in his sights, and the mood had turned against Macedonian outsiders.

What the two possibilities have in common is that the facts of Aristotle's birth—which had made him neither Plato's kin nor an Athenian—caused the life he had made over twenty years to become untenable. At thirty-seven he was starting over again.

Aristotle's departure from Athens marked another new stage of his life, "the period of travels."[15] He headed east around the Aegean

Sea, toward Assos, a city-state in what is today Turkey. The local ruler there, Hermeias, was also a graduate of Plato's Academy, and he had invited Aristotle and several others to establish their own school. At some point, Aristotle married a daughter, or possibly a niece, of Hermeias, named Pythias.[16]

Sources disagree on the timing of the marriage, though Aristotle would later write that thirty-seven was the age at which men had finally matured enough to start their own families, and his views on the subject are unlikely to have been arbitrary. After three years in Assos, Aristotle moved again, to the island of Lesbos, rising from the Aegean Sea five miles out in the Strait of Mytilene, presumably with his bride, and probably with his nephew Callisthenes and his friend Theophrastus as well.[17]

Marriage in ancient Greece meant children, but it would be years, perhaps nearly a decade, before Aristotle and Pythias had a child of their own. On Lesbos, Aristotle began an ambitious new research project, one that in some ways also marked a homecoming for him, as a doctor's son. The subject was what was then called generation—the origins of new life, genesis, parentage, inheritance: how and why "a human being gives rise to a human being or a fish a fish," an Athenian to an Athenian, a Macedonian to a Macedonian.[18] After his marriage, with no children of his own on the way, Aristotle dug into questions of how children came to be.

He found his evidence all around him in nature, collecting and examining hundreds if not thousands of animal specimens, including many native to Lesbos: insects, reptiles, birds, fish, cows, sheep, and especially chickens. The reason for studying so many different creatures was to gain insight into one creature above all: man. Aristotle even seems to have acquired a human embryo, detached at forty days, though he did not say where or how he got it and learned its age. But otherwise, like Hippocratic physicians, Aristotle did not perform human dissections. One of his working models of the human male reproductive system was probably a bull.[19]

The investigations Aristotle began on Lesbos were eventually collected in three volumes: *History of Animals*, *Parts of Animals*, and *Generation of Animals*. These books are the basis for his reputation as the father of biology, the science of life. Aristotle's biology in turn was the basis for his better-known work in ethics and politics. What connected these fields was a novel theory of semen, from which Aristotle developed enduring ideas of fatherhood and politics alike.

For Aristotle, semen was the key to nature's code—the reason why people are who they are. Generation was accomplished through the combination of male and female parts, both of which Aristotle described as seed. Male seed was semen. Female seed was menses. The differences between these forms of seed followed from what Aristotle considered fundamental differences between men and women. Men were hot; women were cold. Semen, relatively scant, was highly refined blood that had been "well concocted" by the heat of the male body.[20] Menses, more abundant, was made of the same stuff but less refined and incompletely concocted, owing to the relative coldness of women's bodies. Semen was emitted in the triumph of sex. Menses was purged as excess, waste, a failure of generation. Semen carried the highest human "principle of soul." Menses, being imperfect, lacked it—"otherwise the male would exist in vain, and nature makes nothing in vain." In Aristotle's view, fathers were the opposite of useless. Fathers were destiny.

Aristotle extrapolated the differences he identified in seed and sex into bigger ones. "A male animal . . . generates in another," while "a female . . . generates within itself," Aristotle said, his certainty undiminished by his awareness of a number of exceptions. This is why, he reasoned, the earth was thought to be a mother, but heaven and the sun were realms of fathers. For Aristotle, a man is by definition a father, an activating agent, and therefore primary: "better and more divine." A woman is by definition a mother, acted upon, secondary, less divine. In these assumptions Aristotle rooted a sweeping theory of life, both its creation and its conduct. His theory was a response to and refutation of core aspects of Plato's *Republic*, and the key difference was the nature and role of fathers.

Aristotle wasn't working in isolation. Many others at the time were also trying to figure out the origins of life through observation of and experiments with nature. These efforts gave rise to a new pantheon of creation stories that went well beyond Gaia and Zeus, and beyond the common convention that women were soil and men were farmers.

Aristotle thought most of the new theories were just as implausible as popular myths, especially the one known as pangenesis. This was the idea that seed is distilled from all the distinct parts of the body, encoding its various characteristics, which were then reproduced in the offspring. From the hands of the parent come the hands of the child; from the eyes the eyes; from the nose the nose. Some theorists of pangenesis even tried to account for acquired characteristics this way, proposing that scars, for example, were also encoded in parental seed.

But pangenesis raised complicated questions about resemblances in secondary characteristics that went beyond the physical—patterns of speech and bodily movement, for instance. And what about cases in which the parent had, for example, lost a hand, but the offspring was born with two of them? What about resemblances to distant relatives, who had contributed no seed to the new child? And what about genitals? Mothers and fathers both had the ability to contribute parts to their children, so why didn't children end up with two sets of everything? Who got what from whom, and why? Existing explanations depended on all kinds of workarounds. One theory said semen from the right testicle produced male children, the left one female. Aristotle wasn't convinced.

So he started over, beginning empirically. Semen was white, he reasoned, because it was a foam: a compound of air and liquid, an *aphros*, as in the goddess of love Aphrodite, born from the foaming of her father's amputated penis in the sea. This foam, Aristotle hypothesized, was alive with invisible yet vital movements that encoded the father's characteristics and imparted them to the embryo—beginning with maleness and extending, potentially, to everything else.

How did semen impart its characteristics to the embryo? What exactly determined how much the child turned out like the father? One of Aristotle's analogies is fig juice splashed into milk, curdling in proportion to acidity. But ultimately this analogy didn't quite capture it, for menses, Aristotle said, was also alive with movements corresponding to the mother's characteristics, beginning with femaleness, defined by Aristotle as maleness minus the highest capacities of reason and the basic elements of the soul. He concluded that the movements of the semen, encoding the qualities of the father, would shape the embryo when they were stronger than the corresponding movements of the menses.

Aristotle presented this theory not as a speculative hypothesis—and unobservable, since the movements of the seed were invisible—but as the very nature of nature. Movements of seed varied with the natures of men and women.

Reflecting the nature of women, menses was colder, thinner, and incomplete, not refined or perfectly concocted, and the movements within it were comparatively weak. By contrast, semen was hot. It "slackened" and became thinner as it cooled. Semen was concocted first from the father's superior internal heat, and then further concocted by the heat generated in sex. The more vital the father, the hotter the sex (though it was possible to be too hot and too strong, burning and violent), the foamier and more lively the semen, the more likely it was to overpower the menses and shape the embryo in the father's image.

In other words, the ideal outcome, the perfect result, was a male child who resembled his father in every way, while "every little girl represents a failure in her father's semen."[21] The best fathers extended a line of great fathers and sons.

Aristotle shaped his study of generation into a pointed response to Plato's *Republic* by using Socrates's semen as an example of the workings of seed and the mechanics of fatherhood. The choice was sensational by design. From the outset, Aristotle framed his work on generation as a challenge to ideas that were characteristic of "the time of Socrates." He criticized philosophers of that age for neglecting the nature of things, and especially nature itself, in favor of principles and values, "useful virtue and political science."[22] The target of these criticisms was not Socrates but Plato: Socrates's student and ventriloquist, Aristotle's former teacher. In *The Republic*, of course, nature had been not just neglected but rejected in favor of the pursuit of a political ideal. *The Republic* was an impossible dream, Aristotle implied, and not even particularly instructive as an ideal, for Plato had misunderstood something about fathers. The biological ties between parents and children could not be erased. The nature of fatherhood was too strong for that.

Aristotle's proof was a nose that didn't exist—a nose belonging to Socrates's daughter, who didn't exist either, for in fact Socrates had only sons. This was a thought experiment of Aristotle's own design, and not one chosen arbitrarily. Not only had Socrates been the speaker in Plato's *Republic*, describing the virtues of the "community of women and children," but Socrates was also, it has often been said, a distinctive-looking man. "Everyone is agreed Socrates was very ugly," Bertrand Russell observed in his history of Western philosophy.[23] In particular, Socrates's nose was decidedly not a classical one—on the contrary, it was compared to a pig's snout. By considering in detail the strength and qualities of the movements latent in Socrates's semen, Aristotle explained how Socrates could theoretically father a female child who was different from him to the extent that she was female, but like him to the extent that she inherited his nose—a female child, in other words, who would be unmistakably his. Whether Socrates's daughter was raised in Socrates's own household or within some ideal "community of women and children," her pig nose would give her away, and mark her publicly as her father's daughter, skewing the common interest toward a private, personal one, undermining the foundations of the ideal republic with her unfortunate, swinish nose.

Effectively exiled from the Academy and Athens, Aristotle undertook a project that demonstrated that, contrary to what his celebrated teacher Plato had proposed, you couldn't get rid of fatherhood. If you really wanted to create good citizens and a just society, Aristotle implied, it was better to work with fatherhood than against it. The appeal of this approach, over Plato's, would have been perfectly clear for patriarchs and their sons to see, whether they had households at stake, or kingdoms.

In 342, after two or three years on Lesbos, Aristotle was summoned to the court of King Philip II of Macedonia. This was another kind of homecoming. Aristotle's father, Nicomachus, had been a doctor at the court of Philip's father, Amyntas. Now the son of Amyntas, Philip, told the son of Nicomachus, Aristotle, that he needed a tutor for his own son, Alexander, then thirteen, not yet known as "the Great" but already showing signs of extraordinary ambition.

Alexander was not the eldest son of Philip, who took at least seven wives—one during each military campaign, it was said, for diplomatic purposes—and kept countless lovers, both female and male. These affairs had produced at least one son who might have had priority over Alexander: Arrhidaeus, who was older but "half-witted," historians say—possibly due to an injury suffered when Alexander's mother, Olympias, tried to kill him to improve her own son's position. Arrhidaeus had been judged by Philip unfit to rule.[24]

In contrast, Philip was proud and protective of Alexander, though it's possible that Alexander did not feel exactly the same way about his father. According to one tale, whenever news of Philip's ongoing conquests reached Alexander, the boy complained that there was now less of the world left for him.

Growing up, Alexander was alternately flattered and browbeaten by court tutors until Philip decided a different approach was needed. He called on Aristotle, then in voluntary exile from Athens, which was increasingly a focus of Philip's expansionist ambitions. Aristotle would have been well paid, and as part of the bargain he seems to have convinced Philip to rebuild his home village of Stagira, which the king had sacked not long before.[25]

For a classroom, Aristotle was granted a lush site outside the Macedonian capital of Pella, called the Temple of Nymphs. Very little is known about the two or three years Aristotle and Alexander spent there together. Surely they studied science, a demonstrated interest of Alexander's too. In addition, Alexander seems to have shared his teacher's misconceptions about the size of India and the location of the edge of the world beyond the Himalayas. Aristotle is also said to have prepared an annotated copy of the *Iliad*—Homer's epic of war and heroism, glory and its costs—that Alexander would later carry with him through Asia. The poem's hero, Achilles, was thought to have come from the north of Greece rather than the more fashionable south, just like Alexander and Aristotle.

In 340 BCE, Alexander was called from his studies with Aristotle to sit on the throne in the absence of his father, then away at the front. Later that same year, Alexander led his own campaign to suppress an opportunistic uprising in northern Macedonia. He celebrated his success by borrowing a custom from his father and naming the city he had defended after himself, the first of many.

Afterward, Alexander joined his father on the march, to learn the practice of warfare, which Aristotle could not have taught him. The long and successful campaign they undertook together culminated in 338 with the Macedonian conquest of Athens. The victorious Philip sent Alexander to Athens with the remains of the city's dead, and he was received with honors and made a citizen. Meanwhile, as the king of a newly subdued and united Greece, and still a relatively young man himself, Philip turned toward Persia and another new bride, Cleopatra.

The marriage meant potential trouble for Alexander, for there was no immutable principle of royal succession beyond paternal preference. The king chose the king. Alexander, whose own status was proof of this, stalked angrily out of his father's wedding feast. His standing as heir apparent had become tenuous. Sure enough, Cleopatra soon became pregnant, and she gave birth to a daughter on the eve of Philip's campaign against Persia. Not long after, Philip, Cleopatra, and their daughter were all assassinated. Despite the strong taboo against parricide in Greek culture, thoughts of a conspiracy were inevitable. Olympias, Alexander's ambitious mother, was positioned to take most of the blame, though the consequences were unlikely to fall on her too heavily, for her son had become king.

Being king meant leading an army. Alexander took his place at the head of his father's and moved quickly to make it his own. In 335, he consolidated Macedonian power over the Greek city-states, crushing Thebes with force fearsome enough to suppress disquiet in Athens too. Then Alexander fixed his sights on the victory that had eluded his father, and left for Persia with forty thousand men behind him.

As Alexander pushed east, Aristotle traveled west to Athens for the first time in thirteen years. He was now fifty, and thanks to his connections to Alexander he had never been more powerful. On the edge of the city, Aristotle founded a school of his own to compete with the Academy, called the Lyceum, set in lush gardens surrounding what was probably the greatest library in the world. Around the same time, Aristotle became a father himself, twice over, by two women.

First Aristotle and his wife, Pythias, had a daughter, whom they also named Pythias. Soon after, the elder Pythias died. Aristotle then took up with Herpyllis, who may have been his late wife's maid and was likely enslaved in his household. Herpyllis became Aristotle's concubine, a common and acceptable position in Athenian society. Before long, Herpyllis bore a son, of whom Aristotle apparently approved, and who was named, in the conventional fashion, after Aristotle's father, Nicomachus.

In these years Aristotle wrote the works for which he is still known and celebrated and sometimes, and not unjustifiably, criticized and decried. Calling his writing philosophy now makes it sound more remote and specialized than necessary. Aristotle's questions are the same ones that shape every contemporary editorial page and bestseller list—how to live a rewarding life, how to build a good society, how to govern a successful state—just as they had shaped Shuruppag's instructions. One difference is that Aristotle lived in and wrote in defense of arguably the most patriarchal society in recorded history, and unlike Shuruppag he never begged for obedience. Instead, he assumed authority, and generally it has been granted to him.

Today Aristotle's works are often read as stand-alone documents of ancient wisdom, with due objections raised to his misogyny and views on "natural slavery." Direct connections between his life and his thought are difficult to establish as matters of historical fact. One famous biography of Aristotle, usually attributed to German philosopher Martin Heidegger, is only fifteen words long: "He was born, he thought, and he died. And all the rest is pure anecdote." Even the biographical facts that can be confirmed are generally pushed to the side by modern readers eager to focus on their own questions and problems. As a result, it has been easy to overlook an intriguing word in the title of what is by any measure Aristotle's most widely read book—his enduring inquiry into how to live a good and virtuous life—which also happens to bear the name of his father and his son: Nicomachus, as in the *Nicomachean Ethics*.

How did their name become a title? What is Nicomachean about the *Nicomachean Ethics*? These are not questions that scholars and historians generally ask. One reason for their reticence is that Aristotle himself didn't call the book by that name. For that matter, it's unlikely that he called it anything at all, or even considered it a book. What we now read as Aristotle's "books" were originally lecture notes for his classes at the Lyceum. These notes were most likely assembled and published after Aristotle's death, probably by his students.

For all these reasons, many scholars have concluded that the title is not only ambiguous and anachronistic but also irrelevant—biographical debris rather than detail. Yet it would be a mistake to leave what little intimate information we have out of the story of Aristotle's ideas, lest they be mistaken for merely ideas, and he be mistaken for merely a thinker.

In the *Nicomachean Ethics*, living a good life is not a matter of following fixed rules with prescribed consequences, as it was for Shuruppag and Hammurabi. Instead, it is a matter of being raised well. Being good starts in the capacities of the soul, shaped by seed at conception. It is deepened by habits imprinted during childhood, but not only at home. It requires education, but not only education, for learning "is not pleasant to most people, especially not to the young."[26] It should be enforced by public law, lest men turn into household autocrats, each making law for his family "like

Cyclops." Yet it also needs to be rooted in something deeper than law, for even great statesmen, Aristotle notes, have failed to make laws that could make statesmen of their sons. What living a good and ethical life ultimately rests on, for Aristotle, is a partnership of fathers and the state, individual patriarchs and institutionalized patriarchy, household and politics, love and power.

This partnership strengthened both fathers and the state. The word of the father alone, Aristotle wrote with confidence, was often resisted by those who stood to benefit from it most. But the state could make fathers stronger by giving them the cover of a greater, public authority. Unlike "a father's orders" to do this or that, "the law has a compulsory power ... which is not hated when it orders what is decent." Conversely, a father could fill in around the edges of the state, promoting "the virtue of his children and his friends," who were already predisposed "to be loving and obedient to him by nature." At the end of the *Nicomachean Ethics*, sons become good by the rule of fathers, at home and in government. That's what is Nicomachean about it.

Whoever created and named the *Nicomachean Ethics* never gave it a proper ending. The last line of the book now published under that title is an invitation to "make a beginning" of another question, one focused on the world beyond the household—how a good state should be governed. With this shift, the *Nicomachean Ethics* becomes a prologue to Aristotle's *Politics*, which begins in turn by announcing itself as a critique of Plato's "community of women and children," in which justice, virtue, and the ideal republic rest on a father's inability to know his children from others.

The *Politics* returns to the topic of Socrates's nose. "Children are born like their parents," Aristotle says again, "and they will necessarily be finding indications of their relationship to one another.... Geographers ... say that in part of upper Libya, where the women are common, nevertheless the children who are born are assigned to their respective fathers on the ground of their likeness." [27] Nature could not be disguised.

The difference between the *Nicomachean Ethics* and the *Politics* is that the latter explains what fathers should do with people who are not their sons—in other words, people who are not capable of becoming entirely good. This is the subject of what may be Aristotle's most infamous sentence. "From the moment of birth," he wrote in the *Politics*, "some are marked out for subjection, others for rule." This marking, according to Aristotle, happened at conception, and was principally done by fathers.

Aristotle allowed that mothers were superior to fathers in at least one way. Mothers loved their children more, he maintained—after all, mothers could be more certain that their children were theirs. But this did not mean, in Aristotle's view, that mothers were better parents than fathers. On the contrary, female biological imperfection—stemming from the original failure of fatherhood to generate a son—led to the incapacities and shortcomings of a woman's character, among which Aristotle numbered "shamelessness, impulsiveness, and lack of control regarding emotions involving pain or anger ... lack of spirit ... cowardice." Unsuited to rule themselves or their children, women, at best, could be trained to be "assistants" to men.[28]

Women shared this quality—congenital incapacity relative to men—with slaves. Perhaps a quarter of the population of Athens was enslaved. Most had been captured in war or raids, others born from enslaved mothers. What these enslaved persons shared, Aristotle said, were slavish natures, and a slave could achieve at best the role of a tool, used by and for the master toward the development of the household. Slaves were, in his notorious phrase, "living tools." Historian David Brion Davis pointed out that by framing slavery as "an essentially domestic relationship Aristotle endowed it with the sanction of paternal authority."[29] He brought it into the home, giving enslavement and mastery a benevolent cast that endured at least until the eighteenth century, and certainly, for some, well beyond.

Unlike the enslaved, in Aristotle's view, children changed and progressed over time, though only sons had the potential to develop into fully virtuous heads of households. By the same figuring, only good men, heads of households, could teach sons everything that needed to be taught. In light of their common incapacities, women, children, and slaves alike required and benefited from the protection and provision of the head of the household, the patriarch, who could make the best of each according to their needs and abilities.

Household forms of authority were related to political ones. The head of a household ruled his slaves as a tyrant ruled the conquered: by force of command. Men ruled wives as an aristocrat ruled over a commoner: by virtue of greater worthiness and rank. Fathers ruled children as kings presided over their loyal subjects: with their interests at heart. Aristotle's ideal state, described in the *Politics*, incorporated elements of all three. Yet he made clear that of all the forms of government, monarchy stood out as the best, due to the paternal care expected of and received from kings. A father's relationship with his children was not only the model for but also the key to successful politics, to a good state. Athens, of course, was then under the command of a king who had been Aristotle's student and was now his patron.

The *Politics* was not merely an extension of Aristotle's critique of Plato. Aristotle had shown why his teacher's version of the ideal republic was flawed. Now he meant to show why it was better to rule through fatherhood than to deny it, and how it could be done. "In a state having women and children in common," Aristotle argued, "love will be diluted; the father will certainly not say 'my son,' or the son, 'my father.'" As a result, "in this sort of community, the idea of relationship which is based upon these names will be lost; there is no reason why the so-called father should care about the son, or the son about the father, or brothers about one another. Of the two qualities which chiefly inspire regard and affection—that a thing is your own and that is your only one—neither can exist in such a state as this." And that would be a poor state indeed.

Where Plato had proposed to sever fatherhood from the private household, care from nature, Aristotle went in the opposite direction. He proposed to heighten fathers' identification with their children through policies designed to create good fathers and children—that is, through eugenics, a word coined in the nineteenth century from a combination of the Greek terms for good and breeding.

In the *Politics*, Aristotle outlined a program in which the state would help men become fathers and bind them to their children as strongly as possible. Good governance would aim to strengthen the movements latent in semen. Marriage and sex would be authorized and encouraged under specific social and environmental conditions. Men should be at their most robust maturity, between thirty-seven and fifty-five—a range that coincided precisely with the likely dates of Aristotle's own marriage to Pythias in Assos and the birth of Nicomachus to Herpyllis in Athens—and women should be older than eighteen. Their bodies should be of vital good health. Marriages, Aristotle proposed, should take place in winter, so suitable couples can mix their seed when the north winds are blowing, the dryness of which would also help with the concoction of strong semen.[30] From this beginning, under good fathers, good citizens and a good state could grow.

In Persia, Alexander the Great, Aristotle's student and patron, also used fatherhood for state building. While his father, Philip, had married many times for strategic purposes, Alexander, then thirty-one and married to Roxana, who was said to be the most beautiful woman in Asia, took it a step further. He not only married (again) into a local dynasty, but had his soldiers do so too. In 324 BCE, having defeated the Persian empire in battle, he arranged for a group wedding of his officers to elite Persian women. His aim was not primarily to mix the races into one, as has sometimes been assumed, but rather to grow the state from sex and seed, cultivating an empire of loyal households and loyal children.

Yet in another sense, Alexander's conquests led him away from the principles that were most important to his teacher Aristotle. Before he set out toward Asia, Alexander's mother is said to have told him that he was begotten not by Philip but by a god, probably Zeus, who came to her as a snake. After Alexander had conquered Persia, he found this account increasingly easy to believe. Received in Egypt as a liberator, he was honored as a Pharaoh, son of the god Amun-Ra, or Ammon, an Egyptian version of Zeus. Inspired, Alexander sought and received confirmation of his divine parent-age from a priest at the shrine at Siwa in the Libyan desert. In 327, he began to insist that he be known, addressed, and treated as the son of Zeus.[31]

In Athens, the response to this request was widespread ridicule. Alexander, feeling that he was not receiving deference appropriate to his divine station, focused his ire on Aristotle's nephew, Callisthenes, then employed as Alexander's field historian. Callisthenes had probably been with Aristotle and Alexander at the temple of Nymphs. But when Callisthenes refused to bow before Alexander as before a god, Alexander had him killed.

And that is when, according to the celebrated biographer Plutarch, Aristotle contrived to poison his former student Alexander, who died under dubious circumstances in 323. To modern historians, such a plot seems beyond unlikely, but that judgment is in some ways less important than the fact that Plutarch thought it plausible. Born in the first century of the "Christian era" (or common era), Plutarch lived in a world in which the stakes of worshiping a man as the son of god were becoming increasingly clear.

After Alexander's death, the mood in Athens turned strongly against Macedonians. "It is hard to live in Athens," Aristotle lamented to a friend. "Pear ripens upon pear, fig upon fig." He was a Macedonian who had never been made an Athenian citizen, and his position had become untenable once again.

Aristotle had spent much of his life studying and promoting the power of fathers. But at the end of it, he sought refuge among women. In 323, Aristotle moved his household out of Athens, to his mother's childhood home on the island of Euboea, where he lived out his last days under the care of his concubine Herpyllis.

CHAPTER TWO

GOD: Augustine of Hippo

In the spring of 391, thirty-six-year-old Aurelius Augustinus stepped off a ship in Hippo, a busy port city in Roman North Africa, alone and without a single piece of luggage. Hippo was only about fifty miles from Augustine's hometown of Thagaste, but that was far enough. Augustine was afraid of the sea, lonely, isolated, and looking for a place to start a monastic community where he could begin a quiet new life.[1] Not long before, his old life had collapsed, and he had "given up all hope in this world."[2]

Augustine's parents were dead. He had split from his longtime love, the mother of his son Adeodatus, whose name is lost to history, to marry a younger and richer woman, only to back out at the last minute. He gave up his prestigious but unfulfilling job as a professor of rhetoric in Milan to become a writer, but his books on beauty and happiness did not sell.

In 388, Augustine had left Italy with the teenage Adeodatus, and returned to his hometown, Thagaste, as an unemployed single father with only the sketchiest of plans. They settled in Augustine's boyhood home with a small group of friends, so Adeodatus could grow up there too. Then Adeodatus died suddenly, and Augustine had to start over again.

The only thing he didn't want to be was a priest. Christian churches on the fringes of the Roman Empire were chronically understaffed. With over seven hundred positions for bishops in Africa alone, there were always jobs to fill. Highly educated Christians such as Augustine, formerly a distinguished professor, were not so much called into service as they were conscripted by a community in need.

Shortly after arriving in Hippo, just as he feared, and against his wishes, Augustine was ordained as a priest. He resigned himself to the job and moved into the Spartan house, more like a shed, in the garden surrounding his church.[3] There he founded the monastery he had sought, a community of celibates, segregated by sex: a "family of God," as Augustine called it, his own days as a father behind him. Among the men who moved there with Augustine were poor laborers, too old to work for themselves, and enslaved men, many also aged, given to the church by their masters. In a separate building nearby, Augustine's sister led the church's female community, but he never entered it.[4]

In 396, Augustine was made bishop, and he began to spend his days attending to duties he dreaded and loathed. Once a week, from early morning to late afternoon, wrapped in a plain black robe, he perched on a hard chair and listened as residents of Hippo laid their grievances and disputes before him. Many of the conflicts focused on inheritance, grown children squabbling over the distribution of their father's estate. It was a bishop's responsibility to resolve such disputes before they opened into larger divisions within the Christian community, and to do so for free, and without taking bribes, and even on behalf of those who weren't members of the church, to help bring them into the fold. It was exactly the sort of work Augustine had hoped to avoid, and all the sitting, combined with fasting, gave him hemorrhoids so painful that for days at a time he could manage only to lie in bed and dictate.

On one such occasion, while bedridden, historians think, Augustine began to compose his *Confessions*, laying out the foundation of one of history's most consequential ideas of fatherhood: Original Sin, the cornerstone of modern Christianity.

The ideas of Saint Augustine gained such extraordinary influence in part because he lived in an extraordinarily perilous time. Thagaste was an agricultural backwater when Augustine was born in 354, at the start of a volatile period for the Christian church and the Roman Empire alike. When the Roman Emperor Constantine had begun to favor Christianity in 312, perhaps between 5 and 10 percent of the empire's population belonged to a Christian church. Over the next century, nearly half of Rome would become Christian.

But a bigger church was not necessarily a safer one. The growth of the church heightened internal divisions over questions of what it meant to be a Christian. At the same time, Christianity's official prominence made it a target for jealous factions within imperial politics, as well as for raiders who struck from outside, especially on the edges of the empire where Augustine lived, and where he died, in 430, as his adopted city of Hippo fell to raiding Germanic Vandals.

The work of priests and bishops—the work Augustine had wanted to avoid—was to keep their churches alive and growing. The task was endless because the hazards were ever present. In his day-to-day affairs, as Augustine confronted existential threats to the Christian church, he formulated practical survival strategies into enduring theological principles that would help to make the church what it aspired to be, universal, or "catholic"—and none more so than his concept of Original Sin, which was based on a new idea of what it meant for God to be a father, and for a man to be one, too.

The *Confessions* is addressed to God, but it was inspired in part by parents—parents in his church, Augustine's own parents, and his intimate personal experiences as a father.

At first, when Augustine was made bishop, he was especially dubious about one part of his job: the practice of baptizing babies. He himself had been baptized as an adult, after a somewhat wayward and lustful youth followed by an intense conversion experience and a painful struggle to commit to God. How could a baby make such a commitment? How could the baptism ritual be meaningful if the person being baptized didn't understand it?

Yet infant baptism had become particularly important to the growth of Christianity, in part because Romans were obsessed with the vulnerability of their children. According to pagan beliefs, children were especially susceptible to harmful curses, including the evil eye, which was often blamed for infant deaths. To keep their children safe, Romans tried to ward off the evil eye with the only thing they believed could match its power: the phallus.

The empire and citizens were bedecked with penis figures and symbols. Small phalluses shaped from gold, bronze, brass, bone, coral, antler, and other materials were strung onto necklaces, bracelets, and horse's harnesses. Phalluses were fashioned into delicate rings too small to have been worn by anyone but children. Boys especially were known to wear phallic pendants around their necks for protection. Phallic mobiles hung in the courtyards of homes. Phallic lamps lit interior rooms. Among the well-preserved ruins of Pompeii can be found phallic carvings and ornaments that were built into and painted onto the architecture of private and public buildings, like the bull horns of Çatalhüyük, and especially at dangerous spots around the city, treacherous corners, bridges, and passageways.[5]

This veneration of the phallus may have had a kinship to Roman law, one of history's most robust systems of patriarchal privilege. To be a Roman meant that you either were a father yourself or fell under the power of the father.

But even veneration of and deference to the phallus wasn't enough to keep families safe, in Pompeii or anywhere else. Perhaps half of Roman children died by age ten. Many Roman pagans believed that some chosen dead watched over the living with protection and blessings. For Rome, the pagan afterlife was a comparatively democratic institution, theoretically open to women and the poor, but not guaranteed to anyone, even the most powerful.

In 45 BCE, when Cicero's favorite daughter, Tulia, died after childbirth, the celebrated politician fled public life and holed up on a remote island estate. There he poured his despair into the writing of a lost masterpiece on grief, an attempt to put himself back together. When Cicero finally emerged from isolation and returned to Rome, he was determined to secure immortality for his daughter. He made plans to build her a columned shrine on the outskirts of Rome, near what is now the Vatican. But then Julius Caesar claimed the land for development, and that was the end of that. And if Cicero—who had amassed more power than anyone in Rome but Caesar—couldn't secure immortality for his beloved child, then who could?

Christianity promised something more definitive: salvation or damnation. As bishop, Augustine, who idolized Cicero, did not use the Christian "terror of the Last Judgement" to bully his congregation, as others would and do. Instead, he used it to enhance his power to set them at ease.[6] He understood that his congregation only wanted for their children the same thing that Cicero had wanted for Tulia, the same thing Augustine himself wanted for Adeodatus.

So Augustine gave them a way to get it. In the *Confessions* and beyond, he articulated a justification for infant baptism that he would develop into his idea of Original Sin. As Augustine conceived it, Original Sin is a patrilineal legacy of evil—a vision radically opposed to Aristotle's idea that fathers were the origin of good. According to Augustine, everyone is born with a sin inherited from the father, and the only way to get rid of it is to accept God as the Father and Jesus as his Son and be born again to him through baptism. Amid the peril and uncertainty of the late Roman Empire, Augustine redefined the meaning of fatherhood in a way that held out the appealing promise of eternal life, and in turn helped to transform the Christian church from one small and defensive sect among many into one of the world's most powerful institutions.[7]

The story of how God became a father in the Christian tradition begins with two sons. As historian Michael Peppard has described, only two men were known as the son of god in the ancient world, and by no coincidence their lives overlapped. The first was "the most honored and celebrated, most famous and powerful person in the world" at the time—Gaius Octavius, grandnephew of Julius Caesar, and best known by the honorific he turned into a name, "revered one," or Augustus. And the second man, of course, is also known by an honorific, the Greek word for "anointed": Christ.[8]

Gaius Octavius—the future Augustus—called himself the son of god because technically he was. Born in Rome in 63 BCE, he rose to power in 44 BCE, following the assassination of his great-uncle, the Roman Republic's "dictator for life." In a surprise, Julius Caesar's will posthumously adopted his nephew Gaius Octavius and designated him heir, and soon Gaius Octavius started calling himself Julius Caesar, too, continuing the line. When his dead uncle Caesar was subsequently deified in 42 BCE by the Roman senate, the same institution that had murdered him for acting too godlike, Gaius Octavius adopted the title son of god.

The fact that he was not his uncle's son was not an obstacle. Adoption, like divorce and remarriage, was common among the Roman elite, who "considered the bonds of family and kinship to be biologically based but not biologically determined."[9] This view was useful for plugging holes in succession and securing ancestral claims to property and status. Adoptees were incorporated into the adoptive father's gens, or ancestral line, without prejudice or disadvantage. In fact, often adoption was a leg up, for adopted family members had been chosen precisely because they were appealing in some way. Even so, just to be safe, Gaius Octavius eventually ordered the assassination of his seventeen-year-old adoptive half brother, Caesarion, son of Julius Caesar and Cleopatra, on the famous principle that two Caesars are one too many.

The killing was a step toward ending divisions within the Roman Republic that had bred decades of civil war, started by Julius Caesar himself. In 29 BCE, with an eye toward reinforcing the depleted ranks of the military, Gaius Octavius tried to push through a new law to increase the population by penalizing celibacy. The proposal proved highly unpopular with the elite, some of whom could not see the benefit of having more heirs, and before long it was withdrawn.[10]

Two years later, in 27 BCE, Gaius Octavius declared the Roman Republic an empire, ruled not by a class of patrician elites but by a single imperial family: Caesars. He adopted the names Augustus and "Caesar Imperator"—Augustus Caesar, the first Roman emperor—and tributes to him were raised across the empire: "To the Emperor Caesar, God, Son of God." The city of Mytilene, on Lesbos, where Aristotle had investigated the mysteries of reproduction, was ready to go further. They sent ambassadors to Rome to proclaim their worship of Augustus as a god, and added, for good measure, with an eye to Augustus's own shifting self-conception, that "if something more splendid should be found later on, the city's eagerness and piety will not neglect whatever can be done to deify him even more."[11]

But it was not clear that Augustus could be more deified. A story had circulated of his divine birth. According to this tale, at a time of many natural portents, including notable stars, Augustus's mother, Atia, had attended a ceremony for Apollo. In the middle of the night, inside the temple where the ceremony was held, Apollo assumed the form of a snake and slithered into her. Afterward an image of a snake appeared on her body, and though her husband was away fighting in Greece, Augustus was born about ten months later.

Being known as the son of Apollo didn't hurt Augustus's reputation, but he didn't need it. Many gods, including Apollo, had children, both divine and mortal. By some counts, Zeus (and his Roman counterpart, Jupiter) had more than one hundred children. The story of Augustus's divine birth did not trump his having been made the son of Caesar, deified by law.

The fundamental principle of Roman law was the *patria potes-tas*, the power of the father. Roman subjects either held the power of the father themselves or were subject to someone else's. This power gave a sharp edge to inherited Babylonian and Greek legal traditions, granting to the "paterfamilias," the oldest surviving male in a line, absolute authority over his household for as long as he lived. This grant included a monopoly of property rights in the household and, theoretically, the power of life and death over its members, his dependents. He could kill them if he wished.

Yet in practice there is no evidence that such powers were exercised. By all indications, Romans understood fatherhood to be a reciprocal obligation. The term "paterfamilias" seems to have been used primarily to refer to those who owned estates and enslaved people—implying less a paternal license to harm and more a paternal duty to cultivate resources, to increase the patrimony.[12] By one standard, the measure of a man was how many people "greeted him with the title of 'father'"—a group that would include not only his own children but also their spouses, as well as their grandchildren and beyond.[13]

More than money was needed to earn the title "father." Ultimately, "the honor of the paterfamilias depended upon his ability to protect his household, and in turn the virtue of the household contributed to his prestige."[14] Censors, public officials who conducted the census, monitored moral conduct within households. Fathers whose households showed, for example, evidence of excessive cruelty or lenience, insufficient deference to ancestors or officials, or disorderly sexual or financial affairs could be fined or even bumped to a lower political and social status. Similarly, fathers who failed to hand down a patrimony could be sued by their children.

For all these reasons, the exercise of unfettered *patria potestas* was not considered the most effective way to govern a household. Horace, Seneca, and Plutarch each emphasized the need for fathers to rule by praise and punishment both, including moral instruction, lest they turn their children against them.[15] Within the household, it's probably true that only the enslaved, who were tasked with most of the day-to-day labor of childcare, were frequently subject to physical punishment, their beatings serving as vivid reminders of the father's legal capacity for worse.[16]

By the time of Augustus the *patria potestas* was not as powerful as it once had been. Looking back on decades of civil war, Horace blamed the destructive conflict on "disrespect for the gods and a husband's lack of control over his wife's sexuality." Men, in his view, had been too weak to control willful and licentious women. Fathers had been too soft and undisciplined to win the obedience of their sons, who turned murderously against them. The age was condemned as indulgent, licentious, decadent: "a time of moral crisis, a period of tradition-breaking and boundary-crossing in many areas of life, including gender roles."[17] Horace wrote: "He who wishes to be father of this country must have the courage to curb vice."[18] Augustus wished to be.

Augustus was a paradigmatic autocrat in claiming that the ideal future for Rome existed in the past. Everything that had happened since had been worse—but he had arrived to reverse the decline. Augustus's vision of greatness wasn't utopian, like Plato's, or technocratic, like Aristotle's. Instead, the birth of the Roman Empire was celebrated as the fulfillment of the oldest values of the Roman Republic. Befitting an empire based on hereditary succession, these were modest household values. Augustus venerated "the strong and stubborn peasant of Italy, laboriously winning by the cultivation of cereals a meagre subsistence for himself and for numerous virile offspring."[19] To make Rome great, as it always had been, Augustus set out to restore the primacy of the family, which to him meant reestablishing patriarchal privileges and increasing the population by force of law.

Beginning in 18 BCE, marriage was legally required of men between twenty-five and fifty and women between twenty and fifty.[20] Children were implied. Men with children, even just one, were favored with tax advantages, while women with three or more children were rewarded with the opportunity to control their own lives and property, outside of the immediate authority of men. By contrast, childless men were punished with restrictions on inheritance and officeholding. There were even proposals to prevent them, along with childless women, from watching the games or going to the theater.[21]

At the same time, senators were prohibited from marrying women of ill repute, including ex-slaves, actors, the children of actors, and convicted adulteresses: "women whose chastity had proven uncontrollable."[22] Adultery was recast as a public crime rather than a private transgression. "If a father caught his daughter and her boyfriend in the act on family premises, he could legally kill his daughter on the spot." According to historian Robin Lane Fox, this was intended more as a threat than a real punishment. But if a father were to kill his daughter in such a case, then he could legally kill her suitor too.[23] A husband couldn't simply kill a wife who cheated on him, but he could imprison her suitor while he attempted to extract a confession. Those convicted of adultery stood to lose half their property. Spying on neighbors was encouraged.

As might be expected, these laws, which brought the emperor and the state directly into the household and infringed on the traditionally autocratic authority of fathers, proved highly unpopular—even within the imperial family itself.

In 12 BCE, Augustus's daughter, Julia, his only child, was widowed. Her father's law forced her to remarry quickly. To demonstrate his family's virtue, Augustus arranged what proved to be an unhappy marriage.

Ten years later, in 2 BCE, Augustus was honored as the "father of the fatherland." Similar honors had been granted to Julius Caesar and to Cicero as well, but in a slightly different form. They had each been recognized as the "parent of the fatherland," highlighting their caring qualities, probably in the hope of overshadowing their rough and ruthless ones. Augustus, as emperor, the patriarch of the ruling family that monopolized state power, was the father of the fatherland in a more concrete sense. So scandal ensued when, in the very same year as Augustus was honored as "father of the fatherland," Julia, then pregnant and long the subject of rumors and accusations, was charged with adultery and arrested under the law her father had established.

Julia is said to have admitted her guilt, brushing off the affair by explaining that she "invited another pilot only when the ship was full"—when she was already pregnant.[24] For Augustus this was not a compelling excuse. He had raised Julia to play a public role in his political life: to live as a "model of feminine chastity," spinning and weaving at home, conducting herself with "propriety" even in private quarters, where she was sequestered from encounters with strangers.[25] Augustus could not be seen trying to evade the exceptionally unpopular law he had made. He treated Julia's offense as not only a moral one but also a crime against the state—treason.

First Augustus forced through Julia's divorce. Then he exiled his daughter to a remote island, Pandateria. Traditionally fathers held the power to relegate their troublesome children to out-of-the-way, unappealing places for offenses as vague as "bad character." But Augustus's banishment of Julia was the first time, scholars think, that exile to a specific island was used as a criminal punishment.[26] Men were barred from Julia's island, with the exception of guards. Augustus demanded a full physical description of these guards, including complexion, distinctive marks and coloring, even tattoos and scars, to discourage additional transgressions and bastards.

Augustus's laws on marriage and family remained in place for three centuries, but their endurance was not necessarily a sign of their effectiveness. Rome was not morally reconstructed. And just as the Roman elite were relatively liberal on questions of adoption when it benefited them, so they were maniacal about paternity when it threatened to cost them money.

In Rome, by the baseline legal principle, a child's father was presumed to be its mother's husband, who was therefore responsible for the upbringing of the children his wife bore. This was a strong incentive for husbands to police the sexuality of their wives, though exposure of unwanted or unviable children was also practiced by the Romans as by the Greeks. According to the same principle, the children of unmarried women were automatically bastards, "filius nullius," sons of no father.[27]

Yet in some cases the legal presumption of paternity was not sufficient certainty. When paternity was in doubt, Romans went far beyond the Athenian practice of having a doctor attend the birth as a representative of the father. In Rome, suspicious births were held on neutral ground: ideally the house of a "very respectable woman" chosen by a state official. The families of expectant fathers and mothers alike sent representatives "to guard the womb"—searching any guests and keeping a watchful eye on the activities of the mother-to-be. The birthing room was to be well lit, and the event itself could be attended by up to five women from each party. Afterward, the newborn was subject to inspection by all concerned, to see if any resemblance to the father could be detected.[28] And to this anxious people, under the most suspicious circumstances, a child was born.

Anything that can be written about the life of Jesus can and will be disputed. He was a preacher from a rural corner of the Roman Empire who was tortured and executed, accused of having claimed to be king of the Jews. After his death, he came to be known both as the Son of Man and the Son of God. Historically both titles have been ambiguous and contested. The first, Son of Man, is taken by scholars to mean everything from "human" to "herald of the apocalypse" to "heavenly being."[29] There is no consensus in part because there need not be. "Son of Man" has long since been trumped by the second title, "Son of God," the meaning of which has been officially settled for nearly two thousand years, because it was the most divisive and therefore most important issue facing early Christians, up to and including Augustine.

"Son of God" is a common phrase in the Old Testament, where it does not refer to Jesus, who had not yet been born, but to the people of God, the Israelites. Later, when followers of Jesus used the term to identify their prophet as God's son, they made a novel claim: that "God is who he is by virtue of his relation to his Son."[30]

That is the core belief of Christianity: that God is the father of his son.

Yet early Christians did not agree on what that meant. Had God, the "father without a father," become a father only when he had a son? When exactly had God's son been born? Many of the first followers of Jesus contended that he had become the Son of God at the moment of resurrection. Others said it had happened at the moment of Jesus's baptism. Many early Christians believed, in other words, that Christ was a mortal who had been "adopted" by God and lifted to heaven, where he now lived at God's right hand.[31]

By the second century CE, these beliefs had raised questions of their own. One prominent Christian leader had suggested that there must be two Gods, for the severe God of the Old Testament was very unlike the caring, paternal one that Jesus described.[32] Others suggested that God must have made Jesus from a part of himself, that the two must be identical in substance. Especially controversial was the seemingly logical belief that if Jesus was God's son then he must be younger than God and therefore junior to him in some indefinite but essential sense—a potential demotion for Christ, his church, and its members.[33]

The competing theories mattered because they shaped the way people worshiped—who they worshiped and how. Early on, distinct Christian traditions took shape around diverse ideas about of the relation of Jesus to God. In particular, the "Gnostic Gospels" treated Jesus as a living person, viewed his resurrection as symbolic, drew connections to Eastern religious traditions, and recognized a "feminine element in the divine, celebrating God as Father *and* Mother."[34] To the extent that such differing traditions divided Christians from one another, they were a source of vulnerability. While Christians began as one small sect among many, as their numbers grew, and especially after AD 250, they were increasingly persecuted within the Roman Empire. After all, they honored Jesus, not Caesar, as the Son of God.

Under persecution, the priority of early Christians was security. The basic tenets of Christian morality evolved, in part, to promote unity and limit the internal conflicts and divisions that arise in the everyday life of a group, the perils of which were clearly demonstrated by the example of Jesus. Christians eagerly took up the project of family values from Augustus, and surpassed him with the zeal of converts. The church succeeded where the state had not, in establishing and enforcing the purportedly traditional moral codes of sex and the household that were supposed to underpin the empire.

Observing the success of the church, the Roman Emperor Constantine came to believe that Christianity could also be a unifying force across his increasingly fractious domain, especially if Christians stopped arguing with one another too. He ended official persecution and, without fully understanding why the nature of God's fatherhood was such a contentious issue, encouraged Christians to figure it out for themselves once and for all.[35] The result was the Council of Nicaea, which in 325 produced the Nicene Creed, a formal statement of God's fatherhood: the three-in-one, one-from-three model of the Trinity. There is one God who exists in three persons: Father, Son, and Holy Spirit. In 380 and 381, Nicene Christianity was declared the official, orthodox belief of the Roman Empire.

The authors of the Nicene Creed worked hard to piece together the unity they achieved in trinity: "We believe in one God, the Father, maker of all things visible and invisible; and in one Lord Jesus Christ, the Son of God, begotten from the Father, only-begotten, that is, from the substance of the Father, God from God, light from light, true God from true God, begotten not made, of one substance with the Father, through whom all things came into being, things in heaven and things on earth, who because of us humans and because of our salvation came down and became incarnate, becoming human. . . ." That is a lot of dependent clauses.

Historian Karen Armstrong has said the Trinity "was not a logical or intellectual formulation but an imaginative paradigm that confounded reason."[36] Yet there was an underlying logic to it: safety in numbers. The paradoxes it outlined were large enough to encompass almost everyone—except for those who would contest or deny that God had begotten a Son who had always existed, God from God, made incarnate in Mary by the Holy Spirit, born in the form of Christ, who was of the same substance and nature of God and was one with him. Those who denied the Trinity were out—in the language of the Creed, they were "anathematized"—no longer welcome within the church. At the heart of the growth, solidarity, and survival of Christianity was God's impossible, undeniable fatherhood.

Yet the elevation of the Trinity meant a demotion for the earthly family. Father, Son, and Holy Spirit now took precedence over father, mother, and child. God displaced Joseph, and Joseph raised no cry. The spirit came down and moved in Mary, its invisible movements rendering unnecessary the invisible movements of semen Aristotle had described.[37] The Gnostic idea of God's motherhood having been discarded, women were no longer made priests and bishops, for Jesus—that is to say, God—had welcomed no female disciples.[38]

*   *   *

As a bishop, the leader of a Christian church in the decades after the imperial adoption of the Nicene Creed, it was Augustine's job to demonstrate and clarify for his congregation, men and women alike, what worshiping the trinitarian God meant in practice.

The phrase "Original Sin" appears in his writing for the first time in 396, the year he was made bishop, and the year before he began working on his most famous and influential book. But it does not appear in the *Confessions* itself.

The *Confessions* is often described as the first memoir. The book may in fact be unique in the ancient world in telling the story of its author's life since birth. But this is also precisely what makes it, more than a memoir in the contemporary sense, an argument, or polemic—one made by showing rather than telling, but made in the service of a larger idea, nonetheless. To present his idea of Original Sin, Augustine told confessional stories not only about himself, but also and especially about his father and his son, who were both, by then, dead and defenseless.

The details were mercilessly unflattering. Augustine's father, Patricius, had been a minor imperial official in Thagaste, a pagan for most of his life, and, Augustine emphasized, not a good father, at least not in the Christian sense. Yes, Patricius had stretched his limited means to send Augustine to school, first in a nearby town, then in Carthage, the capital of Roman Africa. But in Augustine's telling, Patricius had done it for the wrong reasons. He wanted a son who was employable and upwardly mobile, one who would bring credit to his household, and reflect well upon him as pater-familias. Yet Patricius had made no allowance for the soul.

Patricius was thrilled when he and Augustine went to the baths together and he saw that his son was growing up, old enough to give him grandchildren. Even more people might soon call Patricius "father," and raise his status and standing. Augustine despised this crude talk, and his mother, Monica, a devout Christian, took his side. She did everything she could to make sure Augustine understood that God was his true father, not Patricius. Augustine's rejection of his father in favor of God would be the seed of much of his thought, and Monica would later be made a saint herself.

Yet Patricius was right. Not long after he visited the baths with his father, Augustine became a father, too, at age seventeen. At first, he wasn't a good one, either. At the time, Augustine and his partner, whose name is lost to history, had only just arrived in Carthage, where they had moved so Augustine could continue his studies. They weren't married or betrothed and had no plans to be. Their families didn't match—hers was of a lower class. But they were deeply attached to each other.

Augustine admitted in the *Confessions* that when his partner became pregnant, he didn't want to be a father. He wanted to be young, and spend his days with friends, and have carefree sex, and study and work and gain renown—all the things he would later condemn as lust and pride and sin. But Adeodatus, a "gift of god," had made his parents love him. As Augustine rose from student to teacher to one of the most prestigious posts in the empire, professor of rhetoric in Milan, the three lived together as father, mother, and son.

When Adeodatus was around thirteen, the hardest work of raising him over, Augustine's mother, Monica, decided that it was time for her son to finally make an advantageous and profitable marriage. Augustine deferred to his mother's wishes, but unhappily. Monica sent away Adeodatus's mother, never to be seen again, and Augustine felt that something had been ripped from his body. In accordance with Roman law and custom, which attached custody to fathers rather than mothers, Augustine kept Adeodatus with him in Milan.

But ultimately Augustine rejected the marriage Monica had arranged. He converted to Christianity, quit his teaching job, and tried to make a career as a writer instead. During this time, he and Adeodatus were constant companions. In 387, they were baptized together in Milan, and Augustine tended to his son's education, even featuring his precocious son in one of his earliest books, a group dialogue on the subject of happiness—which was to be found, Augustine proposed, among family and friends, in prayer, contemplation, discussion, and gratitude.

Adeodatus died about two years after his baptism, near the age of seventeen—the very age Augustine had been when his son was born. Around that time, Augustine wrote a book about what it meant to be a father, called *The Teacher*. The book was a dialogue between Augustine and Adeodatus; no other characters or voices intrude. Augustine insisted on its accuracy as a transcription of their conversation—it was likely composed just after Adeodatus's death—but its polish and precision suggest painstaking rhetorical crafting. Father and son choose their words with extraordinary care, and understandably so. Their conversation stands as a testament of belief, and evidence of Adeodatus's eligibility for eternal life in heaven.

Fittingly, the book's central question is how we know meaning and truth. Augustine and Adeodatus explore this question by taking up a line from Virgil's *Aeneid*. The line is spoken by Aeneas, Virgil's hero, who gives "all his care to his cherished son," and whose descendants, "the sons born from his sons," are the Romans.[39]

From Virgil's text, nearly ten thousand lines in total, Augustine chooses this line to discuss with Adeodatus: "If it pleases the gods to leave nothing of our great city standing." Augustine asks Adeodatus if he understands what it means.[40]

It's not just any line. Augustine pulled it from a pivotal moment at the beginning of Virgil's tale—Aeneas's account of the fall of Troy. First Aeneas describes rushing over to his parents' house with his wife and son during the siege to try to get his aged father out to safety. But his father refuses to go: "My father, whom I was so keen to carry to the mountain heights, the one I looked for first of all—refused to leave or suffer exile now that Troy was lost." It's a wrenching scene: everyone crying and pleading, the old man still resisting. "Did you think I'd run off, father, leaving you?" Aeneas asks. And then Aeneas delivers the line Augustine chose:

If it pleases the gods to leave nothing of our great city standing,
if this is set in your mind, if it delights you to add yourself
and all that's yours to the ruins of Troy, the door is open
to that death: soon Pyrrhus comes, drenched in Priam's blood,
he who butchers the son in front of the father, the father at the altar.

Yet even faced with threat of execution, Aeneas's father still refuses to go—until at last the old man sees a falling star that he interprets as a sign, and finally agrees to flee.

As violence closes in, Aeneas puts his father on his back, takes his son's hand, and leads them out of the city, only to lose contact with his wife on the way. He never sees her again or learns what has become of her, a loss that only heightens the meaning of his commitment to his father and son. Aeneas carrying his father on his back was the very ideal of *pietas*, the duty performed to gods and parents.[41]

In *The Teacher*, Augustine—who had also lost a partner, and Adeodatus a mother—asks Adeodatus to tell him how he knows the meaning of Aeneas's words to his father. When Adeodatus struggles to answer, Augustine explains that the difficulty was the point. He wants Adeodatus to understand the impossibility of knowing the truth with certainty except by knowing for ourselves. From this beginning, they work toward a larger lesson: We know that Christ is God's son not because he is called that, or because we are instructed to call him that, but only because we know it to be true internally. Such inner meanings and truths, Augustine explains, come from God. In other words, Augustine, the former professor of rhetoric, who had overseen Adeodatus's education, wasn't his son's teacher. God was. That was the lesson.

At the very end of the book, as Augustine concludes their discussion, he asks Adeodatus not what he has learned but rather what he knows to be true. Augustine emphasizes that the answer Adeodatus is about to give is crucial. The stakes could not be higher. If Adeodatus gets it wrong, then he must not be a true follower of God. He will not be ready to live forever with God in heaven. And he is about to die.

In the end, Adeodatus gives his father no reason to worry. "For my part," he says with his last words, "I have learned from the prompting of your words that words do nothing but prompt man to learn. . . . Moreover, I have learned that it is He alone who teaches us whether what is said is true." Augustine recorded his son's answer faithfully. Adeodatus had accepted God as the only teacher, in place of his father.

This was the solace that Augustine found after his son's death, and he never let it go. "There's a book of mine entitled *The Teacher*," Augustine reminded God years later, in the *Confessions*, "and in it my son himself converses with me. You know that all of his own thoughts are represented there. . . . In other respects as well, I found him to be astonishing: his mind actually made me shudder."[42] For this reason, Augustine assured God, the early death of Adeodatus had been a blessing. Before the brilliant boy could be caught up in the perilous world of adults, where he would be tempted by the lust that Augustine himself had struggled to break from, God had claimed him. "You quickly removed his life from the earth," Augustine thanked God, "and I'm more carefree in the memory of him, not fearing any danger to him in boyhood or in youth—fearing nothing at all for that person." Augustine had not been able to protect Adeodatus in life, and for that reason it was even more important to protect him in death.

In this way, Augustine had done his job as a father, delivering his son to the true fatherhood of God. Adeodatus was in heaven, and if Augustine could get there, too, they would never lose each other again. The transformative drama of Augustine's adult life is not that his beloved son died, but that he found a way to ensure that Adeodatus would live forever.

For Augustine, a father's ultimate deference to God was especially important because the first thing that fathers gave their children, inevitably, was sin, passed down from Adam.

One of the most unusual passages in the *Confessions* is Augustine's made-up account of his own infancy. Augustine's writing helped to establish the cradle as the literary starting point of autobiography, but for him this was much more than storytelling and character building: it was the foundation of his idea of Original Sin. Augustine reports that, as an infant, he cried at annoyances—and that, when there was no response to his cries, he turned "wrathful that my elders wouldn't submit themselves to me, and that free people wouldn't be my slaves, and I wreaked vengeance on them." He lashed out, "greedily drooling and wailing, toward his nurses' breasts . . . striking at and struggling to hurt" those around him, "bitterly angry" at those who were taking care of him.

Obviously, Augustine could not have remembered these incidents from his earliest childhood. But he knew they were true, and he knew what they meant, from his experience as a father. "I myself have observed (carefully enough that I know what I'm writing about)," he claimed, "a tiny child who was jealous, he couldn't speak yet, but his face was pale and had a hateful expression as he glared at the child who shared his nurse." The child Augustine had observed most closely—so closely that observations of this child could stand in for his first memories of himself—was Adeodatus. "Being weak, babies' bodies are harmless," Augustine wrote, "but babies' minds aren't harmless." They were just as sinful as anyone else's. "No one is clean of sin in your eyes," he affirmed for God, "not even a baby whose life on earth is only a day long." Newborns, too, needed baptism in order to be good.

What made a baby sinful? Not God, who had made the child, but not its sin. Nor anything that had happened in the first moments of life. The stories Augustine told about his father, himself, and his son in the *Confessions* were meant to show that sin was ancestral, inherited, and congenital. More specifically, it was patrilineal, passed from fathers to children through the act of sex. The sin of newborn Adeodatus had come from Augustine. The sin of Augustine had come from Patricius. And before that, it had come from Adam, the father of all mankind. Augustine's primary evidence for Original Sin, and his justification for infant baptism, were his memories of the infantile wickedness of his dead son.

Thirty years later, in *The City of God*, Augustine claimed that reproduction and procreation would technically have been possible without sin. God's design would have allowed Adam to relax on Eve's bosom, controlling his penis by rational exercise of will. But it had never happened—not then and not since. Eve had been fooled, but Adam had chosen lust. Since that day, Original Sin had been passed down by fathers to their children through the act of sex.

Original Sin recast fatherhood. Augustine shared with Aristotle a concept of patrilineal inheritance as the basic foundation of human life individually and collectively, but Augustine gave it the opposite meaning. For Aristotle, good came from fathers. For Augustine, evil did. Aristotle said that fathers created good children, good households, and a good society through favorable reproduction and the teaching of virtue. Augustine said that was impossible. Through the sex necessary for reproduction, fathers invariably passed on Original Sin. Nor could fathers teach goodness, which came only from accepting God's word and son. Remembering his dead son, fondly and proudly, in the *Confessions*, Augustine wrote: "I gave nothing to him but my sin." Everything else was God. Begetter, teacher, master, origin of all good: Augustine ceded to God the Father all the roles Aristotle had reserved for fathers.

Augustine's duties as Bishop of Hippo, the post he held for the last four decades of his life, involved not only building his church and community, but also defending it. At one time Hippo, located in modern-day Algeria, had prospered as an outgoing port for the agricultural products of North Africa, especially wheat, barley, olives, and figs. But its distance from the centers of power in the

Western Roman Empire had grown as those centers faltered. Out on the ragged edge, Hippo's population was increasingly vulnerable.

Rival Christian sects had thrived on the imperial frontier, some outgrowing Augustine's own church. To hold them off, Augustine honed his concept of God's fatherhood into a weapon that could be used against challengers who worshiped differently. Most of the more than one hundred books he wrote in his lifetime are arguments: for or against a particular point of doctrine and worship. Against those who believed that newborns didn't have to be baptized. Against those who believed that Jesus had been adopted by God instead of begotten. Against those who blamed the sack of Rome in 410 on Christianity, which, they claimed, had softened its defenses. As Augustine was drawn into doctrinal disputes and worked to fend off threats to his church, he articulated the ideas that lifted him to prominence as a theologian, secured him sainthood, and came to define Christianity.

Augustine's theology gained prominence in part because it was practical and useful in its time. His vision of Christianity was rooted in a muscular notion of the church's role in the world that was analogous to a father's role in the household, including the administration of physical punishments. Augustine wrote in *The City of God*:

> Those who are true fathers of their households desire and endeavor that all the members of their household, equally with their own children, should worship and win God, and should come to that heavenly home in which the duty of ruling men is no longer necessary, because the duty of caring for their everlasting happiness has also ceased; but, until they reach that home,

masters ought to feel their position of authority a greater burden than servants their service. And if any member of the family interrupts the domestic peace by disobedience, he is corrected either by word or blow, or some kind of just and legitimate punishment, such as society permits, that he may himself be the better for it, and be readjusted to the family harmony from which he had dislocated himself.[43]

The job of fathers, and of the church, was not just to shepherd people toward God, but to keep them from evil until they could see good for themselves. It was a sin not to stop someone from sinning. Violence could be a force for good, and synonymous with care and service. Through violence for the good of others, fathers would ultimately liberate themselves from the duty of ruling and the burden of authority.

Augustine developed this paternalistic logic into a doctrine of "just war." As he framed it, war was "an act of loving punishment" carried out by caring fathers in the name of God the Father, against fathers who gave their children sin but no hope of salvation.[44] "If we are taught to render help to orphans," Augustine reasoned, "how much more ought we to labor in behalf of those children who, though under the protection of parents, will still be left more destitute and wretched than orphans, should that grace of Christ be denied them?"[45]

This call for salvation by force and conquest positioned the church well for the fall of the Western Roman Empire, which Augustine could see out the window as he died amid the siege of Hippo.[46] For the next thousand years and more, upstart bands and states competing for territory, resources, and power went into battle in alliance with the Catholic church on behalf of God, as a mercy to their opponents, a grace for their enemies, a crusade, a holy war. And everywhere that armies marched and rode and sailed in the name of the Father, the Son, and the Holy Spirit, the cross, rather than the phallus, served as a totem of good fortune and divine blessings, raised high over town squares and strung around the necks of beloveds.

CHAPTER THREE

KING: Henry VIII

By the time Lord Henry Fitzroy awoke on the morning of June 18, 1525, preparations for his sixth birthday had been underway for months. Fitzroy was lodging with his godfather, Cardinal Thomas Wolsey, in Durham House, the grandest residence on London's Strand. Many of its best rooms overlooked the Thames, and a long central hall, lined by marble columns, led directly from an interior courtyard to the river. There, on the bank, well before nine, Fitzroy stepped aboard a barge and floated downriver to Bridewell, a relatively new palace, parts of which were even younger than he was.

In medieval Europe, where perhaps half of all children died by the age of five, six was considered something of a milestone year.[1] At this point, the hazards of early childhood were increasingly remote, infancy passed, and a proto-adulthood began. Now there was some expectation of contributing to the household by labor. Now, theologians said, children became capable of mortal sin.[2] For both reasons, six was often the age when children began to spend more time with their fathers, who were thought to provide more rigorous guidance. And in the case of Henry Fitzroy, bastard son of Henry VIII, the stakes of that guidance were higher than usual.

The day's events were set for the main hall at Bridewell, a striking space even by palace standards. Its vaulted gallery, hung with silks and perforated with large windows, shone with light. At one end, a golden canopy and chair had been positioned in the very center of attention. By the time Fitzroy and his party arrived, the room was already crowded with onlookers and attendants. To the right of the canopy stood the boy's godfather, Cardinal Wolsey, and a battery of clergymen. To the left, a squadron of nobles, knights, and squires. In the center, directly under the glowing gold fabric, waited Fitzroy's father, the king of England.

Henry VIII was over six feet tall, his chest nearly five feet around. By the end of his reign, the king would be so heavy and hobbled by gout that he had to be carried around his palaces in a chair. But at the peak of his vitality—on this occasion, he was just days away from thirty-four—his figure was monumentally imposing: handsome, strong, and vested with extraordinary power.

At the king's command, trumpeters raised their horns and announced the entrance of his son. Most in attendance would have struggled to see Fitzroy in the middle of his procession. First came the Earl of Northumberland, carrying a sword. Behind him, eight heralds bore a patent of nobility and a new coat of arms that had been designed by the king himself. Then, walking between the Earl of Oxford and the Earl of Arundel, came the miniature guest of honor, dressed in the robes of an earl. When he reached the end of the hall, six-year-old Henry Fitzroy knelt at the feet of his enormous father, who had decided to show his bastard son to the world, to see if he could make him king.[3]

*   *   *

The bloody story of Henry VIII's campaign to father a son has often overshadowed the fact that he had one all along. In most histories of the Tudors, Henry Fitzroy appears as a bit player, if at all. Justifiably, the focus is usually on the wives and advisors who paid for the king's mania with their lives. Yet at the time, during the most turbulent years of Henry VIII's reign, it hardly would have been possible to overlook Fitzroy, for the king saw to it that the boy was always on display. At least two years before Henry VIII became infatuated with Anne Boleyn, his hopes for succession centered on his son.[4]

"My worldly jewel," Henry VIII called his son, and unfortunately for Henry Fitzroy the king meant every word. He treasured the boy—in part because Fitzroy was living proof that he could father a son—and proudly put him on a pedestal for all of Europe to admire. Yet to a medieval king, a "worldly" jewel, no matter how lovely, was not as precious as one that could be said to be "divine."

In the days of Aristotle and Augustine, Henry VIII would have had no trouble making Henry Fitzroy king. Ancient history was crowded with handpicked successors, illegitimate princes, and adopted rulers, including Alexander the Great and Augustus Caesar. Yet by the late Middle Ages, the rules had changed. Alongside property, seed, and sin, another strand of inheritance now connected fathers and children: nobility of blood.

Like Aristotle's biology and Augustine's theology, nobility was entirely fictional and enormously consequential. And even as elaborate plans were set into motion around Fitzroy's sixth birthday, it was not at all clear if the king would be able to bend the conventions of nobility to the shape of his agenda. To do so, he would have to claw back some of the power of fatherhood from God and the church. That was a lot to ask, even of a king, yet the first half of the sixteenth century was a good time to try, and Henry VIII did have help, though sometimes inadvertent, from two other powerful fathers.

Henry Fitzroy had not been born to his part in this anxious drama of church and state. On the contrary, he was born a secret, at the start of the summer of 1519, perhaps June 18, though the precise date is obscure, because the birth was, by design.

The secrecy surrounding Fitzroy's birth had little to do with the affair that preceded it. As far as the sex was concerned, there was nothing to hide. Fitzroy's mother was a blond nineteen-year-old named Elizabeth Blount, often called Bessie, who had been born to an ambitious and upwardly mobile family. In 1512, when Bessie was twelve, her family won her a coveted role as maid of honor to Henry VIII's wife, Queen Catherine of Aragon. At court, Bessie's days were light domestic work, and her nights were parties and entertainments in the service of the queen—and, eventually, sometimes the king too.

For kings, ladies-in-waiting served as a favored pool of potential mistresses. This was a key part of the appeal of such positions for families like the Blounts. Should something pass between their daughter and the king or another powerful member of his court, their status would increase.[5] If she also made a marriage connection, so much the better. By all indications, Bessie's chances were as good as anyone's. One observer of court considered her "the beauty and mistress-piece of her time."[6]

Contrary to reputation, Henry VIII conducted "ludicrously few" extramarital affairs, especially measured against his obviously "vigorous" marital life with Catherine. After they were married in 1509, they were constantly together "at the hunts, the jousts, the feasts and the religious observances" that crowded their daily lives. [7]

Catherine of Aragon was the youngest child of the rulers of Spain. Initially, in 1501, she had been wed to Henry's older brother, Arthur, when both were fifteen and unable to speak the other's native language. Just months later, Arthur fell ill and died—still a virgin, Henry VIII long insisted, having failed to consummate the marriage. The connection to Spain had been a boon for the Tudors, and Henry VII was eager to salvage the alliance. The king is said to have considered marrying Catherine himself following the death of his wife. Instead, he promised Catherine to his younger son, the future Henry VIII, then around ten. At some point, the idea began to please the young prince. He held on to it even when his father turned skeptical. Not long after ascending to the throne in the spring of 1509—having secured special papal dispensation to get around the religious prohibition against close marriage, put in place in part to grow the church by forcing Christians to marry beyond their immediate communities—Henry VIII wed his late brother's widow.

Whether Henry and Catherine loved each other was not the question. What mattered was that they reproduced.

The title "king" derives, through lost connections of ancient German and Old English, from the same root as "kin." There is some evidence that the suffix "-ing" meant "son of": the king is the "son of the family."[8] But if the title itself implied ancestry, the office required heirs. In the Middle Ages, "sire," originally a title of distinction and nobility, also became a verb meaning "to father."[9]

A father was the one thing a monarch had to be, and not only for succession's sake. Without an heir, a king was thought to be more vulnerable to challenge. A failure of reproduction amounted to a failure of rule, and the Tudor dynasty especially needed buttressing. Its founder, Henry VII, had claimed the crown in 1585 by right of conquest, his victory at Bosworth Field putting an end to the War of the Roses, more than three decades of civil war in England that had spilled over into France. Even when the fighting was done, hostilities endured, in part because Henry VII took revenge on his enemies, seizing their estates to enrich his new dynasty, which was the target of early challenges and rebellions. With Henry VII possessing a tenuous claim to the throne by inheritance, the establishment of a royal Tudor bloodline was vital.

In the first decade of her marriage to Henry VIII, between 1509 and 1519, Catherine was pregnant at least six times. Five of the couple's children died before birth or soon after. Two of them had been boys, one of whom had lived long enough to be named Henry. The one child who survived was a girl, born in 1516 and named Mary. Even by the grim standards of the day, this was a troubling record, a source of great concern in England and among Catherine's relations in Spain.

It was not that Mary, or any woman, could not be a monarch. There was no fixed rule against a daughter inheriting a throne, just a strong belief that it was not a good idea. Ancient prejudices about female physiological and moral weakness were widely held by rulers and their subjects alike.[10] There were also ominous precedents at home and abroad. Small kingdoms, Burgundy for instance, had been overrun on the watch of female monarchs. In England in 1135, the crown had in effect been snatched from Matilda, the only legitimate child of Henry I. Passing the crown to a woman was virtually the last thing a precarious dynasty like the Tudors would have risked.[11]

By 1518, Catherine was pregnant again. Sex during pregnancy was thought to imperil the fetus, and Henry VIII may have had this in mind when he took up with Bessie Blount. There was no reason whatsoever to conceal the affair with Bessie, or the fact that it resulted in a pregnancy. Yet there was every reason to conceal the possibility that the pregnancy might not result in a living, healthy child. Henry was already on shaky ground.

Medieval science was perfectly aware that both men and women could be infertile. In the late fourteenth century, one treatise noted that "when sterility happens between married people, the males are accused by many people of not having suitable seed."[12] The influential monk and physiologist Albertus Magnus was among those who blamed most failures of generation on men. Nevertheless, women's bodies remained "at the center of questions about fruitfulness" within the household, and men often took on the job of monitoring the schedule and quality of their wives' periods.[13]

Lest he appear unfit to rule, Henry VIII had no choice but to blame Catherine for their sonlessness and hope that he would be proved right by Bessie Blount.

In the late fall of 1518, Catherine suffered another miscarriage, at least her third. Around the same time, Bessie Blount, newly pregnant, was installed in a high-walled, wide-moated house in Essex known as Jericho. The house was an Augustinian priory established in the twelfth century and recently acquired by the king. The monks stayed on even as Jericho gained a reputation as a place Henry maintained for private assignations. The logistics of Bessie Blount's stay in the winter and spring of 1519, and of the birth itself in June, were orchestrated by Cardinal Wolsey, then Lord High Chancellor and the highest-ranking figure in the English church. Wolsey managed virtually everything of importance for the king, but he had some special experience in this area, having fathered children of his own by mistresses, as many clergy did.

That summer, after months of secrets and worry, Bessie Blount gave birth to a healthy boy with red hair, just like his father's. Henry named the newborn after himself, twice. He named him Henry—as he had once before named a son—Fitzroy, derived from the French *fils* and *roi*: in effect, "Henry, son of the king." Cardinal Wolsey attended the boy's baptism and christening as his godfather. Afterward, Wolsey arranged for Henry Fitzroy to remain at first with his mother, who was from that point on referred to not as Bessie but instead as "the mother of the King's son," and who never returned to her position as a maid of honor.[14]

Like "Fitzroy," "bastard" has French origins, deriving from *bast*: pack saddle. Mule drivers were known to use this sort of saddle as a makeshift bed when they stopped in roadside inns, and not just for sleeping.

Bastardry had not been a terminal condition in the ancient world, nor in the many kingdoms that mushroomed up across Europe after the fall of the Roman Empire. Anglo-Saxon England was home to twelve monarchies in 600 CE, some of which had traditions of multiple kings reigning at once. These diverse monarchies were united in the tenth century, but even then there was no expectation that an Anglo-Saxon king would be succeeded by his eldest son, or for that matter by a son at all: successors were named.[15]

By the sixteenth century things had changed. In England, ironically, the changes had arrived with William the Conqueror, son of a king and a commoner—and known in his lifetime as William the Bastard.

The Norman Conquest started the clock on England as we know it. In January 1066, the Anglo-Saxon king Edward died without an heir. Across the Channel in Normandy, William the Bastard claimed that Edward, a distant relative, had promised him the English throne. Edward's brother-in-law Harold disagreed, and claimed the throne for himself. William crossed the Channel in September of 1066, killed Harold at the Battle of Hastings, and conquered England in a matter of months. He was crowned on Christmas. Every English monarch since has claimed a blood connection to the ruling line established by William I, first of the firsts.

Having conquered, William governed by spoils of two kinds. First, his soldiers were rewarded with noble titles and lands taken from Anglo-Saxons. Nobility was an ancient tradition. In Greece and Rome, powerful patrician ruling classes had traced their lines to the "first fathers." Far beyond the Greco-Roman world, societies shared a similar structure based on rank, but the rules changed somewhat in medieval Europe. One historian describes the form of nobility established after 1066 "as a hierarchy of doing, rather than being."[16] At the time, "doing" meant "fighting." A noble bloodline could be created by the king as a reward for military service. Victory in battle translated to land. Control over land translated to control over resources and labor, which led to wealth. Wealth meant the ability to raise and fund armies for more of all of the above.

The second beneficiary was the church. The pope was said to have blessed William's expedition across the Channel, guaranteeing those who killed in his name safe passage into heaven. In return, as king, William I appointed Norman bishops who helped to advance the agenda of the Vatican, which aimed to increase the power of the church in England by tightening laws around sex: ending priestly concubinage, marriage, and fatherhood, and making marriage rites a sacrament—a ritual monopoly of the church, like baptism. Once marriage was made a sacrament, children born outside it were delegitimized, and divorce was effectively outlawed for centuries.

The idea of legitimate birth fused the nobility and the church into a single system of government based on blood, land, title, and wealth: feudalism. On their grants of land, the Norman nobility founded houses. The house was different from the clan. A clan was horizontal: leadership and resources moved laterally within a group. A house was vertical. William introduced to England the Norman custom of primogeniture, in which the eldest son inherited everything, to bind blood to land over time. Lands and their titles were passed down from father to son, rather than across kin groups, prioritizing parentage over other kin relations. Families took on surnames derived from their most important property.

This was a strictly patrilineal system, for nobility was a masculine condition. Wives and daughters were noble only by their relationship to male titleholders.[17] A woman might be of noble birth, but she could not pass on to her children her title or the land and status it was attached to. Instead, wealth, power, and authority passed intact from one generation of men to another alongside indebtedness to the king: a fundamentally conservative system dedicated to the defense of what had been won and the possibility of winning more. But without a legitimate male heir to inherit land, title, and the obligation to serve the king, a noble line went "extinct."

Yet there had been exceptions, and there were a few loopholes. Henry VIII's own great-great-grandfather was a bastard who had been decreed legitimate by the pope after his previously unmarried parents wed.[18] Then again, that was why the Tudor claim to the throne by blood was so weak. As a practical matter, any royal claim was only as strong as its defense, and the strength of its defense was in part a question of how strong the claim itself appeared.

The legitimacy of Henry Fitzroy was not in dispute. His illegitimacy was plainly indicated even by the coat of arms his father had designed for him, sliced in two by a silver band: the "bend sinister," the mark dividing a bastard from the legitimate branches of his family. Yet ultimately the strength of Henry Fitzroy's claim to the throne was not a question of legitimacy. Instead, it was a question of how strong his father could make any such claim appear. And that was the reason for the big birthday party.

In the hall at Bridewell Palace, Henry VIII commanded his bastard son, kneeling before him, to rise. The king then turned to his friend and advisor Thomas More, who not long before had ascended to become one of the most powerful men in England. More was to play a crucial role in Henry Fitzroy's birthday celebration, and also in Henry VIII's campaign to redefine fatherhood, though at great cost to More's own family.

The king handed More a patent and bid him to read. Now a patent documents the invention of a thing. Then it announced the invention of a person. Men became noblemen either by paternity or by patent, deriving from the Latin *patere*, meaning "to display or present for inspection." The words "paternity" and "patent" bear a striking resemblance at the root and in their meaning, pointing back across thousands of years toward the historical conjunction of breeding, marking, and owning. This deep connection is expressed in colloquial language, too, in which the creator of a thing, whether the holder of its patent or the person most associated with its invention, is commonly known as its father.

As Thomas More read out the patent creating Henry Fitzroy the Earl of Nottingham, the king draped a girdle and sword over the boy's shoulders. It was the first time in more than three centuries that an English king had elevated a bastard son to the nobility. But Henry VIII was not finished.

After he was made an earl, Henry Fitzroy and his procession left the hall—and then the boy returned, now dressed as a duke, flanked on either side by the only men who then held that rank in England, the Duke of Suffolk and the Duke of Norfolk. Fitzroy again knelt before his father. When he stood, another patent was read out, making Henry Fitzroy, already Earl of Nottingham, the Duke of Richmond and Somerset. Duke was the highest rank in the peerage—a rank created in 1337, when Edward III made his six-year-old son, Edward, Duke of Cornwall, an office meant to be held by the heir apparent. But a double dukedom was something new.

To clarify Henry Fitzroy's position, two more grants were issued. One of "pre-eminence over all other dukes, except the King's legitimate issue"—meaning that Fitzroy was now the highest-ranking male in England, apart from his father.[19] And another as "Captain of the Town and Castle of Berwick upon Tweed and the Keeper of the City and Castle of Carlisle." For more than a century, that office had been held by every heir apparent. Fitzroy would now be addressed as the "right high and noble prince Henry." Afterward there were feasts and masquerades to fit the occasion.

It was a lot—arguably too much, perhaps not enough. The king had not made his son Prince of Wales, nor Duke of Cornwall, nor Duke of York, other offices traditionally held by heirs apparent. Having proven that he could father a son, Henry VIII may have been reserving the prime real estate for the legitimate heir whose eventual arrival was implied by Henry Fitzroy's existence. Yet these underlying tensions and ambiguities only underscored the questions that Fitzroy's creation had been meant to answer. And of all the people present at Henry Fitzroy's sixth birthday celebrations, no one was as keenly attuned to the ambivalence and absurdity of the occasion as Thomas More, who read the words that had made the boy a nobleman—that had made the king's son a prince.

Though he had the king's ear, Thomas More was in some ways an unlikely choice to read out Henry Fitzroy's patent. In the first place, he was a commoner. Second, and more damningly, he had become famous across Europe for writing a book critiquing nobility as a foolish, corrupt, and unjust institution.

More was born in 1478 to a prosperous London family. His father, John, was an accomplished lawyer and judge who had been knighted, and his mother's family owned a successful brewery. When More was twelve, he served an apprenticeship in the household of John Morton, a lawyer and cleric whom Henry VII made Lord Chancellor and then Archbishop of Canterbury, and who taught More to see religion and law, church and state, as inseparable. In 1492, More went to Oxford, on scholarship, to study Greek and Latin. Two years later, at the age of sixteen, he returned to London to study law, joining his father's chancery, the Lincoln Inn.

Even as a young man, More was old-fashioned. He made his studies into a form of spiritual discipline, wearing a hair shirt to keep himself awake over his books. He took a special interest in the works of Augustine, even giving a course of lectures on *The City of God* in 1501, the same year that he qualified as a full member of the bar. At the start of his law career, More lived next door to—possibly in—a monastery, where he often attended prayers. More contemplated joining a religious order himself, but in the end, according to his close friend Erasmus, the Dutch theologian and philosopher, he couldn't let go of the idea of marriage and children. (Actually, Erasmus put it more crudely than that.)

Owing to the influence of Augustine and the Catholic church, all sex, and therefore all marriage, had acquired the stain of Original Sin. Playing it safe, elite families often shepherded their children into the celibate life of the religious orders, as monks and nuns: the surest path to heaven. In cases when the temptation of sex was too strong for celibacy, the church prescribed family life, administered in regular doses of sacrament: marriage, baptism, communion, confirmation, confession.

Thomas More married in 1505, and in the next six years he and his wife, Jane, had four children, three girls and a boy. When Jane died unexpectedly, More quickly remarried, and his new wife, Alice, immediately moved in and began to care for his young children. More himself oversaw their educations: Greek and Latin, philosophy, theology, logic, and astronomy, for girls and boy alike.

More once instructed his son that his role was to delight his father without ever offending him. More himself kept to the same standard. Even as an adult, whenever More happened to pass his father in the halls of state, he would always kneel down before the older man, a distinguished judge whom More nonetheless outranked, and ask his blessing. At home, More lavished all his children with gifts, and when he had to discipline them, he beat them with peacock feathers.[20]

In 1515, Henry VIII sent More on an important diplomatic mission to Brugge (or Bruges). His assignment was to renegotiate the wool trade between England and the Low Countries. The deal was a proxy for the alliance with Charles, cousin of Catherine of Aragon, soon to be made king of Spain and Holy Roman emperor. For six long months More was away from home. Missing his children dearly, he began to write what would become his most famous book. More called it *Concerning the Best State of a Commonwealth and the New Island of Utopia*, but it's generally known simply as *Utopia*: a play on the Greek terms for "good place," *eu topos*, and "no place," *ou topos*. A good place that doesn't exist.

Utopia was inspired by the European encounter with the lands already then known as America. More had read the accounts attributed to Amerigo Vespucci, contested and at least partly discredited almost as soon as they had begun to circulate in Europe. More's brother-in-law John Rastell was among those eager to raise funds for an English expedition to the "New Found Lands."

More's imaginative journey to Utopia was risky in its own way. His book is an account of a voyage that discovers in the "new world" a second chance for the old one, in the shape of a thriving island. In Utopia, as in Plato's Republic, property was held in common, not monopolized by wealthy families. Similarly, More's commonwealth was secured by a social order that extended ideas of fatherhood beyond the household. But sexually speaking, Utopia was no Republic. Unlike Plato's citizens, Utopians made the nuclear family their basic social unit, monogamous marriage its generative core. Divorce was available by mutual consent only after an official investigation, for fear that men and women would be eager to find a new spouse if they thought it was easy to do. Perpetrators of adultery were to be punished with "the strictest form of slavery," and two-time offenders were executed.[21] One way or another, marriage was meant to end in death.

Order at home was the foundation of the island's prosperity, and prosperity was the key to order at home. Fathers directed a household's economic activity: "Here the head of each household looks for what he or his family needs," More imagined, "and carries off what he wants without any sort of payment or compensation. Why should anything be refused him? . . . Why would anyone be suspected of asking for more than is needed, when everyone knows there will never be any shortage." As a safeguard, an extra layer of governance was set up beyond the household. Magistrates were also called fathers and were expected to act as such: in other words, tending to the commonwealth, in the interests of all.

More's idea of Utopia, conjured out of the doldrums of an interminable work trip to Brugge, was an island paradise where home and work were identical, and father was a special rank in the family and the community alike. And it wasn't only that Utopia was organized around the power of fathers: life on the island also had very specific benefits for them. In Utopia, More wrote, "no man is bothered by his wife's querulous entreaties about money, no man fears poverty for his son, or struggles to scrape up a dowry for his daughter. Everyone can feel secure in his own livelihood and happiness, and of his whole family's as well: wife, sons, grandsons, great-grandsons, great-great-grandsons, and that whole long line of descendants that gentlefolk are so fond of contemplating." In Utopia, as in Saint Augustine's *City of God*, one of the books More most admired, fathers were liberated from the burden of ruling, for everything was already good. This fanciful vision, which some readers mistook for a factual description of a place that actually existed, made More famous across Europe.

In a roundabout way, More's fame made him the perfect choice to announce Henry Fitzroy's ascendance to the world. Coming from a master storyteller capable of convincing men that Utopia was real, who also happened to be a prominent critic of adultery and hereditary privilege, the words that created Fitzroy as a prince might sound especially true. More than once, when Henry VIII had something to say that had to sound just right, he asked Thomas More to say it.

So it was that when Henry VIII, seeking favor with Rome, wanted to write a book condemning the rebel monk Martin Luther's attacks on the pope, he got More to help. And when Luther responded with his own book calling Henry "a damnable and offensive worm . . . without a spark of human reason alive in him," the king instructed More to answer in kind. Someone "should shit into Luther's mouth," More wrote in Latin in 1523.[22]

Along with Thomas More, Martin Luther, father of the Protestant Reformation, was the second man who, at times unwittingly and unwillingly, helped Henry VIII redefine the power of fathers.

Though they came to be mortal enemies, Luther and More had a lot in common: a reverence for Saint Augustine, fathers who wanted them to be lawyers, and a talent for profane insults sharpened by a lifetime of self-laceration. While Thomas More learned to punish himself from books, Martin Luther had been taught by his father.

Luther was often keen to point out that his father, Hans, had been a tyrant, and his mother, Margarete, was no saint, either: He was a copper miner, she ran a household of eight children, and they both beat their son, sometimes severely. Rather than heed their wishes and pursue a profitable career in the law, Luther did what Thomas More had not and entered an Augustinian monastery, where he sometimes spent six hours a day in confession. His parents were not impressed. "You learned scholar," Hans complained at a dinner in honor of his son's ordination, "have you never read in the Bible that you should honor your father and your mother?"[23] For years they were estranged, reconciling only after Martin and his wife named their first son Hans.

The story of how a monk came to have a wife and child—in fact six of them—is the story of the Reformation. Luther wholeheartedly accepted Augustine's belief in innate human sinfulness, but he rejected celibacy as a false solution—the easy way out, like buying your way into heaven—and ultimately quit the monastery.

Nowhere had the Bible said anything about vows of celibacy, about monks and nuns, or even about the pope, for that matter. On the contrary, God's word had been fruitfulness. The frequent, if not ubiquitous, failures of priests to heed their vows only proved that celibacy was unnatural. Luther said it was like trying to keep "water from wetting."

This applied to men and women both. "Unless she is in a high and unusual state of grace," Luther wrote, "a young woman can do without a man as little as she can do without . . . other natural requirements. Nor can a man do without a woman."[24]

In 1523, a group of nuns living in a convent in Nimbschen, Germany, near Leipzig, risked prison and worse to get a letter to Luther, asking for his help in planning their escape. Luther, then teaching in the university about thirty miles away in Wittenberg, arranged for a friend to smuggle the twelve nuns out among the barrels in his fish wagon.

When the nuns arrived in Wittenberg, Luther tried to send them home to their parents. But, having broken their vows, the nuns weren't wanted, and they didn't want to go anyway. Luther then paired them off with his university colleagues in marriage. Only one of the escaped nuns, twenty-four-year-old Katharina von Bora, is known to have protested. She didn't like Luther's matchmaking but made it known that she wouldn't mind marrying Luther himself.

Despite his theological advocacy of marriage, Luther had avoided it. At forty-one he lived in constant expectation of being arrested for heresy or worse, and he paid no mind to housekeeping. His straw bed, untended and unchanged for years, had gone dank with mildew. Undeterred, Katharina married him on June 13, 1525, the week of Henry Fitzroy's sixth birthday. A year later, their son Hans was born.

Martin and Katharina came to believe that "God had ordained them to be parents."[25] This was not quite as sweet as it may sound. Luther viewed celibacy as a form of cheating, for it dodged the exalted work that God intended man to perform: parenting. What made raising children so holy was its awful difficulty. The lower the service, the greater the exaltation. "When a father goes ahead and washes diapers or performs some other mean task for his child," Luther wrote in 1523, the year he helped Katharina escape her convent, "God, with all his angels and creatures, is smiling."[26] Rejecting the celibate family of the Catholic church, Luther made homes into churches, families into congregations, and parents into clergy: "Most certainly father and mother are apostles, bishops, and priests to their children, for it is they who make them acquainted with the gospel."[27]

Luther may have equated mothers and fathers with clergy in his writing, but in practice fathers presided over Protestant religious life. Vastly more men had been taught to read, and moreover women were often tarred with blame for Adam's sin. In Protestant homes, "daily public readings from the Bible by the head of household" became "the main vehicle of religious expression."[28] Luther never expected that the elevation of fathers to priestly roles at home would make for a life of joy and ease and peacock-feather spankings. On the contrary, historian Lawrence Stone concluded, "the identity of the husband and father with the family religious confessor placed severe strains on many wives and children, who found themselves trapped in a situation where they had no one to turn to for escape or alternative counsel."[29] The Protestant home was like a church or convent, but harder to leave.

Martin Luther's own household was no exception. "I readily believe that my son turned soft through the words of his mother," Luther wrote to his son Hans's teacher. "Order him, therefore, to curb that womanish feeling, to get accustomed to enduring evil, and to not indulge in that childlike weakness. For this is the reason that he has been sent away, namely, that he learn something and become hardened."[30] Luther only meant to help. Hans was around seventeen, and nearing the age of fatherhood himself.

For centuries, Luther's approach to fatherhood has been summed up by a grim epigraph: "I would rather have a dead son than a disobedient one." There is no evidence that Luther actually said this, yet he was said to have said it, in a talk: "The Discipline and Punishment of Children." After Luther's death in 1546, his followers spread the remark around as an advertisement for the Protestant church.[31]

The motto of Henry Fitzroy's household, probably composed by his father, was much the same: "Duty Binds Me." So it did. Despite the boy's exalted titles—duke, duke, and earl—there was no expectation that he, at age six, would be able to fulfill his duty to raise an army. Yet there was every expectation that an army might be raised on his behalf. This was exactly the message that Henry VIII meant to communicate by sending his son to Sheriff Hutton Castle, outside of York, and putting him in command of all military operations in the unruly north of England, which the king hoped to bring under greater, more taxable control.

In July 1525, a few weeks after the ceremonies at Bridewell, the little prince was sent north with a battalion of attendants and advisors, plus their horses, all dressed in blue, yellow, and white, the colors of Fitzroy's noble houses. Packed and piled into trailing carts were all the practical makings of a new household: pots and pans, table linens and settings, Fitzroy's extensive wardrobe, plus a knight's armory, more than a hundred sheaves of arrows and nearly seventy javelins. Hauling heavy weapons and seeking maximum visibility, the procession crawled north through the countryside. Fitzroy started out riding in a luxurious crimson and gold carriage strung between two horses, but this displeased him, and after a few miles he switched to his pony.[32] The trip to York took the better part of a month.

Fitzroy couldn't yet fight for the king, but he could act as if he were preparing to. The nobility had developed elaborate protocols by which heirs could demonstrate military power at a safe distance from the battlefield. The ability to command was expressed in a thousand intricate ways that added up to courtliness, civility, manners, sophistication, chivalry. Deft dancing and musicianship. Proper use of a fork. Broadness of mind. Fluency of speech. The right clothes, worn the right ways. Posture. Carriage. Being a gentleman. All signaled money and armies at the ready. All could be taught and were.

As Henry VIII was deciding on the parameters of his son's education, he instructed Thomas More to summon his three daughters to
court, to demonstrate the usefulness of Greek.[33] More's daughters
impressed the king, so Fitzroy was also assigned Greek. Graduates
of Cambridge University were teaching him to read and write in an
elegant script, and they reported to the king that his son was the
best student they had ever seen. The boy learned French, even then
a marker of sophistication. He was encouraged to speak without a
lisp. Fitzroy was taught dancing, archery, jousting, and hunting. He
kept fine horses, dogs, and hawks. The king fixed up his son's castle,
patching its leaky roof, rebuilding its crumbling walls, mending its
iron gates, renovating the aging fortress into "princely lodgings."[34]

The king had an interest in showing off how much he cared for
his son. The shine Fitzroy acquired through his expensive education and lifestyle increased his value in the marriage market. In
February 1527, when the boy was not yet eight, English diplomats
in Spain were exploring the prospects for a marriage between Fitzroy and Catherine de Medici, the niece of the pope, who might
then look sympathetically on the issue of the king's own marriage
troubles, already bubbling. Word came back that the pope would
approve of the match.[35]

At the same time, Cardinal Wolsey, Fitzroy's godfather, was
trying to set the boy up with the Infanta Mary of Portugal, niece
of the Holy Roman emperor, Charles V. The match would perhaps help England gain access to America, which had been divided
between Spain and Portugal in the 1498 Treaty of Tordesillas. To
make Fitzroy's case, English diplomats emphasized that the prince
"may be easily by the King's means exalted to higher things."[36]

Still another possibility was marrying Fitzroy to his half sister
Mary Tudor, on the principle that two half siblings would make

one complete plan of succession. At the time religious law held that sex between brother and sister in the missionary position was a lesser sin than any alternative position with any other partner, lest pleasure take priority over the business of conception.[37]

Yet ultimately the king's pride in his son seems to have only bolstered his belief that he could and should have a better heir. In 1529, Henry might have married Fitzroy's mother, Bessie Blount, who had been recently widowed. Combined with an annulment of his marriage to Catherine, a marriage to Bessie Blount would have made a solid case for the legitimacy of Fitzroy. Henry VIII liked his former mistress, and had often favored her with grants and gifts, but he did not want to marry her. He did not want to elevate his "worldly jewel" as much as he wanted to marry Anne Boleyn, the youngest daughter of one of his top diplomats, Thomas Boleyn. Anne, who had also been one of Catherine's ladies-in-waiting, had made clear that she would not be a Bessie Blount. She would not go to bed with the king until she was queen.

In November 1532, Henry VIII and Anne Boleyn wed in secret. Soon she was pregnant, and at the end of January they married again in public. For the next four months, the king was married to two women. In May—citing a precedent that predated the Norman Conquest, before which, a royal team of scholars had found, the pope had had no legal authority in England—Henry had his marriage to Catherine, which had required papal dispensation, annulled. That summer, the pope condemned Henry's solution. In September, Anne gave birth—to a daughter, Elizabeth.

Pushing back against the pope and the Catholic church, Henry signed the Buggery Act, making specific sex acts subject to civil rather than religious law; they were now effectively crimes rather than sins. In principle, the law applied to all nonreproductive sex. In practice, it was used to criminalize anal sex among men, the penalty for which was death—as it remained in England into the nineteenth century. Groups of unmarried men who lived together, namely religious orders, were easy targets. When monks were prosecuted, their property was confiscated by the Crown. Authority and resources were shifted from church to state.

Anne Boleyn was also busy with her own plots. Immediately after the birth of Elizabeth, Anne arranged to marry Henry Fitzroy to one of her ladies-in-waiting, the daughter of the Duke of Norfolk. Sealed in November 1533, it was a local marriage, not a diplomatic one that would have increased Fitzroy's standing as an heir. By January 1534, Anne was pregnant again.

That spring, the king prepared for the arrival of a new heir by signing the Acts of Succession. The law declared that the crown would belong to: "The first son of your body between your Highness and your said lawful wife Queen Anne." In the absence of a son, then the crown would go to "the eldest issue female, which is the Lady Elizabeth now princess." By the summer, Anne had lost the baby.

Without the new male heir he had envisioned, the king had good reason to worry about potential challenges to his rule. The pope was preparing to offer his blessing to any aspiring king of England who could take the throne by force. Henry VIII drew up a loyalty oath to compel his advisors to honor his stated plan of succession.

Thomas More, who by then had become both Lord High Chancellor of England and a close friend of the discarded Catherine of Aragon, knew that he would be called to take the oath. He knew that he would refuse to put the king before God. So More got ready to resist. He gathered his family for a big dinner. In the middle of the meal, there was a knock at the door, and one of the king's messengers came in and summoned More to take the oath. His family was hysterical with fear. But then More announced that he had staged the scene, playacting this fateful moment to get his family ready for the real thing.[38]

When the real day of oath taking finally came, More left his house early in the morning, without saying goodbye to his wife and children. Ordered to swear to the lawfulness of the king's marriage and the succession of Anne's children, More offered to swear to succession only. The king insisted on everything or nothing. More was condemned to die.

Having failed to give birth to a boy, Queen Anne also felt time running out. She protested her husband's increasingly frequent habit of hanging around with women at court. In response, he told her to "remember where she came from," which was precisely what she was worried about.[39] Already Henry had raised the possibility of divorcing her. At the end of 1534 Parliament confirmed Henry's self-appointment as the "Supreme Head of the English church." That year, the king requested that Henry Fitzroy spend the winter holidays with him.

Fitzroy was back in favor. In May of 1835, Henry VIII sent his son to attend the torture and execution of three monks charged with violating the king's new religious authority. Two months later, Fitzroy sat in for his father ceremonially, taking the "Sovereign's Place" at the feast of Saint George, a major occasion at court. The king was absent because Anne was pregnant again and facing possible complications. Henry was expecting the child to be a boy, but the baby was stillborn in the eighth month. Just over a year later, on the day of Catherine of Aragon's funeral, Anne suffered another miscarriage.

Henry Fitzroy was then sixteen years old. He was educated, accomplished, sophisticated, chivalrous, and popular. Most importantly, he was a man. His stepmother's failure to deliver a living male heir had been good for him. Yet Fitzroy also had something to lose if Anne was cast aside, because his father might try again.

According to one account, the night before Anne's arrest for adultery, Fitzroy went to say good night to his father. When Henry VIII saw his son, he broke into tears. They were tears of relief, the king explained, for Fitzroy and his half sister Mary had so narrowly escaped the fate that their stepmother had designed for them: poisoning.[40]

When Anne was tried by the peerage, Fitzroy was excluded from the jury, but he did attend her execution. It was said that when his stepmother was killed "a malign smile seemed to pass over [Fitzroy's] features."[41] Eleven days later, on May 30, 1536, his father married Jane Seymour.

Nevertheless, Henry Fitzroy was on the rise. In June, the king forced his daughter Mary, against her own interests and her Catholic faith, to renounce the authority of the pope, declaring that her parents' marriage had been unlawful and retroactively making herself a bastard too. In early July, a Second Succession Act was passed establishing the king's marriage to Anne as unlawful and its issue, Elizabeth, illegitimate. In this status she now joined her half brother and half sister. All the king's children were bastards. Yet the Second Succession Act added a provision not included in the first: the king now held the sole and unlimited authority to designate whomever he chose as heir, either by patent or by his last will.[42] Of the three bastards, Fitzroy, who had recently turned seventeen, appeared to be first in line. When this was noted at court, the king did not dispute it.

But just as a new path to the throne opened before him, Fitzroy fell ill with a respiratory infection that may have been tuberculosis, or plague, or something less fearsome but still serious. When Henry VIII left London for the summer in July, he left his son behind to recover. But in this, too, the king's plans were foiled. By the end of the month, Henry Fitzroy was dead.

Henry Fitzroy's death was an echo of his secret birth. In life, he had been put on display for all to see. But once dead he became again a potential liability for his father.

Fearful of being seen as heirless and vulnerable, Henry VIII tried to hide his son's death from the world. He ordered Fitzroy's father-in-law, the Duke of Norfolk, to arrange a clandestine burial. The body was wrapped in lead to contain the smell of decay and loaded in the back of a farm wagon under straw. Two men who had been employees of Fitzroy's household were assigned to accompany the undistinguished vehicle on its journey to a rural priory, following at a distance that did not draw attention to its cargo or purpose—no carriages, no banners, no colors, no wardrobe, no plates, no silver, no arms, no ponies.

Yet even the most elaborate concealments could only be temporary. When word of the prince's death got out, Fitzroy's half sister Mary was reportedly elated at her good fortune and increased prospects. Then, only days after his son's sorry funeral, the king changed his mind. He sharply rebuked the Duke of Norfolk, threatening him with imprisonment and execution for having arranged such an unworthy burial. When his anger cooled, Henry arranged for his son's body to be reburied in Framingham Church, a traditional gravesite for the family of Norfolk.[43]

In July 1536, the month Henry Fitzroy died, Henry VIII made his first statement of doctrine as the head of the Church of England. In August, the king began to dissolve the monasteries, clearing out the remains of the pope's authority in England. Henry VIII and his former enemy Martin Luther had found common ground on the question of a father's authority to interpret God's word in his own house—or kingdom. As church properties were confiscated and sold off, the military budget of the Crown grew. Thousands of people were displaced—not only members of religious orders themselves, but also the many poor people who had depended on the church for aid.

Before the end of the year, this economic discontent fed into the largest English rebellion of the age: the Pilgrimage of Grace, centered in the north, around York. Thousands of protestors drove out the new tenants from the properties seized from the church and reinstalled the holy orders. As many as forty thousand people gathered to deliver demands to the king, highlighting the comparative weakness of the royal forces.

In 1540, to shore up the support of the elite, Henry signed the Statute of Wills, which made it possible for the first time since the Norman Conquest to pass down property to heirs by "devise of will" rather than the previous rules of inheritance, such as primogeniture. Henry had remade the alliance of church, state, and family that had taken shape since 1066 by putting himself in charge of all three, an expansion of the power of fathers that had an impact far beyond the royal household. Rich men across England and its colonies—having now gained the authority to interpret the Bible for their families and to distribute their estates as they saw fit—claimed a share of the singular patriarchal power Henry VIII had made his own.

So began an age of "paternal absolutism" in Europe.[44] "The law which enjoins obedience to Kings," wrote Sir Robert Filmer, seventeenth-century defender of absolute monarchy and author of the appropriately titled book *Patriarcha*, "is . . . 'Honor thy Father.'" In 1689, John Locke, who saw Filmer as a slimy flatterer, pointed out that in fact the Bible said "and thy mother," and that the very existence of the rule underscored the fact that children couldn't be expected to defer to their parents forever.

CHAPTER FOUR

NATION: Thomas Jefferson

Thomas Jefferson could be obsessive about detail when a subject caught his interest, especially natural history. He recorded the weather twice a day for forty years, noting faithfully that on the afternoon of July 4, 1776, when the Declaration of Independence was adopted by the Second Continental Congress, it was a fair seventy-six degrees in Philadelphia, though clouds were moving in. From 1801 to 1809, while he served as president of the United States, Jefferson also kept a chart of the earliest and latest appearance of every vegetable in the market in Washington, D.C.[1] Yet by comparison he had very little interest in the origins of his own family, the original Jeffery and son.

One of the only times Jefferson showed any active curiosity in his ancestry was in the winter of 1771, not long after he had started courting the wealthy widow Martha Wayles Skelton. That February, Jefferson wrote to a friend in London, consigning to him two hogsheads of tobacco and asking if he might search "the Herald's office for the arms of my family." Jefferson already had a copy of what he had "been told were the family arms," but worried that he had no authority to back up the claim.[2]

Fifteen years later, in March of 1786, those worries about authority had disappeared. While living in Paris as the ambassador of the United States to France, Jefferson traveled to London on diplomatic business. Officially he was there to negotiate a treaty with Morocco, but unofficially the trip turned into a shopping spree. Among Jefferson's many purchases in London was a seal he had made of his own coat of arms, to stamp on letters and documents. The coat of arms he used was identical to those of an English family of Jeaffresons, with one notable exception.[3] The arms of the English Jeaffresons featured a motto that read: "Virtue survives death." Aristotle, Augustine, and generations of fathers would have agreed. Yet Thomas Jefferson of Virginia went in a different direction, with a motto he seems to have written himself: "He who gives life gives liberty."[4] To father was to free.

That phrase tells the story of a transformation in fatherhood that is at the heart of not only Jefferson's own life, but also the history of the United States, a nation founded on the "revolutionary insight" that "the title of the father was transferable."[5] Jefferson's generation did not exactly think of themselves like many think of them now, as founding fathers. But, inspired by the parenting advice and political philosophy of John Locke, they relied on newly flexible ideas of fatherhood to create and govern the new United States.

Jefferson especially stood out among the nation's founders for the way he manipulated fatherhood to fit his own personal and political desires. Whether he was asserting generational independence from the overbearing patriarch King George, claiming the title of "great father" for himself when he wanted to send a message of benevolent power over American Indians, or denying paternity of his enslaved children when acknowledging them would have cost more than he was willing to pay, he used fatherhood to shape the nation as well as his own home and family.

The familiar story of the birth of the United States is that Puritans migrated across the Atlantic in the first half of the seventeenth century to escape religious persecution. In fact, they did it for their children. Their primary motive was "to protect their children from [the] moral corruption" they perceived all around them in England, where the king had been ruling church and state according to his own priorities, the Puritans thought, rather than God's.[6]

Once settled in New England, Puritans went to extraordinary lengths to restore an idealized version of the old England. Like Aristotle in Athens and Caesar Augustus in Rome, their strategy was patriarchy: "the right of domination called generation," as Thomas Hobbes put it. In the seventeenth century, the Puritans wrote more manuals on child-rearing than any sect in the wider European world, and all were addressed to fathers.[7]

Puritan fathers were God's front-line troops. In 1642, a Massachusetts statute "required heads of households to lead their households in prayers and scriptural readings; to teach their children, servants, and apprentices to read; and to catechize household members in the principles of religion and law," just as Martin Luther had prescribed. Fathers held a monopoly over property ownership in the household, and used it to control their children, including their trades and marriages. Kin groups generally lived close together, and over successive generations they grew to populate entire villages and towns where the conduct of each household was a public affair of the utmost significance to the godly favor and survival of all. To the Puritans, "independence" meant living free from outside interference in their religious community.

Thomas Jefferson's Virginia, named for the virgin Queen Elizabeth, was always distinctive from Puritan New England. At first, mere survival was so difficult in Virginia that the colony often seemed like a kind of hell, yet settlers there hardly spoke of sin. They had come, as Annette Gordon-Reed says, under the auspices of a company, to make a killing, and most of them had no children to worry about anyway.[8]

The first English settlers to arrive in Virginia, disembarking in the place they named Jamestown in the spring of 1607, were a group of 104 men and boys. They were shareholders, employees, and servants of the Virginia Company, the corporation that held a royal charter on the land and was eager to find treasure there, which soon meant cultivating tobacco. The first two women arrived more than a year later, in the fall of 1608: Margaret Foxe Forrest, wife of Thomas Forrest, a settler and shareholder in the Virginia Company, and Foxe's maid, fourteen-year-old Anne Burras, who was married three months later. In 1619, the year Virginians introduced a representative government—the first in the English colonies in America—as many as thirty enslaved African laborers arrived in the colony, as well as ninety women, who were shipped over from England by the Virginia Company in the hope that male colonists might work harder to produce tobacco if they became fathers. Women of childbearing age were available to be ordered from company headquarters in England at the price of 120 pounds of tobacco, six times the cost of a male indentured servant.[9]

But it was not easy to populate Virginia with British families. Infants and children there died two or three times more often than in England and New England. As many as one-third of children born in Virginia died before age one. Half died before age twenty.[10] Their parents went almost as fast. In one Virginia county, nearly three-quarters of all children had lost a parent before the age of twenty-one, and a third had lost both.[11] When fathers died, children became "orphans" even when their mothers were still alive. For these orphans, broader kin networks often filled the role of the father, though not out of simple charity. The labor of children, along with the labor of the enslaved, was one of the most valuable resources a man could possess.[12]

With a clear-eyed view of the fragility of their own lives and authority, fathers in Virginia often tried to provide for their children by deeding them cattle at birth. As the cattle were bred, the bulls could be sold to pay the costs of bringing a child up, and the cows would form an investment herd to help a child get started in adulthood. As historian Edmund Morgan noted, children ranked among Virginia's principal cattle owners.[13] With so much property in the hands of young people, so much open land to the west (the colony's charter was literally borderless), and so few surviving elders, the traditional model of patriarchal authority didn't apply. To many Virginians, including Thomas Jefferson, John Locke's ideas on family and politics made much more sense.

The first of Locke's *Two Treatises of Government*, the 1689 book that lays out his famous theory that government rests on the consent of the governed, is almost entirely dedicated to proving that popular arguments for monarchy and patriarchy—that kings have the same natural right to rule their subjects as fathers do over families—were based on a fundamental misunderstanding of parents and children.

Locke was born to Puritan parents in 1632, near Bristol, England. His father was a committed parliamentarian who fought in the English Civil War under a commander who later helped Locke get to Oxford on scholarship. At Oxford, as at Cambridge, it was then customary to refer to a teacher as father and a student as child.[14] Locke found traditional philosophical lessons, often centered on Aristotle's logic, terminally dull, but he thrilled to the philosophy of nature, science, and medicine.

After graduation, Locke was hired by the Earl of Shaftesbury, and his jobs included both serving as the earl's personal physician and helping to write the laws of the Carolina colonies. Locke would be a lifelong bachelor, with no children of his own. Yet his experiences in medicine and politics, tending to individual and political constitutions, made him a sought-after authority for questions about fatherhood among his friends and colleagues. In 1693, Locke collected years of letters he had written to his cousin, the anxious father of an unpromising young man, as a book on parenting, *Some Thoughts Concerning Education*. Generally considered to be one of the foundations of the modern British educational system, the book was influential in the colonies as well, where Locke's popularity as a parenting expert initially exceeded his reputation as a political philosopher.

To Locke, a child was a "white paper" to be filled up with knowledge, as he put it in his 1689 *Essay on Human Understanding*, a blank slate. Not all papers and slates could fit the same amount of knowledge: Abilities and temperaments, Locke said, naturally varied. Even so, nine out of ten people, he thought, became who they were because of education or lack of it.[15]

The best education, Locke advised, began with the teaching of hardship. Dress the child in thin clothes and shoes. Dunk its small feet in the iciest water each morning, for a shock of cold was good preparation for a world of hazard. Though Locke recognized an important role for mothers in bringing up children, he believed that mothers would shrink from the sterner duties, the ones that made their children cry and howl. This most important work fell to fathers, who could recognize that long-term benefits outweighed the short-term pains.[16]

This was different from tyranny. The goal of fatherhood was not to dominate one's children and hold them in subordination, but to provide them with whatever they would need to eventually thrive on their own. "The power ... that parents have," Locke wrote, constitutes "a temporary government" meant to prepare children for independence when the time was right.[17]

Though his mother, Jane Randolph Jefferson, would live until 1776, Thomas Jefferson considered himself to be alone in the world after his father, Peter, died in 1757. "At fourteen years of age," he later recalled, "the whole care and direction of myself was thrown on myself entirely, without a relation or friend qualified to advise or guide me."[18] From his father Jefferson had inherited perhaps forty enslaved people. Two years later he entered college at William and Mary in Williamsburg, Virginia. While a student, he began to dunk his own feet in cold water each morning, just as Locke suggested fathers do for their children, and to study the origins of the English monarchy.[19]

Historian Gordon Wood points out that in England and its colonies alike the language of power was paternalistic. According to the conventions of British law, the king was "the *pater familias* of the nation," and each head of household was a kind of "miniature king."[20] In turn, opposition to the king invariably took on the tone of a "family squabble."[21] Colonists of diverse beliefs and experiences, those who prioritized religious freedom and economic opportunity alike, those from Massachusetts, Virginia, and everywhere else, found common ground by describing themselves as siblings, brothers. Jefferson in particular believed that each generation had a natural right to rule itself, and thought of his compatriots in the Revolution as a "band of brothers."[22]

Leaders of the most radical colonial protests, including the Boston Tea Party, cast themselves as "Sons of Liberty." Great Britain remained the mother country, but the king, Thomas Paine wrote in *Common Sense* in 1776, was a failed patriarch, "with the pretended title of Father of his People." Paine challenged his fellow colonists to take charge of themselves: "Is it in the interest of a man to be a boy his whole life?"[23] Locke had firmly answered no, it was not—children were meant to grow up to govern themselves, and only a tyrannical father would say otherwise. Much revolutionary rhetoric carried a flavor of patricide, the murder of the father.[24]

Yet if each generation had a right to rule itself, so was it also responsible for what became of its inheritance, and some observers of the American experiment expected trouble. One of the most prominent skeptics was Count Buffon, director of the royal botanical gardens (Jardin du Roi) near Paris. Buffon had talked his way into the job in 1739, and once installed he began to catalogue the gardens' many specimens. A decade later, he published the first volume of a work titled *Natural History*. By the time Buffon died in 1788, the project had grown to thirty-six volumes in total, twelve times as many as Aristotle's *Generation of Animals*.

There was also a notable difference in the worldview of Buffon's work. While Aristotle had seized on nature's perfection, Buffon fixated on the possibility of decline. In particular, the cold and wet climate of the American continent, Buffon claimed, had led to the *de*generation of animals. In the "new world," he pointed out, there were no tigers, no lions, no elephants, no rhinos—anymore. The great beasts had been replaced by underwhelming impostors, jaguars and tapirs, for example. The bears were smaller in America, and the deer, the wolves, and the foxes too. Even the livestock of European origin had been diminished once they were domesticated in America.

Buffon's volume on the subject was a surprise hit in European capitals, where its conclusions confirmed what many had suspected about America all along.[25] Particularly intriguing was Buffon's portrait of the American human being. He classified humans as a single animal species, with a common point of origin, who had come to differ by virtue of their distinct environments. As wet and cold had worked their degradation on successive generations, Buffon said, American Indians, individually and collectively, had been diminished relative to "polished societies." "In the savage," Buffon wrote, "the organs of generation are small and feeble. He has no hair, no beard, no ardor for the female.... He remains in stupid repose, on his limbs or couch, for whole days.... Their love to parents and children is extremely weak. The bonds of the most intimate of all societies, that of the same family, are feeble. Hence no union, no republic, no social state can take place among them."[26] The implication was that the very environment that had caused this outcome in the American Indian would eventually and inevitably take its toll on European settlers, too, cooling their ardor, stifling their productivity, eroding their family bonds and their republic.

After the Revolution, Jefferson became obsessed with proving that American parents were not doomed to produce lesser children. In 1780, while serving as governor of Virginia, he received some questions about the state from a French minister scouting for economic resources and businesses opportunities, and Jefferson leaped at the opportunity to prove that Buffon had been wrong, and the future of the United States was bright.

The same day Jefferson acknowledged receipt of the inquiries from the French, his wife, Martha, went into labor and very nearly died in the process of delivering their fifth child, Lucy, who was named after Jefferson's sister and lived only five months. Each of Martha's pregnancies had been more difficult than the last, and this was cause for concern. Jefferson knew as much medicine as any doctor at the time, and he often functioned as one around Monticello, his expansive mountaintop plantation in Virginia where hundreds of people lived and worked, the great majority of them enslaved. Martha's string of difficult pregnancies gave Jefferson good reason to fear for her health and life, and he did, to a point. Just six months after Lucy's death, Martha was pregnant again. In May of 1782, she gave birth to another Lucy. For months after the delivery, Martha's health deteriorated, and in September she died.[27]

Distraught and blaming himself, Jefferson went into isolation at Monticello, avoiding even his children. When he finally emerged from his rooms, he began to work seriously on his survey of Virginia and its prospects. Appointed ambassador to France in the summer of 1784, and eager for a change of scene, he took the manuscript with him to Paris but left his children behind. That October, the second Lucy Jefferson, who had stayed in Virginia under the care of her aunt and uncle, died of whooping cough. It was three months before the news reached her father in Paris.

In the spring of 1785, grieving and desperately lonely, Jefferson had his manuscript on Virginia privately printed and distributed to friends in France and the United States. At the same time, he anxiously began to ask for his six-year-old daughter Polly to be sent to join him in France. She arrived there two years later, on July 15, 1787, in the company of a fourteen-year-old enslaved girl called Sally Hemings. *Notes on the State of Virginia* had just been published two days earlier.

The argument of the book was that America could grow great things: plants, animals, people, families, fortunes, civilizations. Jefferson made his case in part through exacting comparisons of European and American animals, and admittedly there were some tricky ones. He had to concede Buffon's claims that livestock in America had "become less than their original stock." But Jefferson attributed this shrinkage not to cold and wet conditions but to the fact that the animals had not been properly managed. The population of the country was so small, and the open land so vast, that stock animals had generally been allowed to wander about free-range. If only American animals were bred and raised in the European way, the results would be different.[28] Already, where there had been good management, there had been good results: bulls weighing over two thousand pounds, hogs over one thousand. It wasn't a problem of American nature's miserly hand, but rather a problem of nature's abundance, which had given men little cause to improve it. In other words, it was a problem of men, not nature, and that was the sort of problem Jefferson, through John Locke, knew how to solve—with education, governance, and good fatherhood.

The stakes of the problem were heightened by Jefferson's work to change inheritance laws by eliminating primogeniture and entail (ended in Virginia in 1785), which had constrained the distribution of property within and beyond families. In America, even bastards were to be given a fair shot, through the right to inherit from their mothers.[29] For these reasons, along with the country's abundant land, property ownership was more open in the United States than in Europe. But would this ultimately prove a blessing or a curse—a spur to economic development or an excuse for laziness?

Jefferson answered the question by blaming American underdevelopment on the nature of Indigenous family life. He explained that American Indians were not, as Buffon had claimed, "defective in ardor," nor were they "more impotent" than Europeans. On the contrary, Native Americans were plenty "affectionate" with children, with "even the warriors weeping most bitterly on the loss of their children." But, Jefferson acknowledged, American Indians "raise fewer children than we do," limiting their population and economic activity. He saw two clear reasons for this. First, the tendency of the men to go off hunting and fighting had made pregnancy and parenting more difficult and encouraged many women to abort pregnancies. And second, because they were dependent on the "gleanings of the forest," as Jefferson put it, many American Indians experienced famine at least once a year. In such conditions of want, it was no wonder that "generation becomes less active, less productive."[30]

Jefferson had seen that Indigenous women could be very fertile, under certain circumstances. In particular, when married to European traders, whom Jefferson thought better husbands and fathers—"who feed their children plentifully and regularly, who exempt them from excessive drudgery, who keep them stationary

126

and unexposed to accident"—Indigenous women were known to produce and raise as many children as white women. Jefferson's conclusion was that American Indians, like the land they inhabited, could be improved through new models of fatherhood.

In the first years of his presidency, Jefferson often referred to Native Americans as "My Brothers." Before and during the Revolution, some American Indians and colonists had called each other brothers—although their relationships were complex and sometimes hostile—in part to build common cause against their overbearing father, the king. But the terms of this relationship changed with American priorities. Eager to claim more land, many settlers gave up on the idea of brotherhood in favor of force. When this proved a perilous strategy—the Indigenous nations were often stronger militarily—settlers changed tactics again, adopting what historian Richard White has described as a new "fiction of conquest": paternity. As early as 1794, U.S. officials began to inform Indians that President George Washington was "your father," just as the king had once been.

This idea, too, had been taken from the Indigenous. At least since the late seventeenth century, American Indians had called French and British officials by the name of father.[31] They were asking for consideration, resources, and protection by using the title they would have addressed to any elder male of their tribe. Indigenous families were often organized along the mother's line. The most powerful man in a child's life was usually an uncle, a brother of their mother who was called a father, which had often been a source of confusion for European settlers when it came to land rights and sales.

During treaty negotiations in 1793, Tarhe, chief of the Wyandots, urged his "brother Indians" to acknowledge "the fifteen United States of America to be our father . . . you must call them brothers no more." For Indigenous "children," this meant that they would "be obedient to our father; ever listen to him when he speaks to you, and follow his advice." For the white father, this meant taking "care of all your little ones . . . and do not suffer them to be imposed upon . . . have pity on them, and relieve their wants."[32] Many tribes would do as Tarhe advised, but fewer benefited from the reciprocity he foresaw. "In becoming fathers," Richard White observes, "the Americans switched the actual pattern of property exchange. Instead of receiving the continent from the Indians, the Americans possessed it and could bestow it, or fail to bestow it, on their deserving or undeserving metaphorical children."[33]

Particularly after the Louisiana Purchase of 1803, which doubled the size of the United States and increased the challenge of populating and improving it, Jefferson addressed American Indians as "my children." In some letters and documents, he repeated the phrase at the beginning of virtually every paragraph, and not just as a formality. Jefferson was always trying to tell "his children" to think of their children, to adopt new models of fatherhood and manhood. He wanted them to settle down in one place and become small farmers with conjugal families, which he assured them would be peaceful and productive. "If you will cease to make war on one another," he instructed a delegation of chiefs in 1806, "you will live in friendship with all mankind, you can employ all of your time in providing food & clothing for yourselves and your families. Your men will not be destroyed in war and your women & children will lie down to sleep in their cabins without fear of being surprised by their enemies & killed or carried away. Your numbers will be increased, instead of diminishing, and you will live in plenty & in quiet." That was what they should want, for the alternative was painful. "My children," Jefferson went on, "we are strong, we are numerous as the stars in the heavens, & we are all gun-men."[34]

Jefferson also promised his "children" that if they followed his advice and reorganized their families and livelihoods onto small farms, they could look forward to the day when they joined white society, mixing with whites by marriage and children. Yet the reality of continental empire and expansion bore little resemblance to Jefferson's optimistic rhetoric. When Native Americans resisted his suggestions to abandon their familiar ways of life, he "was prepared to ride roughshod over Indian desires" by threats, bribes, and unyielding pressures that were justified in his mind in order to feed the dynamic economy and the fast-growing population of the United States.[35]

Fittingly, Jefferson seems to have been the first man to be called "Great White Father," a double-edged title that first shows up in an 1806 translation of an Osage song purportedly sung about visiting Washington, D.C., to meet with the president. Native Americans learned to be wary of such ceremonial occasions, but Jefferson relished them. He had great memories of his father hosting parties of American Indians at their plantation on Virginia's western frontier. As president, Jefferson welcomed Indigenous leaders and representatives to Washington with official banquets and celebrations that were always punctuated by the firing of enormous guns.[36] At dinner, Jefferson would gather his guests at a round table in the President's House, and sometimes he served the food himself.[37]

On at least one evening, he invited the wives of Native American dignitaries to dine too. Also in attendance that night was a scandalized Louisa Adams, wife of John Quincy, who could only wonder what President Jefferson would do next—whether he would ever be so bold as to welcome to his table "the incomparable Sally," meaning Hemings, who at the time may have been the most famous enslaved person in the world.[38]

When fourteen-year-old Sally Hemings first arrived in Paris in the summer of 1787, Thomas Jefferson had already been living there for three lonely years as the U.S. ambassador to France. When the time came for Jefferson to return to Virginia five years later, Hemings was pregnant with their child. If Hemings had stayed in France, she and their baby would have been free. According to historian Annette Gordon-Reed, Hemings agreed to return to Monticello and live as Jefferson's slave because Jefferson promised her, or she extracted from him the promise that, eventually their children would be free in Virginia, too, though the law of the land had been specifically written to say the exact opposite.[39]

More than a century earlier, in 1662, Virginia's colonial government had broken from the English legal tradition to the advantage of its slaveowners. By force of a new statute, mothers would pass their legal status—enslaved, indentured, or free—on to their children. This was a radical departure from England, where skin color was not a conventional marker of legal or social status, and "you 'were,'" writes Gordon-Reed, "what your father 'was.'"[40] Now, in Virginia, you were what your mother was.

This principle became known as *partus sequitur ventrum*—the child follows the womb. There is some evidence that the formal

Latin was added to the text of the legislation decades later, by a close colleague of Jefferson's, to give the law the authoritative stamp of ancient history, which was a great obsession of the Revolutionary generation.[41]

The new principle soon became precedent. Over the next two centuries, the law of *partus* spread to slaveholding societies across the Western Hemisphere. In the process, it joined blackness to enslavement. Because slavery was defined as heritable and congenital, rather than a consequence of capture, military defeat, or indebtedness, it became affixed to African descent.[42] "These two words, *Negro* and *Slave*," wrote the Reverend Morgan Goodwyn, who lived in Virginia in the years after the law's passage, are "by custom grown homogenous and convertible."[43]

What prompted Virginians to break from the English legal tradition they knew? The economic incentives were obvious. The colonial government included the largest slave- and landowners in the colony, and in the middle of the seventeenth century their wealth was principally invested in the slave production of tobacco. By the law of *partus*, a government of slaveholders created a new way to grow the population of enslaved people, including through the rape of enslaved women. The law also increased the market value of women who had already been enslaved. For example, a ten-year-old girl in Virginia was sold along with the right to enslave "her successors forever."[44]

Moreover, if in Virginia the status of a child had matched the status of the father, as it did in England, sex between masters and women they owned as slaves would have produced free children, who were expensive not only in terms of the resources they would consume as they grew, but also in terms of the labor time lost to pregnancies and inevitable maternal deaths. Such costs would have been all the more intolerable to slaveowners if an enslaved woman owned by one white man were impregnated by another.

In effect, Virginia masters gave up one power of the father—patrilineal transmission of status and resources—in order to gain a new power to increase their holdings in people and property through legally nonexistent fatherhood. In 1650, there had been perhaps three hundred enslaved people in Virginia. By 1680, there were three thousand. In 1700, there were sixteen thousand.[45] During this period the increase in the enslaved population largely came from greater imports from Africa, which were outlawed in 1808. But well beyond that date, there were thousands of mixed-race people born who, legally speaking, had owners and masters instead of fathers. The children of Thomas Jefferson and Sally Hemings were among them.

The term "raise," as it applies to bringing up children, is an Americanism. In England, crops and animals were raised, but not people. This usage seems to have originated around the turn of the nineteenth century, and particularly in the southern states, where it referred to the breeding of enslaved people.[46]

By all indications, not long after Jefferson and Sally Hemings returned from France and settled at Monticello, Hemings gave birth to a daughter who lived only briefly. If Jefferson was home at the time, he soon left for New York City, then the United States' capital, with Sally's brothers Robert and James, to serve as secretary of state in George Washington's cabinet. Sally remained behind at Monticello, where she served Jefferson's daughters.

In the next two decades, Hemings was pregnant at least seven times. After Jefferson resigned as secretary of state at the end of

1793, he returned to Monticello eager to be out of public life. "I am going to Virginia," he wrote to a friend at the time. "I have my house to build, my fields to form, and to watch for the happiness of those who labor for mine.... I shall imagine myself as blessed as the most blessed of the patriarchs," invoking the ancient identity of man and household, including women, children, and all forms of property—people and things.[47]

Yet in the summer of 1800, despite his strong desire to stay at Monticello, it was clear that Jefferson would be a candidate in the upcoming presidential election. By August, Hemings was pregnant again. During the campaign, one of the most bitterly contested in U.S. history, Jefferson's opponents claimed he kept a "Congo harem."

Jefferson was elected in February 1801 and inaugurated in March. Two months later, at Monticello, Sally Hemings gave birth to their daughter Harriet. In September, a newspaper in Virginia published rumors that Jefferson was "addicted to golden affections" and had "a number of yellow children."[48]

Detailed reports were published the next year, 1802. Her name was Sally; she had gone to France with him; they had five children; including a teenage son, named Tom, of course; and this "sable" Tom went about acting as if he were president, or would be. In fact, at that time, Jefferson and Hemings had two children—three of the five born to that point had not survived—and neither was named Tom.

Well aware that Alexander Hamilton's career had been irreparably harmed by admitting an affair, Jefferson said nothing in public.[49] Nor is there evidence that he said anything in private, to his daughters.

The presidency kept Jefferson away for most of the next eight years, except for summer vacations and family emergencies. In

the spring of 1804, his daughter Polly lay weakened after a difficult pregnancy and labor. In early April, Jefferson traveled from
Washington to her bedside at Monticello. She improved when he
got there, but only briefly. Nearly inconsolable after Polly's death,
Jefferson stayed home at Monticello with his loved ones through
the middle of May. By the time he was inaugurated for his second
term in March of 1805, Sally Hemings had given birth to another
son, James Madison Hemings, probably named by Dolley Madison,
Jefferson's friend and the wife of his protégé, the future president
James Madison.

In 1808, the final year of Jefferson's presidency and the year of
James Madison's election, another child was due. Sally Hemings
was then thirty-five, two years older than Martha Jefferson had
been when she died. Since Paris, Hemings had survived at least
seven pregnancies. Every reasonable standard suggested that this
pregnancy would be the last. When Hemings gave birth to a healthy
baby boy, it was the first time that Jefferson had been home for the
birth of one of his surviving Hemings children. Jefferson always
called this child Eston, after one of his favorite cousins, Thomas
Eston Randolph.[50] Yet evidence from the Hemings family suggests
that Eston's full name was in fact Thomas Eston—that, in other
words, Jefferson had also named his son after himself.[51]

Jefferson left Washington for good immediately after James
Madison's inauguration in March of 1809. "Never did a prisoner
released from his chains feel such relief as I shall on shaking off
the shackles of power," he wrote to a friend. When a snowstorm
delayed the progress of his carriage on the road to Monticello, he
went ahead alone on horseback.[52]

*　　*　　*

Jefferson returned to a Monticello that was very different from the one he had originally planned and built decades earlier. Beginning in 1796, the year after Harriet, his first daughter with Sally Hemings, was born, Jefferson had undertaken a comprehensive renovation project that transformed what had been an eight-room house into a three-story, twenty-one-room house full of hidden spaces and passages. Sally Hemings lived in a windowless room on the ground level of the south end of the house, that is, under Jefferson's own room, which Hemings could enter easily from the outside. Jefferson also had John Hemings build wooden blinds that enclosed the porches off his bedroom and blocked the view into it.[53] For nearly two decades of retirement he lived as the patriarch of two families in one household.

In the winter of 1815, Jefferson hosted a young Massachusetts lawyer named Francis Gray at Monticello. Gray, from a prominent Salem family, had served as private secretary to John Quincy Adams and would have been well aware of the rumors about Jefferson and his family.

Jefferson resented the endless stream of visitors who came to stay at Monticello in his retirement. Left alone for long stretches of his stay, Gray found plenty to scorn about Jefferson's house—worn furniture, "miserable prints" hung everywhere, "careless" editions in the library—which at that point was almost entirely staffed by enslaved members of the Hemings family.

One day, Gray was prompted to ask Jefferson about what it meant to be mulatto under Virginia law. In response, Jefferson told his guest that, starting from "pure Negro," up to four generations could be crossed with "the whites" and still be considered legally mulatto, with the offspring of the fourth generation becoming white. But it wasn't true, and Jefferson knew it.

After Gray left and returned to Boston, the conversation stuck with Jefferson. It bothered him enough that, though he insisted that the issue was "of little importance," he wrote to Gray to set the record straight. After some additional research, Jefferson explained, he had realized that it was the third cross, not the fourth, that "clears the blood," and then he went to entirely unnecessary lengths—"Let us express the pure blood of the white in the capital letters of the printed alphabet. . . ."—in unspooling a complex algebraic equation showing how black could become white across generations.[54]

There was a good reason why Gray's question mattered to Jefferson. As Jefferson was well aware—and as the Hemings family certainly would have been aware—his "cross" with Sally Hemings was the third in her maternal line, going back to her grandmother. On a page crowded with numbers, letters, and symbols, Jefferson translated the truth of his secret family life into an elaborate mathematical abstraction that happened to culminate in a legally white child, "e.," the initial of Jefferson's namesake, his youngest son, Eston, then seven, who would grow up to be "a near copy" of his father in appearance and build. In the 1850s, after the passage of the Fugitive Slave Law, Eston took his father's last name too. He worked as a professional musician, and one of his trademark numbers was also one of his father's favorites, a song called "Money Musk."[55]

In his letter to Gray, Jefferson was careful to point out that by law a generational change in racial classification from "black" to "white" did not mean emancipation. The child "e." in his equation was no longer legally a mulatto but was still enslaved. "Observe," he invited Gray, who had done just that at Monticello, "that this does not reestablish freedom, which depends on the condition of the mother, the principle of the civil law, partus sequitur ventrem, being adopted here. But," Jefferson continued, "if [the child] be emancipated, he becomes a free <u>white</u> man [the underlining was Jefferson's], and a citizen of the US to all intents and purposes—so much for this trifle, by way of correction."

Jefferson knew his children were legally white, and they probably knew it too.[56] But whatever he had promised Sally Hemings in Paris, his need to keep their secret made their children his slaves. Three of their children, all girls, would die as Jefferson's slaves, soon after birth. The four children who lived to adulthood were raised as slaves and compelled to work as their father's property.

As a subscriber to John Locke's ideas of parenting as education, Jefferson had long been worried about the influence of the master-slave relationship on children. "The whole commerce between master and slave is a perpetual exercise of the most boisterous passions," he wrote in *Notes on the State of Virginia*. "The most unremitting despotism on the one part, and degrading submissions on the other. Our children see this, and learn to imitate it, for man is an imitative animal. This quality is the germ of all education in him. From his cradle to his grave he is learning to do what he sees others do. . . . The parent storms, the child looks on, catches the lineaments of wrath, puts on the same airs in the circle of smaller slaves, gives a loose to the worst of passions, and thus nursed, educated, and daily exercised in tyranny, cannot but be stamped by it with odious peculiarities."[57] When Jefferson advised masters to moderate their behavior around their children, he did not account for the fact that some of the enslaved people they owned were their children. But in the case of his own children—enslaved by the law of *partus*, legally without a father, but white by the twisted algebra of race—Jefferson tried to prepare to them to be free men and women in the world. He did not want them to learn "degrading submissions."[58]

Many slaveholders set out to emasculate men they owned in part by refusing to recognize them as fathers. According to southern law, enslaved men were not necessary to make enslaved children and not permitted to make free ones with white women—an offense so threatening to the structure of slaveholding society that it was probably acknowledged and prosecuted less often than it occurred. Masters often identified enslaved children only with their mother, one piece of a larger strategy of taking reproductive power away from enslaved men, not only by denying them fatherhood and policing their relations with women but also by limiting their ability to provide for others in the ways that white fathers did, for example by prohibiting them from owning livestock.[59] Denying Black men manhood, Edward Baptist observes, was a cornerstone of white manhood.[60] But even under constant pressure, as historian Libra R. Hilde has shown, enslaved and Black fathers found and improvised ways to protect and provide for—and also sometimes to dominate and control—kin, lovers, and children, their own and others, from scavenged food and toys, to guiding prayers and lessons, to, in precious few cases, buying or escaping with their children into freedom.[61]

Jefferson took a different approach at Monticello. As Annette Gordon-Reed has described, he recognized "enslaved men as the heads of their households. His farm book listings of slave households begin with a male's name, followed by a female's, and then their children's. When they do not . . . it was because the father of the children was a white man, and could not be listed as living within the woman's household"[62] And in such cases, the children of enslaved women and white men, including Jefferson's own Hemings children, gained a father in the form of an enslaved uncle. In other words, Jefferson set up, at Monticello, for his enslaved children, a family structure that was like the one he worked to eradicate among American Indians.

Jefferson's enslaved children, along with the rest of the Hemings family, were favored with special status at Monticello that largely exempted them from field work and the most violent forms of discipline. Once Jefferson's enslaved sons turned ten, he placed them under the tutelage of his "best slave artisan," John Hemings, their uncle, who became a "surrogate father" to the boys.[63] In his plantation records, Jefferson referred to the boys as John Hemings's "assistants" or "apprentices" in carpentry, which was the craft Jefferson most admired and valued. Some of Jefferson's grandchildren, the youngest of whom were around the same age as his enslaved children, also learned to call John Hemings "Daddy."[64]

Hemings and his three "assistants" worked in the joinery at Monticello as well as on the construction of Poplar Forest, a secluded second home, away from visitors, that Jefferson used as a retreat from Monticello. In the woods at Poplar Forest, Jefferson could have stood by and watched as John Hemings, along with Beverly, Madison, and Eston Hemings, built his secret home.[65] He might have even joined in the labor, for he loved woodworking.

The boys shared more than carpentry with their father. All three were shaped, Annette Gordon-Reed has written, into versions of the "private self" Jefferson had longed to cultivate his whole public life.[66] They all played violin and loved music, like their father. Eston made his living as a professional musician. Beverly, like his father, had a great interest in hot-air balloons. And

Madison, like his father, knew how to put words together into a memorable phrase.

The girls were different. For all his daughters, Jefferson believed that a woman's education and training "should be geared to making them amiable companions for men."[67] Jefferson's youngest daughter, Harriet Hemings, worked on sewing and mending at Monticello. Harriet was said to be "nearly as white as anybody," and "very beautiful," like her mother. Jefferson had reason to believe that would take her far.[68]

Jefferson's Hemings children knew that their master was their father, and that certain privileges derived from this fact.[69] Yet they also knew, and had learned by experience and lesson, that he did not treat them in the same way that he treated his other children and grandchildren. Jefferson "was not in the habit" of displaying "fatherly affection" toward his Hemings children, though he was known to emerge from his private study in the evenings to play games with his other family, as the toys carefully strewn across the parlor floor in Monticello today represent.

Beverly Hemings, the oldest, left first. In 1822, he departed Monticello for the port city of Baltimore, probably with the expectation that his sister would follow soon after. Harriet left two months later, when Jefferson directed his overseer to put her in a stagecoach bound for Philadelphia. "Ran away," Jefferson lied in his ledger about Beverly and Harriet, a bit of false accounting to help free his children from him, their father and owner.[70]

In the spring of 1826, his health failing, Jefferson willed to John Hemings his freedom and "the service of his two apprentices, Madison and Eston Hemings, until their respective ages of twenty-one years, at which period, respectively, I give them their freedom." After Jefferson died on July 4, 1826, Madison Hemings rented a house in Charlottesville and lived with his younger brother, Eston, and their mother, Sally, until she died ten years later. After Sally Hemings died, Madison and his wife—the free black granddaughter of a white planter and the enslaved woman whom he had freed and married—moved to Ohio. They had ten children, and seven of them survived, including three sons. Like his father, Madison named his boys William Beverly, James Madison, and Thomas Eston.

But unlike his father, Madison used his skill with words to put the story of their family into print. In 1873, his recollections of growing up as his father's slave were published by a small Ohio newspaper, the *Pike County Republican*. "About his own home," said Madison Hemings of his father, Thomas Jefferson, whose words had given birth to a nation, "he was the quietest of men."

CHAPTER FIVE

MONEY: Emerson and Thoreau

T hirty-three-year-old Ralph Waldo Emerson wanted to a be a writer, but especially after the birth of his first child and namesake, Waldo, in October 1836, the pressure of supporting a family with words weighed heavily on his mind. Too often Emerson found himself sitting in the study of his big new house in Concord, Massachusetts, notebook open, pen quiet, not working. On one particularly low day, the anniversary of his first marriage, which had ended in his wife's death from tuberculosis before her twentieth birthday, Emerson managed only to scrawl her name three times: "Ellen, Ellen, Ellen."[1]

Emerson's second wife, Lidian, lived under the burden of a painful self-consciousness that she projected onto everything around her. She had "a mania for straightening things: a chair askew, unevenly laid silverware, a crooked picture, a rug misaligned with floorboards."[2] She awoke in the middle of the night to the thought that she had left a larger book on top of a smaller one. She doubted that she could ever be worthy of her husband and feared that, in heaven, he would end up with Ellen after all.[3]

One morning in January 1837, while Emerson sat in front of an empty page, Lidian came into his study, took up his pen, and wrote in his notebook their three names: Lidian, Waldo, Waldo.[4] Not long after, Emerson began working on material that he would eventually shape into his most famous essay, "Self-Reliance." When Emerson included the essay in his first book-length collection—published in 1841 and self-funded—he introduced it with three epigraphs, the last of which was a poem he wrote himself. The first lines of the verse were "Cast the bantling on the rocks / Suckle him with the she-wolf's teat."[5] A bantling is an infant, who in Emerson's formula would survive by learning nature's unforgiving lessons or not at all. This he saw as exactly the kind of parenting the perilous times required—being raised by wolves, just like Romulus, who killed his brother Remus and founded Rome.

It was an age of being cast on the rocks. In the first half of the nineteenth century, in Concord, across the United States, and around the Atlantic World, Thomas Jefferson's idea of each generation for itself was put into effect by force. A wave of destabilizing economic changes, pushed forward by the Industrial Revolution, swept through as a "market revolution." Capitalism flooded into every corner of life and experience, including family relationships.

Before 1820, almost three-quarters of the American labor force worked in agriculture. Families working at home produced what they consumed, taking very little, and often only imports such as sugar, coffee, and tea, from merchants and stores.[6] By 1860, the world had changed. Steamships and railroads had tapped vast new resources and markets that meant increased competition and volatility for small farms and businesses. Factories, growing cities, land booms, gold rushes, and all sorts of bonanzas—a word that entered English from Spanish in the 1840s, meaning "fair weather for sailing," prosperity ahead—helped to draw the next generation away from home. Even those who stayed behind began to focus on producing just one or two profitable commodities to sell into the wider market, and as a result "the family as a largely self-sufficient economic unit began to disappear."[7]

These changes transformed family life. Traditionally fathers expected to pass a parcel of land or a craft skill onto their sons or their sons-in-law. But now the very things that fathers had relied on to provide for their families—and to exert power over them— were no longer so valuable. One small New England town, Chelsea, Vermont, had fourteen shoemakers and five tailors in 1850. By 1900 there were two and none, respectively.[8] In these same years, many proprietors and tradesman began to add "& Sons" to the name of their business. Before the market revolution this would have been redundant. Now advertising as a legacy business became a testament of staying power—as well as a fading echo of an old tradition, part of a broader nostalgia for bygone days and fathers. More often, the next generation had to find its own way.

In theory, this was just what Ralph Waldo Emerson—born in May of 1803, the same month Thomas Jefferson finalized the Louisiana Purchase—wanted: a chance to go out on his own. "Our age is retrospective," complained the first sentence of Emerson's self-published first book, *Nature*. "It builds the sepulchres of the fathers. . . . Why should we not enjoy an original relation to the universe?"[9] Jefferson would have agreed.

Yet an "original relation" was not easy to find in Concord, Massachusetts, six decades after the town had been the site of the opening battle of the Revolutionary War. In seeking one in the years before the Civil War, Emerson and his friend Henry Thoreau forged the modern philosophy of individualism. Their most famous essays, including "Self-Reliance," "Civil Disobedience," and *Walden*, are exhortations to a private revolution. It is largely because of them that we now feel we have a duty not to abstract notions of virtue, or to God, or king, or ancestral line, or nation, or town, or even household, but to ourselves. "I shun father and mother and wife and brother when my genius calls me," Emerson wrote in "Self-Reliance." Trust yourself. Go your own way. Sing your own song; wake your neighbors up. For Emerson and Thoreau, writes historian Robert A. Gross, the highest purpose of life was to dive into the "inner ocean" and come back up to tell the tale.[10]

Emerson and Thoreau tried to practice what they preached. Their ideas grew out of their personal struggles to live the lives they imagined, and arguably the greatest obstacles they faced on the way were their fathers. Emerson and Thoreau each conceived of freedom as breaking away from the world and institutions of their fathers, particularly the institution of slavery. But each found this more difficult than expected, because, in order to become the sort of individuals they wished to be, they needed money.

Emerson had two fathers he wanted to leave in the past. He was related to the first by birth, the second by law.

Ralph, as he was then called, was born in Boston, the fourth of six children of William and Ruth Emerson. Ruth was the daughter of a prosperous distiller, and William was a minister, as at least five generations of Emerson men had been before him. Yet none of these pious ancestors had risen as high as William. In 1799, four years before Ralph's birth, he was called from an undistinguished rural post to take the most prominent pulpit in Boston, First Church. Former president John Adams and his son John Quincy Adams were among his parishioners, and William Emerson preached what the Adams family and their peers wanted to hear, deference to authority.

At home, William led his family in memorizing Bible verses and poetry, eager to fill his children up with knowledge. "It will grieve me exceedingly to have you a blockhead," William told his eldest son, John, then age six, who would die of tuberculosis two years later. "I hope you will be as bright as silver." When Ralph was two and just starting school, William worried that he was proving "rather a dull scholar." [11] At three Ralph still failed to read as well as his father would have liked. More than once, William forced his son out into Boston Harbor to swim for his life, and Ralph learned to hide from him.

Ralph was seven when his father died in 1811, following years of lung problems. William left his family with debts of nearly $2,500, almost double his annual salary. Ousted from the parsonage of First Church, Ruth Emerson and her six children—five boys and an infant daughter who would live only to age three—moved from one rented house to another. To pay their way, Ruth sold her husband's library, took in boarders, and worked as a maid. Ralph and his younger brother Edward often walked to school on winter mornings sharing one coat between them. Before and after school, Ralph helped his mother tend to their lodgers. When his mother sent him out one afternoon with a dollar to buy shoes, he lost the bill on the way to the cobbler, and she made him go out again to search for it among the fallen poplar leaves.[12]

Ralph and three of his four brothers would eventually earn scholarships to Harvard. The college was then notorious for the meagerness of its accommodations, but the Emerson boys relished it. In his third year, Ralph adopted the name Waldo and started keeping a journal. Yet Harvard was only a temporary break from family responsibilities. The fifth Emerson brother, Robert Bulkeley, known as Bulkeley, was born with an intellectual disability and required lifelong care.[13] Eventually Ruth Emerson required the same.

In need of a steady income after graduation, Waldo decided to train for the ministry, like his father, and his father's father, and so on before him. In October 1826, Emerson was approved to preach in the Unitarian church. Around the same time, he began to feel an indefinite tightness in his lungs, as if having followed his father into the ministry, he would now suffer the same fate.

That winter, Emerson escaped Boston for Florida, where he wrote sermons and preached and felt his lungs get stronger. Within a year he returned to take an interim position in the First Church— his father's church. After just his fourth sermon, his lungs were feeling weak again, and he was eager to flee once more. Instead, in 1829, he was offered a job by the city's Second Church, founded in 1649 where the Puritan ministers Increase and Cotton Mather had once presided. Emerson accepted because he wanted to marry Ellen Tucker.

Emerson's second fraught inheritance came from his other, richer father: his father-in-law.

The term "in-law" refers to church rules designed to enlarge congregations by discouraging marriage within the existing group. Growing up, Waldo Emerson and Ellen Tucker had lived near each other. "She is the youngest daughter of the late Beza Tucker, a merchant of Boston," Emerson wrote of Ellen to his brother William. "She is 17 years old, & very beautiful by universal consent."[14] Ellen wanted to be a poet, she called her dog Byron, and she had a promised income from her father's estate and her choice of suitors—and she was already sick with tuberculosis and coughing blood. Waldo and Ellen wed at the home of her wealthy stepfather in Concord, New Hampshire, in the fall of 1829, when he was twenty-six and she was eighteen.

Ellen's coughing punctuated their marriage. Even as she got sicker, Waldo continued to send her out on winter days to ride in her carriage, believing that exposure to cold would strengthen her. On Wednesday, February 2, 1831, Ellen went riding twice. She died six days later.[15]

Ellen's trustees contended that, at nineteen, she had been too young to inherit when she died, and therefore Emerson had no claim on her share of the Tucker family money. Over the next year, Emerson came unmoored. To still his grief, he got into the daily habit of walking several miles from Boston to Roxbury to visit Ellen's grave. In March 1832, he opened her coffin and inspected her body.[16] Many New Englanders then believed that those who had died of consumption—one of the most common causes of early death—could literally suck the life out of their loved ones from beyond the grave. The only solution was to exhume the body, check it for undecomposed flesh, turn it facedown, and bury it again.[17]

Emerson was no longer finding solace in the rituals he led in his church. He told his parishioners that he would not offer communion. He could not believe in the literal truth of the gospels. He could not accept Jesus as the begotten Son of God. When the congregation fired him, Emerson impulsively booked a ticket on a cargo ship loaded with mahogany, tobacco, sugar, and coffee, bound for Europe.[18] He was so weak that the captain hesitated to let him onboard. They sailed on Christmas 1832.

In Paris, Emerson visited the Jardin des Plantes, Count Buffon's collection. There Emerson was overwhelmed by the "upheaving principle of life" on display. "I feel the centipede in me," he wrote in his dairy, "cayman, carp, eagle, and fox."[19] When Emerson returned to the United States in 1833, he sued Ellen's family for her inheritance.

In the meantime, without any money of his own, he moved in with his mother in Concord. Ruth had taken a job as a maid in a house that Emerson's grandfather, Reverend William Emerson, had built in 1769. The upstairs rooms overlooked Concord's North Bridge, site of the opening battle of the Revolutionary War, and William Emerson had been an avid supporter of the patriot cause. Now his grandson Waldo hoped his writing would thrive there. "Hail to the quiet fields of my fathers!" he wrote at the end of 1834.[20] He had reason to celebrate. Not long before, Emerson had won his case against the Tuckers, and he was set to receive about $23,000 from his late wife's family. Paid in two installments, it would be enough to generate an annual income of $1,200 from dividends and interest, roughly what he had made as a minister. Like that, on paper, Emerson had become one of the richest men in Concord.

Emerson never met Ellen's father, "the late Beza Tucker" whose fortune was the source of this windfall, but knew he was a merchant dealing in what were then called West Indies goods—meaning slave-produced commodities, especially sugar and coffee.[21] Tucker may have even invested in plantations in the Caribbean, and he traveled there in the company of his brother, who certainly did. According to Emerson's biographer Robert D. Richardson Jr., Tucker also owned a rope factory in Boston.[22] Given Tucker's orientation toward the Caribbean, his rope factory may have made rigging for the ships that carried the goods he traded—and restraints for the enslaved people who were forced to work to produce them.

At the time, Emerson was much less concerned with the budding abolitionist movement in the United States than he was with getting himself established. In the summer of 1835, he bought his own large house in Concord—the first one he had lived in that wasn't rented—and settled in the busy market and manufacturing town with his new wife.

Lydia Jackson was the daughter of a merchant and shipowner, too, from Plymouth, Massachusetts, with an inherited income of her own. She spoke French and Italian and read German. Her long hair had never been cut.[23] She loved poetry and Romantic mysticism. Emerson liked her passion for ideas, but not the sound of her name. Not long after they met, he wrote her proposing marriage. She accepted right away, and as soon as they were engaged, he began calling her Lidian. She called him Mr. Emerson.

The same year the Emersons moved to Concord, French aristocrat Alexis de Tocqueville coined the term "individualism" to describe the unique nature of life in the United States, where he had traveled to study the prison system. Tocqueville was referring not to "individuals" in the sense of "selves," but to the small, molecular circles of kin that dotted the countryside. In the absence of traditional hierarchies of authority, including royalty, aristocracy, and guilds that monopolized trades, these small family groups had amassed enough wealth that they could afford to isolate themselves from other obligations and impositions. For many Americans, this freedom was the starting point of the opportunity to make their own way up. "Our children," insisted one American parenting text in 1827, "are born to higher destinies than their fathers."[24] In the United States, fewer social rules and freer access to resources meant that white men especially could be "self-made"—but also unmade, for if family fortunes turned, there was little else to rely on.

Born in the fall of 1836, Emerson's son Waldo shared a birthday with one of the worst financial crises of the nineteenth century. After the celebrated "self-made man" Andrew Jackson, then president, made it clear he would not renew the charter of the Second Bank of the United States in 1836, money and finance became principally a local concern. Hundreds of new and unregulated banks had opened in the previous decades, often printing their own promissory notes secured by investments. The overall money supply of the United States tripled between 1830 and 1837.[25] Boston banks in particular had speculated heavily in remote Maine timberlands, expecting that the forests would soon become new things made of wood all over the country. But by the end of 1836 and the start of 1837, the bubble had begun to deflate. Before it was done, almost half of the banks in the country failed, their promises and their banknotes becoming worthless.

A financial crisis has its own gravity, and economic problems often get heavier closer to the ground. A government goes into debt or exile. A business goes into bankruptcy—a legal protection pioneered in the United States at this time, specifically to mitigate the consequences of real estate bubbles. But a family goes hungry, and an individual, in the language of the time, goes "dead broke."[26]

By the spring of 1837, the value of Emerson's inheritance from the Tucker family, much of which had been in bank stocks, had been sharply reduced, and his income from investments fell short of his expectations. But just then he received the second half of the payment from his wife's estate, nearly $12,000.

Emerson himself became a bank for his friends and family. The Tucker money helped him take care of his mother, Ruth, and his brother Bulkeley, as well as others who hadn't planned on borrowing. When Emerson's friend Bronson Alcott, devoted father of Louisa May and three more daughters, fell into a deep depression, Emerson bought him a ticket to Europe, which he knew to be a treatment for despair. On a lark, Emerson bought a stretch of land outside Concord, and permitted his younger friend Henry Thoreau to build a house there, on the shore of Walden Pond. When Emerson's older brother William, who had been speculating in real estate, fell thousands of dollars in debt, he arranged a loan for him.

Generous as he was, money and finances made Emerson anxious, and during the panic of 1837 he despaired to read the news of hardship all around. Men were standing "like daylabourers idle in the streets," and "young men have no hope."[27] Whenever his bank accounts ran uncomfortably low, Emerson would get started planning a lecture tour. He would set the dates, sell tickets, compose his talks, and then "make the plunge into this great odious river of travelers, into these cold eddies & boarding houses."[28] He much preferred to stay home in Concord, writing in his study, playing with and marveling at his young son, Waldo—though that was increasingly seen as the sort of work men had no business with.

Human spermatozoa, swarming and frantic, were first seen under a microscope in the Netherlands in 1677. Microscopy, like all science, was then almost exclusively a male enterprise, and 140 more years passed before the human egg, fulsome and singular, was also observed. By then, the differences in the nature and shape of reproductive cells had taken on a pointed meaning. As fathers lost the security of inherited lands and trades, they were increasingly expected to go out into the world of work, where not all would succeed. Those who did brought home to their families not a harvest but a manufactured good: "bread." The term "breadwinner," which had originally meant something like a marketable skill and was first applied to persons in England at the end of the eighteenth century, raised at the same time the new possibility of being a "loser"—a man who failed economically.[29] Virtually the only thing that fathers could be certain of bringing home at the end of the day were hard lessons, often translated into a language of frustration, anger, and punishment.

The nineteenth-century "domestic sphere," chaste, nurturing, and calm, has sometimes been conceived as a world apart from rough and competitive masculinity, its gentle opposite. But in another way, this concept helped women and mothers claim some of the power and authority that had long been the property of men, and precisely at a moment when men were proving to be unsteady stewards.

Inside the walls of the home, raising children was increasingly the special province of mothers, who gained certain privileges and responsibilities. English common law had once given fathers virtually unlimited custody rights. But in the 1820s, courts began to take into account the well-being of the child when awarding custody. By 1860, some states were already treating the mother as "the default parent," especially during a child's early "tender years."[30] For the first time, parenting manuals were addressed primarily to mothers. Fathers, who had formerly held their children as exclusive property, became the "second" parent.

While men spent more time working outside the home, they were demoted within it. Family portraits, which had conventionally elevated the father above the rest of the household, now put everyone on the same plane.[31] Responsibilities and expectations were shared more evenly among members of the family. Once children were prepared for the world, they, too, were often expected to leave home to work, girls and boys alike. Girls often left even earlier than boys did, possibly because the education of boys seemed a better long-term investment. Women and girls made up more than 80 percent of the industrial workforce in antebellum New England.[32]

Most of the "mill girls" weren't fleeing disastrous poverty, just the increasingly likely threat of it. Their fathers had been farmers, and for that reason many of the young women who left home to work in the mills had their hopes set on marrying "a mechanic in preference to a farmer. They know that marrying a farmer is a serious business. They remember their worn out mothers."[33]

In place of a father he admired, Emerson had Jean-Jacques Rousseau. When Emerson was facing uncertainty and difficulty, he turned to Rousseau for guidance. When he was wondering whether to marry the consumptive Ellen, whose fate was evident from the moment they met, Emerson read Rousseau's book *Émile, or On Education*. When he was preparing to leave the pulpit, the last sermon he preached was on the "natural man," a concept adapted from Rousseau. And as a new father, amid a nationwide crisis of money and manhood, Emerson went back to Rosseau again.

Like John Locke, Rousseau was initially more popular as a parenting expert than as a political philosopher. As it had been for Locke, this was an unlikely role for Rousseau too. While Locke never had any children of his own, Rousseau never kept any of his. Instead, all five were abandoned at the door of a home for foundlings in Paris after their birth.

Rousseau had been born in 1712 in Geneva. His mother's family was rich, but she died nine days after giving birth to him. Afterward, his father, a respected watchmaker, took the money that had been meant for Rousseau and his brother and fled Geneva. After a rough apprenticeship, Rousseau made his way to Paris. There he started a relationship with a laundress, Thérèse Levasseur, whose meager wages were then supporting a large family, including her unemployed father. The role of women, Rousseau wrote in *Émile*, was to help men discover their strength, and he would live with Thérèse for the rest of his life.

Rousseau and Thérèse conceived five children, including at least one son. With every birth, Rousseau persuaded Thérèse, apparently against her wishes, to abandon the baby. In his later autobiography, titled *Confessions* to evoke Saint Augustine—who hadn't wanted Adeodatus at first, either—Rousseau explained that "I trembled at the thought of entrusting them to a family ill brought up, to be still worse educated."[34] He meant his own. He also feared children would get in his way of writing something important. And after all, hadn't Plato himself suggested that ideally no father should know his own children, nor children their parents? When, some years later, Rousseau gave in to regret and tried to track down his children, no trace of them could be found.[35]

By that point, he was famous, or at least on the brink of it, for his book on education and raising children. When the celebrated author of *Émile* was revealed to have abandoned his own children, Rousseau had, as his biographer Leo Damrosch says, some "explaining to do."[36] Voltaire among others disputed his qualifications. Yet in another sense Rousseau had done precisely the thing that authors of successful parenting books must do: he identified something that parents are afraid of.

The fear was sweeping economic change. Rousseau was the first to give a name to the unappealing new character born of the industrializing cities of Europe: "the bourgeois." Indecisive and apprehensive, the bourgeois, Rousseau claimed, "will never be either man or citizen." He wrote *Émile* as an antidote, and it was a hit in the United States especially. The book's radical message was that children were inherently good, if only parents and society would stop messing them up.

Rousseau's argument was the opposite of Saint Augustine's. Children were born good, Rousseau said. It was everything that happened after that ruined them, especially the actions of their parents. And while John Locke encouraged discipline, habit, and reason, parents filling a child's "white paper" with knowledge and virtue and training for eventual independence, Rousseau said that childhood was a special state to be appreciated and extended as long as possible. Locke had advised reasoning with children. Rousseau said that was impossible, since children weren't reasonable, which was one of their best qualities. Instead of time in the schoolroom, he encouraged parents to devise situations in which their children could learn by experiment to trust their instincts rather than external lessons. Not school. Not religion. Not even books. Rousseau said children should learn to read on their own, from the invitations to parties that were sent to them, or suffer the pain of missing out.

Émile was addressed primarily to mothers, who were natural parents, Rousseau said. Men, on the hand, were natural teachers. Having never raised any children himself, Rousseau argued that the worst possible thing men could teach their children was to obey authority.[37] Instead, the role of the father was to be the author of a series of unfortunate but instructive events—as Emerson would put it, to "cast the bantling on the rocks."[38]

At the heart of *Émile* was a cryptic confession. Rousseau's personal experience of fatherhood, or lack thereof, still a secret when the book was published, lurked just below the surface of the story. "He who cannot fulfill the duties of a father," he wrote, "has no right to become one. Neither poverty nor labors nor concern for public opinion exempts him from feeding his children and from raising them himself. Readers, you can believe me. I predict that whoever . . . neglects such holy duties will . . . shed bitter tears for his offense and will never find consolation."[39]

"Imitation is suicide," Emerson wrote in his celebrated essay "Self-Reliance." "Insist on yourself; never imitate." Yet the essay is all Rousseau, in style and substance. Casting the bantling on the rocks, where it survives by learning for itself nature's lessons, was Rousseau. The disdain for bourgeois security was pure Rousseau: "Reliance on Property, including the reliance on governments which protect it, is the want of self-reliance." The emphasis on misfortune as education was Rousseau: "If our young men miscarry in their first enterprises they lose all heart. If the young merchant fails, men say he is *ruined*. A sturdy lad from New Hampshire or Vermont, who in turn tries all the professions, who teams it, farms it, peddles, keeps a school, preaches, edits a newspaper, goes to Congress, buys a township, and so forth, in successive years, and always like a cat falls on his feet, is worth a hundred of these city dolls."[40]

As a boy, Emerson had feared his father's practice of forcing him out into the cold ocean to swim. After his father's death, Emerson had grown up hungry, searching among fallen leaves for a lost dollar. Now, as a father himself, and with some of Beza Tucker's money in his pocket, Emerson had come through the peril and could see the wisdom of it. He was sure that it was better to risk drowning than never to swim at all.

When his son was born, Emerson was pleased but puzzled. "I see nothing in it of mine," he wrote. Even so, instinctively he called the baby by the name he had chosen for himself: Waldo, the boy's "natural name," he thought. When Waldo was a week old, Emerson went into the woods with a friend and hauled back six hemlock trees "to plant in my yard which may grow while my boy is sleeping."[41] The progress of the trees toward the sky would mirror young Waldo's own.

As Waldo grew, he became his father's "constant companion" around their house, inside and out, in the study and the garden alike. The boy played for hours at a time with a globe, a microscope, and magnets while his father worked. Waldo made whistles, boats, popguns, and a toy house with Henry Thoreau. Waldo slept in a trundle that pulled out from under his parents' bed, and he hated the thought of being separated from his family. "He does not want to go to school alone, no not at all, no, never," Emerson wrote in 1841, the same year he published "Self-Reliance."[42] Never mind the rocks and wolves, even the Concord schoolroom was too rough for Waldo.

At the end of January 1842, less than a year after the publication of "Self-Reliance," five-year-old Waldo came down with scarlet fever. Within two days the doctor had given up, and Waldo died on the night of January 27. His younger sister Ellen—whom

Lidian had insisted on naming after Emerson's first wife—got sick herself that same day. That night Ellen slept in her parents' bed, so Lidian could watch her. Emerson stayed up late writing letters, though he had little to say. "Farewell and farewell." "My darling my darling." "My boy, my boy is gone." "Shall I ever dare to love anything again?"[43] The next day, when nine-year-old Louisa May Alcott, whose family were neighbors and friends of the Emersons, knocked on the door to ask about Waldo, Emerson could only tell her, "Child, he is dead."[44] Emerson would spend years trying to make sense of it.

When Waldo Emerson died, Henry Thoreau was in the middle of a family crisis of his own. His beloved older brother, John, had died only two weeks earlier, and just as suddenly. Having nicked himself while shaving, John had succumbed to tetanus. Henry lost not only a brother but also his dearest friend. The two had taught school and had great adventures together, and they had been so close that after John's death Henry himself began to exhibit symptoms of tetanus, which is not contagious. Henry didn't have tetanus, only debilitating grief.

The question of why Thoreau went to live at Walden Pond in 1845 has never been answered definitively.[45] "To write" is the most common answer, and perfectly true as far as it goes. In particular, he wanted to write a book about a canoe trip he had taken with John, a sort of tribute and memorial. In *Walden*, Thoreau famously explained that "I went to the woods because I wished to live deliberately, to front only the essential facts of life, and see if I could not learn what it had to teach, and not, when I came to die, discover that I had not lived."[46] But for Thoreau living "deliberately" in the woods and writing also meant something more specific: getting away from work in his father's pencil factory. Thoreau went to the woods for the same reason that many young men and women left home for cities and towns and factories and western lands—to break free from the old family economy. Yet in Thoreau's case the problem was that the family business was working too well, and it bound him to his father in a way he deeply resented, but has never been fully known by his readers and admirers.

In the first half of the nineteenth century, no one in the United States made better pencils than the Thoreau family, and the reason for their success was Henry. John Thoreau, Henry's father, had entered the pencil business in 1823, after his brother-in-law happened upon a vein of plumbago, or graphite, in the New Hampshire hills. By then, John and Cynthia had four children, including Henry, and needed a lucky break. As a young man, John had borrowed against his expected inheritance to open a store. But the early death of his father, combined with mismanagement of the family estate, meant that John's inheritance never came through. His store failed, and afterward he struggled to earn a living, and was ultimately compelled to sell his gold wedding ring.

Once John got started in pencils, he and Cynthia were determined to recover the economic security and social standing they had lost. Pencils made by the family firm, initially called J. Thoreau & Co., quickly gained local recognition, winning an award in the first year of production.

Even so, more than a decade later, financial security remained elusive. Henry's brother, John, had skipped college to take a job as a teacher, and John Sr. proposed that Henry apprentice himself to a cabinetmaker, sensible training for pencil makers. But when Henry passed Harvard's entrance exams in 1833, Cynthia insisted they make it work. In 1835, near the end of Henry's second year, the Thoreaus gave up their brick house in Concord and moved into a smaller one with two of John's spinster sisters.

Fifteen miles away in Cambridge, Henry felt their sacrifice keenly. In November 1835, the Board of Overseers of Harvard College voted to allow enrolled students to take up to thirteen weeks off to earn money teaching, and Henry Thoreau was one of the first to apply for leave. A month later, he became the master of a one-room schoolhouse and seventy boys in Canton, twenty miles to the south. By the time he returned to Cambridge in the spring, he had acquired a new contempt for Harvard's classical curriculum as well as symptoms of what historians now think was the tuberculosis that would eventually kill him.

In May 1836, increasingly sick, Henry left Harvard again, and this time it wasn't clear whether he would be going back—whether he had the strength, or his family the money. Late in the summer, just before the start of the fall term, Henry and his father packed up boxes of pencils and set out on a trip to New York, where they hoped to earn tuition money.

Henry returned to Cambridge that fall with mixed feelings. He dedicated himself to academic work and performed well enough to win a prize of twenty-five dollars and a speaking role in the commencement ceremony. Thoreau and two other students were assigned to address a theme of special relevance: "The Commercial Spirit of Modern Times, Considered in Its Influence on the Political, Moral, and Literary Character of a Nation." Many members of his class were struggling to find jobs amid the financial panic of 1837. The twenty-year-old Thoreau wondered whether they should even be trying. Imagine looking down at Earth from "an observatory above the stars," Thoreau asked the hundreds assembled for the graduation ceremony. How would this "beehive of ours" appear from that height? Men "hammering and chipping, baking and brewing...scraping together a little of the gilded dust upon its surface"—precisely what his father did all day while mixing graphite powder into pencil "leads." For Henry, these workingmen had given away the most important thing they possessed: their freedom. The commercial spirit, Thoreau argued, was too much "the ruling spirit." Its triumph had made every man "a slave of matter."[47] Henry wanted nothing to do with the pencil factory.

After graduation, he started a teaching job in Concord, only to quit ten days into the academic year when he refused to punish wayward students with lashings, as the Concord school board required. Henry appealed to friends for word of open teaching jobs, but none appeared. Out of options, he joined his father in the pencil factory after all.

That autumn, Thoreau started two new projects. First, he began to dig into the complex technical problems that had made American pencils so inferior to European imports, greasy and brittle. Possibly through research in the Harvard library, Henry developed a formula for kiln-fired pencil leads—a mix of finely ground graphite and clay—that could be reliably graded from hard to soft. The improved Thoreau product appealed especially to engineers, surveyors, carpenters, and artists who valued its consistency.

At the same time, Henry also began a journal that eventually grew to roughly seven thousand pages and 2 million words. In the very first entry, he wished for a writer's room where no pencil making would impinge: where "the spiders must not be distributed, nor the floor swept, nor the lumber arranged." Even as he worked diligently in the pencil factory, refining innovations crucial to his family's livelihood, Henry was eager to get away.

In 1838, Henry went back to the classroom and opened a school in Concord with his brother, John. They taught together until 1841, when John's health—he, too, suffered from tuberculosis—worsened. After John's death, Henry found himself in his father's factory again. "I have been making pencils all day," he wrote with resignation in his journal that March.

In 1844, Henry made another breakthrough, inventing a grinding machine that produced exceptionally fine graphite powder, the key to a strong, even point, and in turn a clear, steady line. On the strength of these innovations, Thoreau pencils won more awards and were celebrated as the equal of any English ones. Around the same time, John Thoreau changed the name of the family business, stamped into their round pencils, from J. Thoreau & Co. to J. Thoreau & Son.

Henry's inventions had helped to lift his family, long accustomed to economy, into Concord's comfortable middle class, yet they didn't address the greatest challenge of pencil making in the first half of the nineteenth century: simply finding the wood.[48] The good red cedar needed to make high-quality pencils was hard to get because at that time it came from only one place in the world: the Gulf Coast of the United States, and especially Florida, where it was harvested and prepared by enslaved workers.

The Thoreaus, writes historian Robert A. Gross, were "Concord's first family of antislavery activists."[49] Their commitment to abolitionism had strengthened on precisely the same timeline as Henry's involvement in the pencil business. His pioneering work on kiln-fired leads in the fall of 1837 coincided with the visit of famed abolitionists Angelina and Sarah Grimké to Concord. Inspired,

Henry's mother, Cynthia, and his older sister, Helen, helped to found the Concord Female Anti-Slavery Society two months later. The youngest member of the Thoreau family, Sophia, joined soon after. These commitments carried over to the Thoreau household, where Cynthia refused to have sugar on her table.[50] Helen quit the Unitarian church because it permitted slaveholders to preach.[51]

In contrast, John Thoreau Sr. was probably the least politically active member of the family. He was a Whig, and his politics were oriented toward economic development, though not at any cost. In 1840, the whole Thoreau family, John included, signed a petition opposing the admission of Florida as a slave state.[52]

Meanwhile, Henry tended to hang back from public politics until at least the mid-1840s, when he moved to Walden Pond, spent the night in jail rather than pay his overdue taxes, and wrote the most influential abolitionist essay in history: "Civil Disobedience." The Thoreau family surely understood where their pencils came from—common knowledge among pencil makers in Concord and beyond. Henry in particular would have had a unique perspective, for he not only lived in the woods but treasured them, delighting in noticing and recording precisely what grew where.

Red cedar, sometimes called pencil cedar in the nineteenth century, is one of the most widely dispersed tree species on the North American continent, covering the Eastern Seaboard from southern Canada to southern Florida. As Thoreau noted in his journals, there was some of it growing around Walden Pond. But the problem was quality. Northern climates compress the growing season, compacting the trunks, cinching and skewing the grain. Exposed to New England winters, the red cedar can grow into a spectacularly gnarled and contorted tree—useless for pencils.

By contrast, in the warmer southern climates, red cedar grows tall and straight, and its soft but durable heartwood possesses a long, even grain, softening as it ages. Florida—acquired from Spain at no cost in 1819, formally claimed as a U.S. territory in 1821, and opened for business especially after the devastation of the Indigenous population in the Second Seminole War from 1835 to 1842—was then home to the richest stands of pencil cedar in the world. Enslaved workers were often hired out from cotton plantations to logging camps in the swamps, feeding felled trees downriver toward sawmills on the Gulf Coast. Particularly in the steam-powered sawmills built after 1830, much of the workforce was enslaved. So absolute was Florida's hold on the global trade in pencil cedar that when the Civil War cut off exports from the state, manufacturers in the United States and Europe alike had little idea where to look for an alternative source or substitute. Generations of historians and admirers of Thoreau's life, writing, and exacting ethical commitments have overlooked the connection between pencils and slavery, though Henry himself surely did not.

Late on a sunny afternoon in the summer of 1846, Henry Thoreau left his house by Walden Pond and walked two miles to the center of Concord to go to the cobbler. On the way, Thoreau happened to run into his hunting partner Sam Staples, the town constable and tax collector.

As he often had, Staples asked Thoreau about his overdue poll taxes, four years' worth, about six dollars. Warning that jail was next, Staples offered to pay the tax bill on Thoreau's behalf. When Thoreau declined, Staples responded, "Well, come along," and Thoreau did, to his famous night in jail.

Neither Thoreau's tax refusal nor his imprisonment was a direct statement on the Mexican-American War, which had begun a few months earlier, or the expansion of slavery and cotton around the Gulf of Mexico. He had stopped paying taxes years before, and the timing of his arrest owed more to the laziness of the collector than to protest.[53] Yet when Thoreau retrospectively described his night in jail as an act of protest in "Civil Disobedience," he highlighted the U.S. war with Mexico to expand slavery around the Gulf—through cedar country. "I love mankind," he wrote in his journal shortly after his night in jail. "I hate the institutions of their forefathers."[54]

John Thoreau makes a brief but noteworthy appearance in his son's essay, which detours through a story that highlights their differences. "Some years ago," Henry begins, "the State met me on behalf of the Church, and commanded me to pay a certain sum toward the support of a clergyman whose preaching my father attended, but never I myself. 'Pay,' it said, 'or be locked up in the jail.' I declined to pay." The anecdote has no known basis in fact. Church taxes had been discontinued by the time Henry was old enough to pay, and jail was not a penalty for unsubscribing from a congregation's rolls.[55]

John Thoreau's presence in "Civil Disobedience" marks the essay as a family matter. Henry turned the story of his opposition to war and slavery into a story about the differences between father and son. John represents his son's presumptive guilt by association. Was there an analogy between John Thoreau and the church and John Thoreau and the state? Did John also "attend" the services of the government that made war in Mexico on behalf of slaveholders? Henry seems to have been saying that, despite appearances and assumptions, J. Thoreau and son didn't worship the same creed, or subscribe to the same institutions.

*　　　*　　　*

Originally titled "Resistance to Civil Government," "Civil Disobe-dience" is by any name and measure one of the most celebrated and influential essays in history, an inspiration for Gandhi, Martin Luther King Jr., and many others. Fundamentally it is an inquiry into complicity in injustice and what to do about it. Thoreau pieced together his answer from metaphors drawn from the pen-cil business. "If I have unjustly wrested a plank from a drowning man," he said, "I must restore it to him though I drown myself." His metaphor for justice was lumber. "Let your life be a counter-friction to stop the machine," the inventor of sophisticated graphite grinders advised his audience.[56]

But Thoreau knew how many people were reluctant to do so, with the livelihoods of their families at stake. He himself was among them. "I do not wish to . . . set myself up as better than my neighbors," he explained. "What I have to do is to see, at any rate, that I do not lend myself to the wrong which I condemn."

After Thoreau was released from the Concord jail—to his cha-grin, someone, probably his aunt, paid his tax and got him out—he went back to Walden Pond and kept writing. By the time he left his house by the pond in September 1847 and moved back in with his parents, he had finished a draft of the book about his brother. The problem was that no one wanted to publish it. Determined, Thoreau kept reworking the manuscript for two more years. In 1849, the same year that "Resistance to Civil Government" was published, Thoreau paid around $300—roughly equivalent to a year's wages—to print one thousand copies of his book, *A Week on the Concord and Merrimack Rivers*. He raised some of the money by making and selling extra pencils. Perhaps he did not "lend himself" to the slavery he condemned, but he did borrow from it once again, and from the hated institutions of his father.

Today Thoreau is almost as famous for hypocrisy as for writing. Even his sympathetic readers and admirers relish charging him with ethics violations against himself, as if his point in moving to Walden Pond was to take a stand against going home for dinner. In fact, his business with his family ran much deeper than that, and Thoreau never stopped seeking rocks to cast himself on, even after he had left his house at Walden Pond and settled in again with his parents in Concord Village.

At the end of 1849, the year "Civil Disobedience" was published, the Thoreau family got an opportunity to untether themselves from the lumber business. They began selling their graphite, ground using the technology Henry had invented, for use in electrotyping instead. By the time Henry spoke on "Slavery in Massachusetts" on July 4, 1854, J. Thoreau & Son had been out of the pencil business for about a year. Of course, the advantages the Thoreaus had drawn from that business—the houses, the educations, the books, the money, the time, the freedom—remained theirs.

"The majority of the men of the North, and of the South and East and West, are not men of principle," Thoreau announced in "Slavery in Massachusetts." Instead, he went on, "it is the mismanagement of wood and iron and stone and gold which concerns them." His strident rhetoric, writes Thoreau biographer Laura Dassow Walls, "propelled him into the most militant ranks of the radical abolitionists." The press covered it avidly, alongside publicity notices and advance excerpts of *Walden*, set to be published a month later. Thoreau was pitched, Walls says, as "the

'Massachusetts Hermit' who had stepped boldly into the glare of radical abolitionism."[57]

He only got bolder. In the fall of 1859, on the night he heard of the militant abolitionist John Brown's siege of the federal armory at Harpers Ferry, Thoreau put a pencil and piece of paper underneath his pillow, as if to ensure that he wouldn't be able to sleep. When he woke up in the middle of the night, he picked up his pencil and wrote: "Our foes are in our midst and all about us. There is hardly a house but is divided against itself, for our foe is the all but universal woodenness of both head and heart, the want of vitality in man, which is the effect of our vice; and hence are begotten fear, superstition, bigotry, persecution, and slavery of all kinds." John Brown was the opposite of a wooden man. Four times in his plea, Thoreau mentioned Brown's role as a father, and the six sons who had fought with him, and "in whom he had perfect faith." Two of Brown's sons had died in the fighting at Harpers Ferry. Brown himself would be hung in December. "These men," Thoreau concluded, "in teaching us how to die, have at the same time taught us how to live."[58] At least for a time, John Brown was Henry Thoreau's idea of a father who lived for principle rather than capital.

Ralph Waldo Emerson, for his part, was a late-blooming, reluctant abolitionist at best. For years his wife Lidian had pushed him to join her, the Thoreau family, and others in Concord in the antislavery cause, but Emerson hung back. He finally spoke up in 1844, when he delivered an address "On the Emancipation of the West Indies"—marking the tenth anniversary of the end of slavery in the place where his inheritance had originated, where the Tucker family had done business. In the speech, Emerson condemned slavery for having left Black men with no financial patrimony to give or receive.

Ever since Waldo's death two years before, Emerson had been thinking about his son and fatherhood, but without arriving at any redeeming insights. On the contrary, he had trouble finding any meaning at all. "In the death of my son," Emerson wrote with unusual directness in his 1844 essay "Experience," "I seem to have lost a beautiful estate,—no more."

> I cannot get it nearer to me. If tomorrow I should be informed of the bankruptcy of my principal debtors, the loss of my property would be a great inconvenience to me, perhaps, for many years; but it would leave me as it found me,—neither better nor worse. So it is with this calamity: it does not touch me: some thing which I fancied was a part of me, which could not be torn away without tearing me, nor enlarged without enriching me, falls off from me, and leaves no scar.[59]

In the end, Waldo had dropped from his father's life like a fallen leaf or a loose dollar. Emerson, who had once identified good parenting with risk and peril, had gained only a rueful perspective on how entangled, and how fragile, money and fatherhood had become.

CHAPTER SIX

FAMILY: Charles Darwin

C harles Darwin spent more than fifty years investigating the connections between parents and children, honing theories of natural selection that have reshaped the world as much as any new idea or discovery of the last two centuries. Yet no one would have been more surprised by Darwin's extraordinary impact than his own father, Robert, who expected little from his son.

As a boy, Charles had proven himself to be an unremarkable student, falling "well below the ordinary standard of intellect," thought Robert, who as a doctor had made something of a practical study. "You care for nothing but shooting, dogs, and rat-catching, and you will be a disgrace to yourself and all your family," Robert scolded his son, and Charles never forgot how ashamed he was to hear it.[1]

Robert Darwin's disapproval hurt all the more because Charles revered his father. All his life, Charles, an avid collector of specimens, believed his father—whom he and his siblings and everyone else called the Doctor—to be the most impressive man in the world. At six feet two, and very broad, Robert Darwin was the largest man

Charles had ever seen. At the same time, Charles also thought his father to be the kindest man, the most astute, the most sympathetic, and the best judge of character—so sensitive that he was effectively clairvoyant, his son said, able "to predict the course of nearly any illness." Moreover, Robert was known to be an exceptionally savvy investor, growing what he had inherited, as well as what he had gained through marriage to a Wedgwood, into a patrimony large enough to grant his children ample allowances and loans that were easily forgiven.

But perhaps the most important thing that Charles Darwin inherited from his father, the Doctor, was a fear of blood. When Robert, expecting to boost his undistinguished son into a comfortable medical career, sent Charles to the University of Edinburgh, where he was meant to follow in the footsteps of his older brother, the lessons proved too grisly to endure.

The anatomy lectures—staged in grimy dissecting theaters, starring maimed corpses and spattered professors with bloody fingers—were bad enough. But the surgeries were far worse. Darwin witnessed two surgeries as a student. In the middle of the second, a gruesome operation on a child, he fled the operating theater, and vowed never to return.[2]

Thanks to his father, he didn't have to. With expectations of a substantial inheritance, Charles's attention wandered away from medicine. Changing course, Robert arranged for Charles to enter Cambridge, where he would study to be an Anglican priest, a reliable fail-safe for unpromising sons of well-to-do families. Securing a comfortable parish post was no more difficult than buying it at auction, which the Doctor was more than happy to do.

The idea of life as a country vicar appealed to the eighteen-year-old Charles. Less so the classical curriculum that would prepare him for ordination. Charles much preferred collecting bugs, especially beetles, and hunting birds.

At Cambridge, while he should have been studying Greek and Latin, Charles spent most of his time in his room with his friends and his gun. He would take up a stance in front of his mirror, double-barreled shotgun in hand, and quickly raise it to his shoulder, targeting his reflection. Or a friend would wave a lit candle about, and Charles would shoot a blank at it, to see if the air expelled from the barrel would extinguish the flame. The frequent explosions caused the housemaster to complain that Charles Darwin spent an unusual amount of time in his room cracking a horsewhip.

In view of his dubious record, when Charles, having recently graduated from Cambridge, received an unexpected invitation to join a two-year scientific expedition around the world, aboard the HMS *Beagle*, the Doctor said no. Then he sought a second opinion and changed his mind.

Though Charles Darwin is most identified with his journey on the *Beagle*, he came up with his best ideas within the walls of his own home, and he explored their implications especially through his experiences as the father of ten children. Studying his own children as if they were specimens like any other, he developed new theories about how creatures become what they are, rewriting foundational stories about the origins and development of the human family—and about the role of fathers.

In the middle of the nineteenth century, the great majority of people living in England would have said God the Father had designed and created each individual being. Darwin was not the first to propose that humans had instead evolved from other creatures, most directly apes. In fact, Charles's grandfather Erasmus Darwin was himself the author of one of the earliest books on the origins and development of life. But Charles's idea of natural selection gave the clearest picture of the process of evolution, and stated most clearly what the monkeys in our family tree revealed about the nature and future of the human species. As he worked out these world-changing ideas, Darwin's family life gave him a vivid window into what it meant to live in a world in which only the so-called fittest would thrive and survive, for he was desperate to make sure that his children would.

The voyage of the *Beagle*—departing from Plymouth, England, at the end of December 1831 and returning in October 1836, three years behind schedule—was for knowledge, but knowledge was for empire, and empire was for money. Done right, geography and science were tools for commerce. The *Beagle* was one small pawn in a British strategy begun in 1821, the same year that many South American republics gained their independence from Spain, setting off renewed competition among European sea powers. The ship's mission was to map the coastline for navigation, chart the winds for sail, sound the harbors for ports, and see what could be got from where, before someone else figured out a better way.

In September and October of 1835, as the *Beagle* plied the Galápagos, Darwin busied himself hunting finches—dozens of individual islands full of finches, the same but different. When the ship turned north and sailed on, and Darwin finally had a moment to organize his finches, he confirmed that the birds varied by island, just as their principal food sources did. But he didn't yet know what to make of these observations.

Darwin sailed back to his home island of Britain in October 1836, the same month Waldo Emerson was born, amid warning signs of an international financial crisis. In England, basic necessities, including food, were increasingly hard to come by. Two years earlier, the British government had passed revisions to England's Poor Laws that aided manufacturers but squeezed the working classes. Gone were long-customary forms of relief that had protected against hunger and privation—and, critics of the old laws claimed, protected people from their obligation to work. Now relief could only be obtained by entering a government-run workhouse, where conditions were meant to be a deterrent against staying.

At the heart of these reforms were the bracing ideas of Thomas Malthus, an Anglican cleric whose father had been a friend of Jean-Jacques Rousseau. Malthus took issue with Rousseau's assessment of human nature—his conviction that fathers could be encouraged to do what was good for their children. Malthus thought the opposite: that as conditions in society improved, men would inevitably take the opportunity to father more children than they could support, no longer feeling any compelling responsibility to provide for them. His 1798 *Essay on the Principle of Population* claimed that if births continued to increase without check, especially among those he judged to be the lowest moral and economic classes, the earth's resources would dwindle toward zero, leading to widespread hunger and eventually starvation. The prediction was meant to be frightening.

Malthus asked, in the absence of painful but necessary checks on population, such as plague and war, what could be done? Birth control beyond basic education and moral restraint was considered too scandalous—for Malthus and others, separating sex from pregnancy was even scarier than starving. Instead, new laws that limited assistance for the poor exerted population control from above, imposing on families and their newborns especially a struggle for survival that for many would end in death, despair, or Australia. At the same time, Britain reached out into the world for more of what it needed via its unmatched empire, an attempt to outrun scarcity to the ends of the earth.

In 1837 and 1838, the same years of economic crisis in which Emerson worked on "Self-Reliance," Darwin hit on the idea that a "struggle for existence" drove the development of life over time. Competition for necessary resources led the victors to pass on advantageous traits and adaptations to their offspring. That was why the finches were different on different islands. Their struggles for existence had varied with local conditions and food sources.

Darwin's grandfather Erasmus had theorized something similar: that natural drives to procreate led male creatures especially to develop useful defenses and adaptations. This was the reason stags had horns and male birds had sharp spurs, while females of the species did not: to fight for paternity. Erasmus Darwin called these drives loves. Charles's concept, developed in the anxious laboratory of the British Empire, was bloodier and more fearsome than his grandfather's. "When two races of men meet, they act precisely like two species of animals," he wrote in his journal in 1838, when he was a bachelor living in London and reading Malthus. "They fight, eat each other, bring diseases to each other &c, but then comes the more deadly struggle, namely which have the best fitted organization, or instincts (i.e. intellect in man) to gain the day."[3]

As he developed these ideas at home, Darwin kept collecting specimens and evidence. He made regular outings to the London Zoo. He wrote to experts in animal husbandry for insights into culling. He studied the breeding of dogs, pigeons, livestock, and horses, a sort of "artificial selection" of favorable traits.[4] Darwin was beginning to see the world as "a constant competitive struggle for survival" whose outcome was not preordained by God, but did have its own coherent logic.[5] He plainly recognized this as a challenge to the image of God the Father as creator, designer, begetter. Airing such ideas publicly would be as serious as "confessing a murder," Darwin wrote to a friend in 1844.[6] Anxiety over the implications of his work and fears about its reception often made Darwin physically ill, and he procrastinated and deferred publication of his most famous ideas for years that stretched into decades.

Darwin's worries were personal as well as professional. If the point of life was procreation, he was missing out. "We poor bachelors are only half men," he wrote in 1838, on the occasion of a friend's marriage. "Creeping like caterpillars through the world, without fulfilling our destination." Darwin's immersion in the natural world led him to the same conclusion that Aristotle had reached on Lesbos: full manhood meant fatherhood, a wife, and children. But Darwin wasn't sure he had what it took to get there. "As for a wife, that most interesting specimen in the whole series of vertebrate animals, Providence only know[s] whether I shall ever capture one or be able to feed her if caught."[7]

Darwin was then twenty-nine. He had never known real scarcity and never would. He could have secured a post as a gentleman vicar with nothing more than his rich father's good word. Yet he was terrified of poverty. Even as his career as a naturalist and author started to take off, he was haunted by the possibility of ending up poor and alone.[8]

Yet he also worried about what marriage and children would mean for his work. As a young bachelor, he feared especially running out of time—so few days on earth, so many things to be done.

In the summer of 1838, Darwin's cousin Emma Wedgwood caught his eye, but Charles was hesitant. To work out the best course of action, he made an accounting of expected gains and losses from family life. His assessment may have been based on a conversation with his father, Robert, and it may also have been informed by a comic drama of the age titled *To Marry or Not to Marry*.[9]

Sometime that summer, at the top of a blank page, Darwin wrote: "This is the question." Underneath, on one side of the paper, was the heading "Not Marry." Here Darwin listed the costs of marriage and fatherhood. He would lose the "Freedom to go where one likes—choice of Society . . . Conversation of clever men at clubs." Having a family meant being "forced to visit relatives," taking on the added "expense & anxiety of children," "perhaps quarelling [*sic*]—Loss of time.—cannot read in the Evenings—fatness & idleness—Anxiety & responsibility," he repeated. Not to mention "less money for books &c—if many children forced to gain one's bread . . . you will be worse than a negro . . . but there is many a happy slave." Glibly and privately, Darwin described fatherhood as a form of enslavement—an obligation to serve the financial and emotional demands of children and family.

Glibly and privately, he thought marriage and fatherhood would be worth it. On the other side of the page, under the heading "Marry," Darwin listed the benefits. "Children (if it Please God)—Constant companion, (& friend in old age) who will feel interested in one,—object to be beloved & played with,—better than a dog anyhow.—Home, & someone to take care of house—Charms of music & female chit-chat." For Darwin, this was a compelling vision. "My god," he concluded, seemingly surprised at himself, "it is intolerable to think of spending one's whole life, like a neuter bee, working, working, & nothing after all.—No, no won't do . . .

picture to yourself a nice soft wife on a sofa with good fire, & books & music perhaps . . . Marry—Mary—Marry."[10]

Darwin tallied marriage and children as time lost and obligations acquired, but that failed to account for the overlap between family and work. His courtship of his cousin Emma was marked by long chats, many about Charles's research and the questions it raised, large and small. At the time Darwin was living in his father's house and working on the problem of how traits, characteristics, qualities, and conditions pass from one generation to the next. Much of his evidence came from his father's anecdotal experience as a doctor, and was filtered through a physician's focus on disease and infirmity. But Darwin had also started writing to friends and relatives who had children, especially newborns, for field reports on child development and insight into what was innate and what was learned. He sketched the outline of a new project in his notebook: "A natural history of babies."

Emma could already see what this would mean for their home lives: "You will be forming theories about me," she wrote to Charles, "& if I am cross or out of temper you will only consider 'What does that prove?'"[11] She was on to something, but it wasn't Emma alone that Darwin would fixate on as a research subject.

Through her father, Josiah Wedgwood II, Emma Wedgwood was the granddaughter of the famous potter, manufacturer, and abolitionist Josiah Wedgwood. Through his mother, Susannah Wedgwood, Charles Darwin was Josiah's grandson. In 1787, amid the campaign for the abolition of slavery in the British Empire and around the world, Josiah Wedgwood created and mass-produced a medallion featuring an image of a Black man on bended knee, bound hands clasped beseechingly, framed by a pleading phrase: "Am I not a man and a brother?" Reprinted on abolitionist pamphlets, reproduced as brooches, pendants, bracelets, and hair clips, the medallion was one of the most widely circulated images of an African person in the age before photography.

Emma Wedgwood and her cousin and husband, Charles Darwin, shared their ancestor Josiah's earnest commitment to ending slavery, which Darwin had observed firsthand during his journey on the *Beagle*. They shared as well the substantial financial inheritance that derived in part from selling Wedgwood pottery to British imperial markets in the Caribbean, where prosperity meant slavery.[12]

Charles and Emma would have ten children. The first one, a boy, was born just after Christmas 1839, eleven months after their wedding. Earlier in the year, Darwin had published his first book, a journal of his voyage on the *Beagle*. Now he started a fresh notebook to record observations of his newborn son, named William Erasmus, after his grandfather, claiming by that name "a right of hereditary descent to be naturalists & especially geologists."[13]

"During first week," Darwin reported, Willy "yawned, streatched [*sic*] himself just like old person—chiefly upper extremities—hiccupped—sneezes sucked, Surface of warm hand placed to face, seemed immediately to give wish of sucking, either instinctive or associated knowledge of warm smooth surface of bosom." For some time, Darwin was content simply to record. At a month and a day, Willy "perceived bosom, when three or four inches from it, as was shown by protrusion of lips—& eyes becoming fixed—was it by smell or sight?—It was not, certainly, by touch." The frame of these observations is extraordinarily intimate—bosom, infant, and observer, pressed so close together that they nearly cease to be recognizable as mother, child, and father.

But before long Darwin grew impatient with observation and began to intervene to advance his research. He touched the bottom of his son's foot with paper, and "it jerked it away very suddenly & curled its toes, like person tickled, evidently subject to tickling. . . . What can be origin of movement from tickling?"[14] When Willy— the "it" who jerked its foot—was four months old, Darwin began to startle him, to learn about the development of reflexes. "I made loud snoring noise, near his face," Darwin noted, "which made him look grave and afraid and then suddenly burst out crying. This is curious, considering the wondrous number of strange noises, and stranger grimaces I have made at him, and which he has always taken as good joke. I repeated the experiment." Three days later, Darwin tried a new approach. "I came to him," he recorded, "with my back to him, & then stood motionless,—he looked very grave & surprised, & would almost have cried had I not turned round, when his face relaxed into smile. These vague fears, curious." Where had they come from?

The importance of learning by imitation was clear. At nine months, Willy was already trying to imitate his father, patting his mouth and making noise. Less than a week later, Darwin was convinced that his son had copied him by saying "poor"—the boy's first word, and one of his father's lifelong obsessions. "Whenever excited, more especially when pleased," Darwin noticed, "he wrings his hands & arms, something like the theatrical representation of grief, in the same manner as I have been assured I did, when very young."

There were also traces of a deeper inheritance. When Willy was a year old, his father held a mirror up to his face. The boy kissed his reflection, and snuggled his face up to the glass—"very like Ouran Outang [*sic*]," Darwin thought. He had been studying them at the London Zoo. The implication was that even the expression of what were usually thought to be uniquely human emotions was in fact shared with, which is to say inherited from, other animals.[15]

For nearly two decades, Darwin continued to observe and chronicle the development of his ten children, overlaying fresh notes from the younger ones onto his records of the older ones, compiling a data set that grew more robust with every conception, pregnancy, and delivery.

Darwin was able to study his children so closely because he was always home. His family's money, combined with his wife's portion of her own family's money, freed him from the need for a teaching position. In 1842, the Darwins moved out of London, settling on a generous estate in Kent, called Down House, that Charles's father helped them buy. There Darwin lived as a self-described "hermit" for long stretches, hardly traveling for years on end, not even to local academic conferences.[16] On the rare occasions when he did venture out, he always got a bad feeling at the start of a trip.[17] This was partly because, though he had once, in theory, feared losing the company of men at clubs, he was by nature a solitary person. And it was partly because he was sick.

Darwin's illness was principally digestive, or at least its symptoms were. They began just after the birth of his son Willy, and they lasted for the rest of his life, with Darwin diligently tracking their ebb and flow: "Extreme spasmodic daily & nightly flatulence," plus "occasional vomiting, on two occasions prolonged during months. Vomiting preceded by shivering, hysterical crying, dying sensations of half-faint & copious very pallid urine. Now vomiting & every passage of flatulence preceded by ringing of ears, treading on air & vision. Focus & black dots, Air fatigues, specially risky, brings on the Head symptoms, nervousness when E.[mma] leaves me." Doctors, Darwin reported, were "puzzled."[18]

When he first got sick, Darwin spent much of his time in the nursery with his son. Emma monitored his health with the same dedicated attention that he had paid to Willy's development. "Pulse 60," she noted one day, "oysters and artichokes." Later: "Pulse 52, partridge and pudding." Then: "Very good day, hare, oysters, pulse about 54." But a meal of "turtle did not agree."[19] Darwin was ill more often than he was well.

But when he was feeling up for it, he loved to play. He would get on his knees and dance while singing opera. He padded about like a bear, growling as his children put their hands inside his shirt to feel his hairy chest.[20] He loved to have his back rubbed and often enlisted his children to do it. Sometimes they all looked through an illustrated book about animals they called "the monkey book," and Darwin's children were rapt as he told them about each one.[21]

Victorian families often celebrated themselves by making a diary of their children. Usually this was the role of mothers, a way to forge warm family bonds in the seemingly heartless world of capitalist industry and competition. By the middle of the nineteenth century, increasing numbers of social welfare laws and services, including public schooling, meant that not every member of the family could be expected to contribute to the household by working. But all could contribute to the family's emotional life, its private mythology, history, culture, and language.[22] Children were increasingly seen in Rousseau's terms, as existing in a special realm of innocence outside the marketplace. They were "precious," even "priceless."[23]

In the Darwin household, these daily observations were recorded in a book called the *Babbiana,* and Charles added to it religiously, especially when Emma happened to be away, so she wouldn't miss a single chapter of their lives. In the *Babbiana,* everyone was a character, and any event could be dramatized. "When I had had him for about five minutes," Darwin wrote of his eldest son, Willy, "I asked him where was Mama, and he repeated your name twice in so low and plaintive a tone, I declare it almost made me burst out crying . . . one could write for ever about him."[24]

But Darwin's favorite was Annie, his oldest daughter, born a year and a half after Willy.[25] When Willy went off to boarding school at age ten, Annie stayed behind. She would sneak her father a pinch of tobacco while he was working, "her whole form radiant with the pleasure of giving pleasure." She would spend half an hour fixing her father's hair and smoothing his collar and cuffs. Her affection was irrepressible and transparent.[26]

Darwin was terrified of anything that might break his family up. He always felt worse when his wife was away. He especially worried that he had passed his own health problems on to his children: his family frailties, plus Emma's, multiplied by the fact that they were cousins. Even before he proposed, he had studied the question of close marriage: "why beauty health and intellect result from certain unions, and deformity disease and insanity from others."[27] Having absorbed his father's anecdotes of heritable disease, this was the most awful thing he could imagine: "Nothing comes up to the misery of having illness amongst one's children."[28] To some degree, this was more fear than reality. Darwin's third child, a girl named Mary, had died at just twenty-three days old in the fall of

1842, but especially for the time, Emma's pregnancies and deliveries had been remarkably successful.

Then, all of sudden, in the summer of 1850, Annie got sick.

All that fall Annie was weak, not quite herself, and her parents sought answers from the best doctors in London. None could provide a definitive diagnosis, but Charles was convinced: "She inherits, I fear with grief, my wretched digestion."

Darwin arranged to bring Annie to his own doctor in Malvern, a hydropathist who administered water cures, including a proprietary "spinal wash" that involved rubbing a cold towel up and down the backbone. Charles loved having his own back rubbed, and often enlisted his children to do it, especially Annie.

For a moment, the water treatment seemed to be working, and then in the winter of 1851 Annie started vomiting. Charles rushed her to his doctor again, a day's journey by coach. "Her case seems to be an exaggerated one of my . . . illness," he wrote to Emma when they arrived.[29]

As long as there was hope, there was news to put in a letter and send home. But when Annie worsened with diarrhea, Darwin couldn't bring himself to write. No letter from him arrived at Down House on Wednesday, April 23, 1851. For Emma, waiting, silence was telling. The next letter she got, the following day, was a memory rather than an update. "She went to her final sleep most tranquilly, most sweetly at twelve o'clock today," Charles wrote of Annie. "Our poor dear dear child has had a very short life but I trust happy, and God only knows what miseries might have been in store for her." He found some solace in the fact that she would not live as he did, chronically ill, but that was not much comfort. He left his doctor's clinic in Malvern before Annie's funeral to get home to Emma as quickly as he could. "We must be more and more to each other, my dear wife," Darwin wrote before departing.[30] For some time he did not know precisely where his daughter had been buried.

One week after Annie's death, Darwin composed a memorial. "Her joyousness and animal spirits radiated from her whole countenance," he recalled. "She seemed formed to live a life of happiness," Darwin wrote, and he had expected that her happiness would be his too. "I always thought," Darwin grieved, "that come what might, we should have had in our old age, at least one loving soul, which nothing could have changed."[31]

Darwin's concept of "natural selection" has sometimes been interpreted as justifying a laissez-faire or hands-off approach to social policy—as if hardship and suffering were diseases best allowed to run their course. Yet Darwin's own approach to fatherhood was the very opposite of Emerson's call to "cast the bantling on the rocks." For Darwin, "the survival of the fittest" only heightened the importance of every parental intervention that might make his children the fittest, that might allow them to be selected and survive.

Annie's death heightened Darwin's fear that he had passed on to his children his own maladies and infirmities, made all the worse by his marriage to his cousin Emma, whom he nonetheless adored.[32] "The worst of my bugbears," Darwin wrote the year after Annie's death, "is hereditary weakness."[33] Someone at Down House was always sick. "For years we have had one or other of our children invalids," he wrote a friend in 1863. "Everyone has his heavy drawbacks & my own health & even more that of my children is our sore drawback."[34]

Illness wasn't the only area of concern. Darwin viewed his oldest son, Willy, much as the Doctor had once viewed him. At twelve, Willy seemed "backward for his age." Like his father, he preferred collecting butterfly specimens to doing schoolwork. Worried that his son was drifting off course, Darwin agonized over where to send him to school, and for a time considered a new, progressive school known for its unconventional discipline and a focus on sciences. Yet ultimately the school's newfangled curriculum seemed too risky, an "awful experiment" to conduct on his son, and Darwin sent Willy to a time-tested boarding school instead.[35]

Work was the only thing that kept Darwin's mind off of worries about his children.[36] Especially in moments of his greatest personal despair, Darwin focused on the problem of heredity and parentage, cultivating "the habit of close mental attention" and making big breakthroughs that led to radical new insights into the question of origins.[37] He abandoned the pretense of churchgoing— on Sundays he would walk his family to the church door, and there he would turn around and walk away.

Despite the worries they provoked, Darwin wanted more children. Emma was forty-three in 1851, when Annie died and their youngest child, Horace, was born. Charles was hoping he wouldn't be the last. In October 1852, he wrote to another cousin: "Emma has been very neglectful of late and we have not had a child for more than one whole year."[38] She miscarried not long after, and again the next year. But in 1856, at the age of forty-eight, Emma gave birth to another son, named Charles.[39]

When Darwin renewed his nursery observations after Charles's birth, he noticed some worrisome signs in his youngest son. The baby was small, slow to walk and talk, and cried less than his brothers and sisters had. But even so he was placid, and joyful, and much loved. Darwin taught him to kiss on command and held Charles on his lap for hours. Biographers have speculated that Charles Junior may have had Down syndrome, first identified and named ten years later.[40] The Darwins' *Babbiana*, the family's journal that lovingly recorded the daily development of the children, ended the year Charles was born.

After years of procrastination and fear about the reception of his ideas, what finally got Darwin working on his theory of natural selection in earnest, more than grief, more than anxiety, was competition. In 1858, he received a letter from a younger naturalist and admirer, Alfred Russel Wallace, laying out a theory of origins, heredity, and evolution much like the one Darwin himself had been developing—in fact sitting on for two decades. "For a moment the news hit him like the death of a child," according to Darwin's biographer Janet Browne. That was the metaphor he used for his idea of natural selection: his child. Now gravely worried over its health, he finally took decisive action.

Alfred Russel Wallace's father, a lawyer, had died young, leaving no legacy for his family. Wallace was in the field, collecting and selling specimens to earn a living, while Charles Darwin sat on the estate his father had bought him and wrote *On the Origin of Species*. The book effectively ended the competition Wallace did not realize he had started. "I am almost glad of Wallace's paper for having led to this," Darwin wrote once he was nearing the finish.

On the Origin of Species was published in 1859, thirty years after Darwin had hit on its core ideas of natural selection and the struggle for existence. For three decades, he had thought obsessively about the implications of these ideas for his own family and children, and yet his book contained only one sentence about the origins of man and human evolution—a closing promise, on page 487 of 489, that, in the future, "light will be thrown on the origin of man and his history." [41]

But readers did not wait until the next volume to apply Darwin's theories to human beings. It was an issue of the greatest interest and importance for the implications of Darwin's ideas went in two radically different directions at once. First, his book made clear that it was very rare for parents to generate an enduring legacy—extinction was much more common. And second, death, Darwin claimed as he concluded his book, was a beneficial and necessary thing. This was "natural selection" at work "solely by and for the good of each being," so that "all corporeal and mental endowments will tend to progress towards perfection." By "the war of nature, from famine and death . . . endless forms most beautiful and wonderful have been, and are being, evolved."

Darwin's conclusion was all the more tantalizing—and worrisome—because he did not explain precisely how inherited traits were transmitted from parent to child on the way to perfection or extinction. In 1867, one anonymous critic of Darwin's theory put the problem this way: Imagine a light-skinned sailor shipwrecked on a desert island populated by dark-skinned natives. The white man, claimed the critic, might well "kill a great many blacks in the struggle for existence." He might well "have a great many wives and children." He might even become king of the island. But its inhabitants, as Darwin's critic imagined them, would never "acquire the energy, courage, ingenuity, patience, self-control, endurance" by which their king had "killed so many of their ancestors, and begot so many children." Nor would these imaginary islanders become white. On the contrary, the skin color of the sailor's children would be darker than that of their father.[42] Perfection, as some conceived of it then, would never arrive. It was easy to see the larger question: Could the so-called heroes of the British Empire manage to save the world, or would they be dragged down with it?

Darwin genuinely believed that the answer to his grandfather Josiah Wedgwood's abolitionist question—"Am I not a man and a brother?"—was yes: All human beings were a family of a sort, descended from a common ancestor in the deep past. He disputed the then-common claim that human "races" were different species, though he did allow that "sub-species" would be a fitting characterization. More infamously, Darwin frequently argued around this time that the world's "savage races," in effect meaning people with relatively darker skin, were less evolved and remained closer to their primate ancestors than the world's most "civilized" race, meaning "Caucasians" hailing from "the western nations of Europe, who now so immeasurably surpass their former savage progenitors."[43]

Darwin was so bothered by the desert-island critique of natural selection that he spent a whole year trying to identify its author. His investigation led him to Fleeming Jenkin, a distinguished Scottish engineer, professor at the University of Edinburgh, and inventor of the cable car. Jenkin was a friend of Robert Louis Stevenson, author of popular adventure stories, including *Treasure Island*, that cast their heroes out to sea in the far reaches of the empire. To answer his critics, Darwin wanted to explain the transmission of traits from parents to children in a way that would clarify the beneficial operation of natural selection, tending toward perfection, even given the survival of, for example, relatively darker skin color. That became the task of his 1868 book, *The Variation of Animals and Plants under Domestication*.

"Domestication" brought Darwin's thinking home. A chapter on inheritance marked the first time that he had written directly of human parentage, and it featured stories about his own family, who remained anonymous. "A boy had a singular habit," began Darwin, who was the boy in question, "when pleased, of rapidly moving his fingers parallel to each other. When this boy was almost an old man," explained Darwin, who was then nearly sixty, "he could still hardly resist this trick when much pleased, but from its absurdity concealed it. He had eight children." Darwin then had seven living children. "Of these, a girl, when pleased, at the age of four and a half years, moved her fingers in exactly the same way . . . when much excited. . . . as her father had done." The girl was Darwin's youngest daughter, Elizabeth. "I never heard of anyone, excepting this one man and his little daughter, who had this strange habit; and certainly imitation was in this instance out of the question."[44] The story of Darwin and his daughter showed the powerful mechanism of inheritance linking parents and children. Traits could be passed down intact and undiluted, and even those that seemed unrelated to survival could help parents recognize and in turn care for their children. Darwin called this mechanism of heredity pangenesis.

When he was looking for a name for this theory, Darwin had written to his son's tutor at Cambridge, where ancient texts retained their central place in the curriculum. Aristotle had rejected the "pangenesis" of his own time, but Darwin liked the word's primordial authority. He hoped its resonances would bolster his theory, which he knew to be speculative, tenuous, and provisional.

Two thousand years separated Darwin at Down House from Aristotle on Lesbos, yet even the observation of human sperm and egg under a microscope had not clarified the workings of generation. Like others of his day, Darwin understood reproductive cells to be made up of "a multitude of germs thrown off from each separate atom of the organism." He called these germs, or seeds, gemmules. He said children got some from fathers, some from mothers, and the strongest of these were passed on in turn, dominating for generation after generation.[45] Yet no matter what it was called, "pangenesis" was still just a theory. Darwin wrote to a sympathetic colleague that he feared his idea would "expire, unblessed & uncussed by the world, but I have faith in a future & better world for the poor dear child!"[46]

Darwin got help from his cousin—not Emma this time, but Francis Galton. Galton was thirteen years younger and in awe of his famous cousin Charles. Taking off from Darwin's work, Galton proposed that intelligence was a heritable form of family property—an ability that "clings" to families. He traced family lines to show that judges begat judges begat judges, and he liked to think that the same was true with natural scientists. In 1869, Galton published a self-congratulatory study called *Hereditary Genius*. He later coined the term "eugenics" to describe his "science of human improvement," and went on to lead the early development of the field until Charles Darwin's son Leonard took over after Galton's death in 1911.[47]

Eugenics wasn't only about intelligence, but also talent and beauty, which Galton also defined as family legacies. "It is not improbable," he wrote, "whether each person may not carry visibly about his body undeniable evidence of his parentage and near kinships." Galton and his fellow eugenicists claimed to have mastered the science behind the idea, now taken for granted, that beautiful people had beautiful children, reorienting romantic love away from the ancestry and legacy of each family and toward its future.

The term "eugenics" was derived from the Greek for "well born," but really it meant well fathered. For Galton, ability, like nobility, was a strictly patrilineal inheritance. This finding, too, was self-interested. Like his cousin Charles Darwin, Francis Galton was a grandson of the learned Erasmus Darwin, but Galton had a different grandmother. Identifying discrepancies between male and female achievement, Galton held that a distinguished mother alone was not enough to make a distinguished child. He seems never to have considered the significance of all the resources and advantages lavished on sons, over and above daughters, from the moment of birth. In this oversight he was hardly alone. "I do not think I ever in my whole life read anything more interesting and original," Darwin said of his cousin's book. Darwin's son George also found Galton's ideas compelling, and helped him work up charts on their family lineage.[48]

Galton's theory of hereditary superiority fit Darwin's tenuous theory of gemmules. Galton's fawning approval fit Darwin's chronic insecurity about the reception of his ideas, and Galton pulled his cousin into an experiment involving rabbits and blood transfusions. Galton injected the "alien blood" of black-and-white spotted rabbits into silver ones, who were then induced to breed with other silvers. He expected to yield proof of Darwin's gemmule theory in the form of a litter of silver rabbit babies with black-and-white spots.

Waiting for the expected litter, Galton was "quite sick with anxiety," the old family curse. Finally, a silver rabbit was born with white markings on its foot. "Good rabbit news!" Galton wrote to his cousin, before learning that this variation was in fact quite common among silver rabbits.[49] Of the eighty-eight rabbits whose births he had contrived to engineer, none betrayed any influence of the "alien" gemmules that might support a hypothesis of blood-borne genius.

After these disappointing results, Galton started to think that characteristics were passed on to children in proportion to their strength in parents, and in 1871 he published his rabbit experiment in *Nature*. Darwin however, with his theory of pangenesis now in greater doubt than it had been at the start of the rabbit experiment, wished Galton would just drop the whole thing. Nevertheless, Charles agreed to move dozens of the crossbred rabbits to Down House.[50] He was always trying to save money on food for his household, to protect and grow the financial legacy he meant to leave his children.

By then Darwin's sensitivity to criticism was four decades in the making, loaded with the anxiety that the idea of "natural selection" had given him from the outset. He knew that to realize the full potential of his insight he had to court controversy and make good on the promise of *On the Origin of Species*: to address the question of human origins and evolution.

Published in 1871, *The Descent of Man*—Darwin called it his "man book"—was arguably even more ambitious than *Origin*. The book was written against "that arrogance which made our forefathers declare that they were descended from demigods."[51] It brought human history down to earth, where apes became a main character.

First Darwin showed that man was an animal like any other. Tracing clear links and likeness from the human body to other animals, Darwin showed that virtually everything that seemed uniquely "human"—the gross anatomy of the skeleton, muscles, nerves, blood, guts, and organs, as well the softer stuff of the brain, reproduction, diseases, instincts, language, emotion, and expression—was more generally "animal." Even the very ideas of parents and children and family were in fact products of natural selection, one animal caring for another, helping it survive. He presented evidence of "parental affection . . . [in] starfish and spiders," concluding that "those communities which included the highest number of the most sympathetic members would flourish best, and rear the greatest number of offspring."

Then, to explain precisely how humans had evolved from "lower forms of nature," Darwin introduced the novel concept of "sexual selection." The "struggle for survival" was not only a question of brute strength and wiles. Physical appearance—beauty—also mattered. He drew analogies to colorful insects and birds with elaborate plumage. Such qualities were irrelevant to nature in general but paramount to mates. To prove it, he had male pigeons dyed magenta to gauge the effect on females.[52]

The magenta pigeons highlighted an important point. There was one thing about sexual selection that set humans apart. Darwin thought that among pigeons, as among most animals, females controlled sexual selection. But in humans, Darwin proposed, selection was the job of men, especially the great ones. "The strongest and most vigorous men," Darwin wrote, "those who could best defend and hunt for their families, and during the later times the chiefs or headmen—those who were provided with the best weapons and who possess the most property . . . would have succeeded in rearing a greater average number of offspring than would the weaker, poorer, and lower members of the same tribes. There can also be no doubt that such men would generally have been able to select the more attractive women," projecting their favorable traits and admirable characteristics into the future. By Darwin's formula, one good white man was enough to improve a world of lesser beings. Through sexual selection, fathers drove society toward perfection.[53]

Darwin continued his interventionist ways even when his children were grown.

William, the oldest, had his grandfather Robert's skill for finance and investment. Leonard would become longtime president of Francis Galton's Eugenics Education Society (sometimes called the Eugenics Society). Horace went to Cambridge and founded a thriving manufacturer of scientific instruments. Two of Darwin's sons, George and Francis, wanted to do serious science, just like their father, who did everything he could to help.

Darwin put the boys forward for membership in learned societies. He sent them to the United States to cultivate professional contacts. He pushed Francis to pick up on some questions raised by his own work on plants. When Francis's paper on the teasel weed was rejected by the Royal Society, Darwin flew into a petty fury, placed his son's paper elsewhere, and then published a letter celebrating it in the journal *Nature*.[54]

One of George's early papers took up the question that had long obsessed his father, cousin marriage. George had a special interest in its effects on the mind. He compiled statistics from society pages, doctors, psychiatric hospitals, and also attempted some field research, circulating questionnaires that returned few results, respondents proving unwilling to report on the mental health of their families. George concluded that cousin marriage was not correlated with infant mortality, yet it did tend to produce offspring of a relatively low vitality. This outcome was not so damning as might be feared, contended George Darwin, the offspring of one such marriage, for it could be overcome by dedicated care and cultivation, such as the type that his own father was known to provide. "Oh lord what a set of sons I have," Darwin crowed in celebration of George's publication success, "all doing wonders."[55]

Darwin's surviving daughters were not educated as formally and expensively as his sons. Even so, Henrietta became her father's most trusted editor, especially as he took on the topic of human origins and wrote publicly about their family life. She read his proofs during the decades of his greatest success and renown. Her brief as editor was not only to fix her father's mistakes and improve his prose but also to ensure that no identifying details slipped out that would harm their family. "Several reviewers speak of the lucid, vigorous style," Darwin wrote Henrietta shortly after the publication of *The Descent of Man*, the book a hit. When he got a check from his publisher for more than a thousand pounds, he wanted to show his gratitude for her work. "Now I know how much I owe to you in this respect," he told Henrietta, and paid her a bonus of thirty pounds.[56]

Charles Darwin transformed our understanding of the ties between parents and children, bringing new clarity to the mysterious workings of heredity. Because he was also such a devoted and loving father, he was feverishly obsessed with the practical implications of his theories: what it meant that his children were his, how they were all bound by the laws of biological inheritance, and what he could nevertheless do—was in some ways compelled to do—to help them thrive. In this fixation and anxiety Darwin was hardly alone. Thanks in large part to his ideas, for nearly two centuries empires, states, nations, and families have devoted vast resources to systematically promoting the survival of those they have deemed "naturally" fittest, their favored sons and daughters. Yet at least as far as his own case is concerned, Darwin may well have been wrong.

Drawing on the insights of modern medicine, historians now suspect that Darwin's chronic fear of passing his ailments on to his children may have been misplaced and overblown. The facts of his case suggest that while traveling the world aboard the *Beagle*, Darwin contracted a parasite or bacterium, perhaps Chagas and possibly others, too, that at least contributed to his chronic digestive problems as well as to the acute heart failure that killed him in April 1882, following a sharp three-month decline. Then again, there are plenty of other diagnostic possibilities, including acid reflux and lactose intolerance, which can indeed have a hereditary component.[57]

"Tell all my children to remember how good they have always been to me," Charles asked Emma while he lay in bed, gravely ill.[58] More than gratitude, this was a fatherly point of pride. Everything could be inherited, Darwin had come to believe, except humanity, which had to be taught.

CHAPTER SEVEN

WAR: Sigmund Freud

Sigmund Freud believed he would die on his fortieth birthday, May 6, 1896, and for years afterward he insisted that his prediction had been sound. No sooner had the anticipated date come and gone than Freud learned that his father, Jacob, was terminally ill. Freud, then a busy practicing physician, took the coincidence as evidence of "heavenly influences." He wrote to his friend Wilhelm Fliess, a doctor in Berlin: "It is the symbolic presentiment of unknown realities."[1]

By that time, Fliess was one of Freud's few remaining doctor friends. Many of the others had been alienated by Freud's fixation on proving the sexual origin of what were then called neuroses. Headaches, chest pain, shortness of breath, fatigue, diarrhea, gas, dizziness, numbness: all the everyday complaints patients brought to Freud's office could be treated as symptoms of deeper ills of mind, spirit, and society. Diseases known as neurasthenia and hysteria were then an epidemic in the industrial capitals of Europe and the United States. The afflicted were often stricken with diffuse neuroses and crippling fatigue and exhaustion. The larger fear in some circles was that European races, empires, nations, and individuals, men especially, were dying from within, victims of their own success. Their societies had become too manufactured and refined, their bodies too soft and unmanly. They could no longer compete in Darwin's "struggle for existence." They were not equipped for life under industrial capitalism. They were not the fittest, and they would not survive.

Most doctors then were conventional Darwinists, believing in the hereditary or physiological nature of illnesses—the existence of viruses was just being discovered. Darwin's influence on Freud ran deeper. As a young man, he idolized Darwin, but not for the technical details of his theories. Instead, what impressed Freud most was Darwin's fame, the scope and impact of his "extraordinary advancement in our understanding of the world."[2] Growing up poor in Vienna, Freud was determined to become a natural scientist in part because he wanted for himself what Darwin had achieved: renown, respect, riches.

Decades later, when he wrote his introductory lectures on psychoanalysis, Freud said that Copernicus had shown that the earth was not the center of the universe; Darwin had shown that man was one animal among many; and he, Freud, had shown that individual consciousness was not so individual or conscious as generally assumed.[3] Instead, it was inherited from the dim beginnings of history, where there loomed a primal father and his primal sons, certain that the world wasn't big enough for two generations at once. In Freud's account of inheritance, more than traits had been passed down across time. The legacies of this primordial generational conflict had been transmitted within families as anger and desire that, when repressed, caused illness and despair. The only way to have peace, individually and across society, was to face the father at last, strike him down, and then give him his due. Freud made it normal, even healthy, to despise your father, for that was part of growing up, and the first step to honoring him. Freud's own case was proof.

Freud was born in 1856 in a one-room apartment above a blacksmith's forge in Freiberg, a small town within the Austro-Hungarian Empire, now the Czech Republic. By then, his father Jacob, a struggling textile merchant, already had two grown sons and an infant grandson. Freud's mother, Amalia, was Jacob's third wife, half his age.

When Freud was three, the family left Freiberg. The reason for their departure is not known, but Freud remembered it as a "catastrophe." They may have gone after a business failure—Jacob was losing out to large textile manufacturers and merchants. They may have been fleeing anti-Semitism, on the rise in largely Catholic regions of Central Europe. Or they may have been helping Freud's older brothers avoid service in the Austrian army—the boys would settle in Manchester, England, and enter their father's trade.[4] From Freiberg, the Freuds first traveled to Leipzig but were denied a permit to stay there. They then made their way to Vienna, where they settled alongside other poor migrant families in the Jewish Ghetto.

"Settled" is the wrong word. The Freuds moved around the Jewish neighborhoods of Vienna at least six times in the next fifteen years. Struggling economically, Jacob provided for his wife and children probably by partnering with his older sons, who did well for themselves in Manchester, allegedly by dubious means. When

Jacob's brother, Freud's uncle, was arrested for counterfeiting in 1865, the older boys were said to be implicated, and according to Freud the stress turned his father's hair gray.

By seven, Freud was an avid reader. Jacob was full of hope that his son would surpass him and grew frustrated whenever he feared it might not happen. At seven or eight, Freud accidentally peed on the floor of his parents' bedroom. "This boy will never amount to anything," Jacob scolded. Amalia disagreed. She called him "my golden Sigi" and believed he was destined to be great, making sure he always had his own room, no matter how cramped the quarters were for his six siblings.

Freud's parents filled his room with books, another luxury his siblings did not enjoy. As a teenager, he often ate meals by himself at his desk, so he could read without interruption. Freud loved two subjects above all, Darwin's natural science and ancient history. His reading gave shape to his interior life and often made the exterior one seem shabby.

Jacob told his son a story about having been bullied by gentiles. "Jew, off the sidewalk!" they ordered Jacob, and knocked his hat into the street. Freud asked his father how he had responded. "I stepped in to the road and picked up my cap," Jacob replied, which to his son "did not seem heroic" at all.[5] Freud longed to set out on an epic sea voyage aboard a ship loaded with scientific instruments, just as Darwin had.[6]

In high school, Freud was perennially first in his class. He translated thirty-odd lines of Sophocles's *Oedipus Rex* for his graduation exam and earned a degree with distinction. In 1873, at seventeen, he entered the University of Vienna, one of the best schools in the world for natural science. Freud wanted to be a researcher, like Darwin, in the fields of zoology and physiology, which had been transformed by *On the Origin of Species* and *The Descent of Man*. But after Freud obtained his doctorate in 1881—with a year off for compulsory military service—his family's economic struggles pushed him toward private practice in medicine. That was the only way he could afford to get married to Martha Bernays, which he very much wanted to do.

The two were engaged in June 1882, mere months after meeting, but Martha made Freud wait until he could support children financially to get married and consummate their relationship, which they finally did more than four years later, in September 1886. By the end of 1895, Freud and Martha had six children. The eight of them lived together in a Vienna apartment, along with Martha's sister Minna, who moved in to help with the babies. Following the birth of their youngest child, Anna, Freud and Martha abstained from sex for the rest of their lives. Freud suffered bouts of impotence, and he wanted to focus on work.

On the lookout for attention-grabbing ideas on a grand scale, Freud zeroed in on sex. Forced by financial pressure to see patients, he turned his clinical work into the basis for sweeping theories that addressed the epidemic of neurasthenia and neurosis.

Freud's first theory proposed that neurasthenia resulted from a failure to father. He claimed the disease originated in men who indulged in nonreproductive sex, especially masturbation, which, he wrote to Fliess, "runs completely parallel with the frequency of neurasthenia in men."[7] Masturbation had long been blamed for female hysteria, but Freud had a different view.[8] In women, Freud suggested, neuroses were often contagious, acquired from impotent neurasthenic men. "The poorer the man's potency, the more the woman's hysteria predominates; so that essentially a sexually neurasthenic man makes his wife not so much neurasthenic as hysterical."[9] Male masturbation was the most common cause, but anything that interfered with conventional reproductive sex could also be a trigger for neurasthenia, including birth control.

Freud claimed that his patients changed his mind on this. He noticed a pattern in the case histories that neurotics brought to his office: an alarming incidence of childhood sexual abuse by their fathers. Considering the widespread occurrence of neuroses, this was an implausible, even sensational theory, and that may have been part of its appeal.[10] When Freud first presented his theory publicly in April 1896, it was ridiculed and dismissed by colleagues. The response to his idea was so hostile that he feared "some password has been given out to abandon me."[11] He was nearly forty, the age at which he expected to die.

Freud was not always proud of his father, Jacob, while the old man was alive. But Freud was impressed that his father had faced his final illness with courage, and died "valiantly," as Freud saw it, in October 1896.[12] After his father was gone, Freud sank into a despair that he didn't fully understand.

"I now have a very uprooted feeling," Freud wrote to his friend Fliess. "Through some of those dark paths behind the official consciousness the old's man's death has moved me very much."[13] That fall, Freud turned inward and began to dig up "the remains" of memories of his childhood.[14] At night he would pour himself wine and replay old scenes in his mind, following connections from the past into the present. He detected traces of his formative boyhood experiences everywhere: slips of the tongue, unintended jokes, double meanings, and compulsive habits, like his own smoking, which he viewed as a proxy for masturbation. But his primary method was interpreting his own dreams.

In May 1897, Freud dreamed of having "overly tender feelings" for his eldest daughter, Mathilde—a compelling piece of evidence, he concluded, for the role of the father in the origins of neuroses. But Freud gave up his theory about sexually abusive fathers as he increasingly understood that, if his theory was to hold, his own father would be implicated along with all others.[15] This required letting go of his hope that his theory would bring him "eternal renown," not to mention "certain wealth, complete independence, travels, lifting the children above the severe cares that deprived me of my youth."[16] But he had run into a wall that he was not willing to break down.

Instead, Freud began to think that his patients who had told him about their abusive father were imagining things. They were having fantasies—dreams. Fueled by wine, he recalled his own youthful "infatuation with the mother" and jealousy of the father. He used "the" rather than "my" because he now believed these feelings to be "a general event in early childhood." Sensing the potential of the idea, Freud put it at the center of the book he was writing, which he had started calling his "dream book."[17] Racing to finish it, he uncharacteristically neglected his children during their summer vacation in the Alps in 1899. Even when Freud made time for his family during the holiday, his focus remained on his work, and he inquired about their dreams and wrote them up for the book, his first as a sole author: *The Interpretation of Dreams.*

Freud put the story of Oedipus into a section of the book about dreams of the deaths of loved ones. Oedipus, of course, had been abandoned, exposed to the elements outside the household like many other children in the ancient world whose fathers judged them more cost than benefit. Oedipus's father, Laius, the king of Thebes, had been informed by an oracle that he would be killed by his son as a punishment for having abducted another man's child. Laius, then sonless, believed it, and for a long time he avoided his wife, Jocasta. When celibacy proved impossible to sustain, Jocasta gave birth to a boy. Laius ordered a shepherd to take the newborn to the mountains and leave him there with his feet nailed and bound together, to prevent the infant from escaping and fulfilling the patricidal prophecy.

But the shepherd couldn't bear to do it. He passed the boy off to another shepherd, who passed him off to a childless king and queen who adopted the boy and named him Oedipus, meaning "swollen feet." Once Oedipus was grown, he heard rumors that the king who had raised him was not his father. Oedipus consulted the oracle at Delphi and to his surprise was informed that his fate was to kill his father and marry his mother. To avoid this outcome, Oedipus left home for Thebes, only to promptly and unwittingly beat his real father, Laius, to death in a dispute on the road.

When he got to Thebes, Oedipus banished a monster that had been tormenting the city. For his heroics, he was rewarded with the city's throne and the hand of Jocasta, widow of the recently deceased king. Son and mother had four children together before discovering the truth. When it came out, Jocasta killed herself and Oedipus blinded himself, and he was nursed thereafter by Antigone, his daughter and half sister.

Freud had come to believe that the extraordinary power of the Oedipus myth, which had endured in culture for thousands of years, derived from its relatability. Everyone was moved by the story of Oedipus because, Freud explained, everyone "was once a budding Oedipus in fantasy."[18] For Freud, homicidal and incestuous fantasies, dreams of the death of a loved one, fueled the competition and conflict at the heart of all families. "It is the fate of all of us, perhaps, to direct our first sexual impulse towards our mother and our first hatred and our first murderous wish against our father," Freud wrote. "King Oedipus, who slew his father Laius and married his mother Jocasta, merely shows us the fulfillment of our own childhood wishes."[19] More than just normal, Oedipal feelings were inevitable. Most people got over them. Those who didn't became "psychoneurotics," patients of Dr. Freud.

But the links between the drama and the diagnosis are not necessarily as strong as Freud made them out to be. Sophocles's story is powerful because the tragedy comes as a surprise. Oedipus's father and mother are unknown to him when he kills the one and weds the other. Freud's story unfolds precisely because our parents are right in front of our faces.

When *The Interpretation of Dreams*, featuring Freud's first mention of Oedipus, was published at the end of 1899, Freud predicted his theory of desire and conflict within the family would set off a storm of controversy. But in this regard Freud was no Darwin, and the book sold only 351 copies in five years.

Soon Freud developed another big idea he was eager to publicize: that children matured by moving through stages of sexual development. Oedipus was not mentioned even once in the first edition of Freud's 1905 book on theories of sexuality. Yet he hadn't completely dropped his Oedipus idea. On the contrary, he had moved Oedipal conflict to the center of his clinical practice.

In 1905, Freud began to publish a series of now-famous case histories that all pivot around the father and Oedipus. Freud's account of treating eighteen-year-old Dora, conducted in 1900 and published in 1905, was among the first to take this shape. She came to his office with common neuroses: stomachaches, headaches, cough, depression, and an addiction to cigarettes. Digging into her family history, Freud determined that she was in love with her father, and jealous of his attention to another woman: a feminine version of Oedipus. "I have learnt," he concluded, citing his own work in *The Interpretation of Dreams*, "to look upon unconscious love relations like this (which may be recognized by their abnormal consequences)—between a father and a daughter, or between a mother and a son—as a revival of germs of feeling in infancy."[20] Inside every adult was a child. If such germs were not completely resolved in childhood, they could lie latent, awaiting activation.

The father was also at the center of Freud's 1908 treatment of "Little Hans." Hans was the five-year-old son of one of Freud's acolytes. Freud had asked his students to take notes on the development of their children, so he could compile a library of evidence to support his theories. Hans's father conducted the analysis on his son according to Freud's methods, and then sent the transcripts to Freud, who wrote up the case and published it in 1909. Hans, his parents had noticed, had developed a fixation on penises, his own and others. His parents tried to prevent him from masturbating, but this, Freud concluded, had only transformed his pleasure into a neurosis. Hans became afraid of horses and their giant penises—and fathers and theirs. Little Hans was a "Little Oedipus" in the making. But while Freud used the boy's story to support his ideas, he offered no treatment or resolution, for Hans was under the care of his father.

The same year, 1909, Freud also published an account of his work with Ernst Lanzer, a capable twenty-nine-year-old lawyer. In their first session, Lanzer had described being haunted by a fear "that something terrible might happen to his father and his beloved." He told of a childhood full of "sexual curiosity, including the pressing wish to see women naked." Yet he also thought that if he failed to suppress his sexual thoughts, his terrible fears for his father and his beloved would come true. In fact, Lanzer's father was already dead, but the fear and anxiety had survived.

The stricken Lanzer told Freud a story he had heard while in the army—of "a particularly horrifying punishment practiced in the Orient" whereby "someone convicted of a crime was tied down, [and] a pot with rats in it was turned upside down on his buttocks," encouraging the rats to eat their way out from the inside. During the telling, Freud registered on Lanzer's face "a very strange composite expression . . . one of *horror at pleasure of his own of which he himself was unaware.*"[21] Lanzer had imagined that his own transgressions, minor though they were, would result in his father and his beloved suffering this punishment. Freud interpreted Lanzer's fear as a wish that his father would die. In response, Lanzer protested that he had loved his father very much. Freud agreed: Lanzer loved his father so much that this love was accompanied by an equally powerful hatred.[22]

Prompted by Freud, Lanzer recalled a dim memory. When he was a young boy, his father had caught him in the act of masturbating and beaten him. In response, Lanzer lashed out, setting the pattern of conjoined love and hate that had defined all his closest relationships since. Once Freud had identified the core problem, the cycle was broken, the patient relieved of his torments. Lanzer, known to history as "the Rat Man," was one of Freud's favorite cases. The account of the case marked the first time Freud had written of "the father complex" as the "nuclear complex of the neuroses"—the central knot of the problem of human development. The term "Oedipus complex" appeared in print for the first time the following year.

In a decade Oedipus had taken over Freud's self-understanding, his concept of human development, his clinical practice, and the field of treatment he had founded, psychoanalysis. He even revised his older work to make his signature emphasis on fathers clearer. In the 1909 edition of *The Interpretation of Dreams*, he recounted that he had begun work on the book as part of his attempt to come to terms with the death of his father—"the most important event, the most poignant loss, of a man's life," as he now described it.[23]

"Every human newcomer has been set the task of mastering the Oedipus complex," Freud wrote in 1914, in a footnote to a new edition of his *Three Essays on Sexuality*, which he also updated to reflect his increased commitment to Oedipus. "Whoever cannot manage it falls prey to neurosis. The progress of psychoanalytic work has sketched the significance of the Oedipus complex ever more sharply; its recognition has become the shibboleth that separates the adherents of psychoanalysis from its opponents."[24] The Oedipus complex was king.

At the same time, its opponents were increasing in number—including some dissenters within psychoanalysis Freud had once thought of as his friends, his disciples, and even his children.

Alfred Adler was an early member of Freud's circle who was named president of the Vienna Psychoanalytic Society in 1910, after Freud gave it up. Yet Adler resented the mistaken assumption that he had been Freud's student and split with him over 1911 and 1912.[25] Afterward, Adler de-emphasized the "Oedipus complex" in favor of what he called the "inferiority complex," an anxiety about fitting in and measuring up beyond the immediate family.

Carl Jung, a Swiss psychologist who was Freud's heir apparent and thereby his implicit rival, was also skeptical of the increasing emphasis on the Oedipus complex. Jung often referred to Freud as his father, and Freud reciprocated by calling Jung his "adopted eldest son." In 1909, the two traveled to Clark University in Worcester, Massachusetts, Freud's only trip to the United States, to present their ideas on psychoanalysis to American academics. While Freud's lectures explained how he had arrived at his theories of dreams and sex, Jung moved in a different direction. The paper he delivered at Clark, "Psychic Conflicts in a Child," proposed that childhood was not in all cases saturated by desire. Instead, Jung claimed, the universal question for children was: Where do I come from, and how did I get here? Jung's paper was based on observations he had made of his young daughters, Agathe and Gretl. To disguise their identities, he gave them the pseudonyms Sophie and Anna—the names of Freud's daughters.

A psychic conflict was brewing between the men. In 1912, it opened into an outright fracture. "Your technique of treating your pupils like patients is a blunder," Jung wrote to Freud. "In that way you produce either slavish sons or impudent puppies. . . . You go around sniffing out all the symptomatic actions in your vicinity, thus reducing everyone to the level of sons and daughters who blushingly admit the existence of their faults. Meanwhile you remain on top as the father, sitting pretty. . . . If ever you should rid yourself entirely of your complexes and stop playing the father to your sons instead of aiming continually at their weak spots . . . then

I will mend my ways."[26] Later in his career, Jung would describe what he called mother and father complexes that were based not only on desire and conflict but also on care and protection.

In the midst of his break with Adler and Jung, Freud tried to make the Oedipus complex even bigger than he already had: not only ancient and enduring but also universal across human societies—as universal as Jung's concept of childhood curiosity claimed to be. Freud began to explore the deep prehistory of the Oedipus complex. Where had the ideas behind the story of Oedipus come from, before Sophocles and the Greeks? How far back could they be traced?

Freud was single-minded in his search for an origin story of what he called "the first heroic deed: the rebellion against the father."[27] When he published *Totem and Taboo* the following year, Freud said that his breakthrough came from a fragment of Darwin. In *The Descent of Man*, Darwin had hypothesized that prehistoric humans, like their primate ancestors, had lived in small groups, or "primal hordes," each ruled by a "violent, jealous" tyrant who claimed all the women and resources for himself. That was as far as Darwin had gone. But how had modern forms of family life and society evolved from that one? Freud's research in the relatively new field of anthropology, which studied existing "primitive" cultures to understand the origins and development of "modern" ones, was no help. No "primal horde" had ever been observed in the actual world, though Freud did find a record of "associations of men" operating under a female leader, in a matriarchy. [28]

Lacking hard evidence, Freud imagined his own origin story for modern civilization and culture, one that went well beyond

Darwin even as it claimed a debt to him. As Freud told it, the tyranny of one prehistoric father had left his sons with no choice but to venture outside the group to find their own women—until, one day, they saw another possibility. Banding together, perhaps motivated by mastery of a new technology or strategy, they used their superior numbers to turn the tables and kill their father. The same process could be readily observed, Freud noted, in herds of cattle. Having dethroned the father they all feared and envied, the sons feasted on his body, united in triumph: "Now, in the act of devouring, they carried through their identification with him; each of them appropriated a piece of his strength." This, Freud said, was "perhaps the first festival of mankind." The sons formed a society. History had begun.

But if the first event in human history was a feast, the second was no fun at all. The mood soon soured with regret. The sons were overcome by ambivalence and guilt about killing their father. To relieve these feelings, they honored the father they had killed as immortal—their totem. To avoid conflict with each other, they foreswore the women their father had denied them—their taboo. On these principles, they formed a commonwealth.

Freud was well aware that his story had not answered all of his own questions. In particular, he had not explained the documented fact of matriarchy. Ultimately Freud dealt with the counterexample of matriarchy by describing it as a temporary, transitory, in-between stage. He suggested that, after the initial killing of the primal father, matriarchy may have arisen from the truce between the murderous brothers—that is, before the brothers had figured out how to rule on their own, by patriarchy of their own design.

But Freud was already looking past this wrinkle. The point of *Totem and Taboo*, as Freud biographer Peter Gay put it, was that "man *makes* his father into a god" so that, after vanquishing him, man himself can rule with a godlike hand.[29] Notably, Freud had offered an account of the origins of civilization that underscored the importance of psychoanalysis as a solution to civilization's ills, individual and collective. One reviewer called *Totem and Taboo* a "just-so story," the human equivalent of Rudyard Kipling's fanciful, nonsense explanations of how animals came to be what they are.[30] Freud had written a new story of human parentage and inheritance, putting at the center a malevolent image of a father concerned not for the survival of his children but who, instead, thinking only of himself, sent them off to die.

Some men viewed the start of the Great War in Europe in the summer of 1914 as a chance to prove that they weren't broken down and softened up by modern life, that their nerve and strength was intact. Initially, Freud was proud of early German successes and proud of his three sons, Martin, Ernst, and Oliver, for serving. Martin especially, then twenty-four and newly qualified as a lawyer, could have easily found a way to stay home, but he volunteered anyway, doubting that he could forgive himself if he hadn't.[31]

But the mood changed as the war dragged on. The brutality of the fighting seemed to prove Freud's theories right, but this gave him no satisfaction. "I do not doubt that mankind will survive even this war," he wrote to a friend in 1914, "but I know for certain that for me and my contemporaries the world will never again be a happy place. It is too hideous. And the saddest thing about it is that it is exactly the way we should have expected people to behave from our knowledge of psycho-analysis."[32] The polite and civilized norms of day-to-day life were thin cover for the repressed violence latent underneath.

Even Freud was surprised by the scope of the destruction. During his time in the Austrian army, he had been a barracks doctor. War had existed for him mostly in books and myths, including his own. Now the combination of catastrophic death and mundane wartime hardships wore him down. The war left 40 million people dead or injured, more than half of them civilians. Freud struggled to find paying clients in Vienna, and he wrote an article in exchange for a bag of potatoes. He dreamed that one of his sons died. He dreamed that his acolytes died. His family and his field were in danger from "the strife of nations."[33] Martin was injured, captured, and imprisoned in Italy.

The bloody prehistory of fathers and sons Freud had described in *Totem and Taboo* had been an invention. But now he saw what it really meant: "a genealogy of murderers."[34] Fathers sent their children off to die, and there children learned how to kill.

While his sons were off fighting in the war, Freud grew close to the only one of his six children who remained at home, his youngest daughter, Anna, eighteen years old in 1914. The Oedipus complex was born from the death of Freud's father, but it grew up with Anna, whom Freud increasingly thought of as his most gifted child.

Anna was born at the end of 1895, around the time that Freud started using the term "psychoanalysis" and began to focus on the significance of dreams. He often said that Anna and psychoanalysis were twins—though she had given him far less trouble. The real difference was that Freud, then desperate for professional distinction, hadn't wanted Anna. Nor for that matter had Martha. Anna was their sixth child. After the fifth, they had tried abstaining from sex. Following Anna's birth, they tried abstinence again and succeeded.[35]

Anna always felt that psychoanalysis got more of her father's attention than she did. Yet she also felt the pressure of being the last of her siblings living at home with her parents, performing what once had been the emotional role of six. In 1913, when Anna was seventeen, she informed her father that she had read his books, but he didn't need to worry about the impact of their content on her, because she was "grown up" and "interested." The next year, she began to train as an elementary school teacher. This choice pleased her father, who was increasingly interested in children as subjects, but he also worried that Anna would never find a husband. His worry was justified. As Freud observed but only partly acknowledged, Anna was more attracted to women.

Freud's working theory of homosexuality was what he and others at the time often described as "inversion," a crossing of the wires of attraction. He didn't object to homosexuality, but he did describe it as disordered development, the result of a failure to confront and resolve the Oedipus complex. Yet Anna's case didn't exactly fit the feminine version of the diagnostic model: a woman who never vanquished her mother. Freud was well aware that Anna worshiped him, and that by aspiring to a scientific career she had rejected her mother.

In 1918, to "awaken her libido," Freud encouraged Anna to become his patient, an arrangement they kept secret, for it was taboo among psychoanalysts, though hardly unprecedented. For four years, they met in Freud's office at ten at night. Anna lay down on the famous couch, and her father went to work.[36] Anna wished to be her father's best patient and student. Freud wished Anna would stay at home with him. They both got their wish. Anna never married—as one of Freud's students remarked, "Look at her father.

This is an ideal that very few men could live up to"—but she did become a world-famous psychoanalyst in her own right.[37]

In 1919, during the course of Anna's analysis, Freud wrote a paper titled "A Child Is Being Beaten." The text explores how pain and pleasure become linked, how suffering could be experienced as satisfaction. Presenting evidence from six cases, one of which was probably a disguised version of Anna's treatment—which had likely touched on a fantasy of being punished by her father—the paper concluded that a father's violence is a form of attention children can learn to crave and covet.[38]

At around the same time, Anna began to train in psychoanalysis. In 1922, she presented her first significant professional paper, on the same kind of "beating fantasies," again probably her own. According to her paper, these fantasies dated from around the age of five or six. "All the sexual drives were concentrated on the first love object, the father," Anna wrote of the patient she described.[39] When the paper was criticized, Freud spoke up publicly in his daughter's defense. He was just then in the process of extending the Oedipus complex into his concept of the superego: an internalized father, ruling over the id and ego, that developed around age five largely through paternal approval and punishment.

The next year, Freud was diagnosed with mouth cancer, the result of a lifetime of smoking, which he did especially while working. He learned of the diagnosis while on a trip to Italy with Anna. Three years earlier she had written to her father from her summer vacation in the mountains, restless and anxious at being away from him. "Promise me that if you should fall ill some day and I'm not there, you will write me about it immediately, so that I can come?"[40] Now she steered them home and took charge of his care.

In October, Freud had two surgeries and was fitted with a prosthetic to close the hole in his jaw. It changed his appearance and voice, which he feared would upset his mother, Amalia. He wrote to her preemptively: "Everyone you ask will confirm the news that on the fourth and eleventh of this month I underwent an operation on the upper jaw which, owing to the skill of the surgeon and the excellence of the nursing, has been very successful so far. It will take me some time to grow accustomed to a partial denture that I have to wear. So don't be surprised if you do not see me for a while and I hope you will be in good spirits when we meet again."[41] Freud's theoretical work almost never dealt directly with mothers. Some critics and historians have suggested that this was because his own, who had championed his brilliance from a young age, was simply too important for him to analyze. While Freud focused on fathers, Jung, not Freud, would describe the controlling figure now known as the "devouring mother."

As Freud kept his distance from his mother, Amalia, he began to depend ever more on his daughter Anna. He wanted her care as much as she wanted to give it to him. In the next sixteen years, he had at least that many surgeries, and Anna tended to him after each one. Even as she established her own psychoanalytic practice focused on children, she nursed her father daily, tenderly packing his decaying mouth with sterile gauze, stanching profuse bleeding from his painful wounds, updating his colleagues on his health, and elbowing her mother, Martha, to the edge of the picture.

In 1927, Anna Freud published *Introduction to the Technique of Child Analysis*, which adapted her father's practice to treat patients as young as six. Though many psychoanalysts, including Freud and

Jung, had used their own children as subjects, there had been no formal associations, journals, or institutions focused on treating children—no common set of questions, problems, approaches, aims. In large part, those would be Anna's contributions, expanding her father's work into a new realm.

Anna argued that the emotional lives of children should be treated just like those of adult patients. This was a logical extension of Freud's argument that childhood experiences shaped adult life, but Anna's techniques departed from her father's. She would allow children to wander around her office while they talked, and focused much of the work on building trust and alliances by playing and spending time together.

Anna's critics, including many of her father's other students, psychoanalyzed her ideas, using her father's theories against her, which was not especially hard to do. They said her own Oedipus complex had not been mastered, and that her ideas were simply reflections of her own desires and repressions. Her opponents attributed whatever mistakes and oversights they could identify to her internal resistances to confronting these repressions. Virtually all of Anna's critics were people known intimately to the Freud family, and vice versa. One of the harshest voices, Ernest Jones, had even pursued Anna romantically, only to be rebuffed by Freud himself, chasing away a potential rival for his daughter's affections.[42]

Even Anna's defenders and advocates, her father among them, recognized a grain of truth in such critiques. Anna herself acknowledged wishing to surpass her father's other colleagues, students, and patients.[43] There was no way out of the personal and professional dilemma of being her father's daughter except to ignore it to whatever extent was possible, and to work, work, work.

As Anna's biographer Elisabeth Young-Bruehl points out, this strategy can itself be described as a kind of "beating fantasy"—a desire for recognition and praise that only comes at the price of great pain, and is never fully satisfied.[44]

In 1927, the same year Anna published her first book, she founded a school in Vienna with two other women. Roughly twenty students, ages seven to thirteen, and some of their parents, too, would undergo analysis alongside their work in the classroom. The school was housed in a backyard cabin in a prosperous, leafy neighborhood of the Austrian capital. Two teachers, including Erik Erikson, then a young art-school dropout and not yet a psychologist in his own right, led the immersive project-based curriculum. If the students were doing a project on the Arctic, the "whole school would for a time become . . . the world of the Eskimos," Erikson remembered.[45]

One of Anna's partners in the school was Dorothy Burlingham, a granddaughter of Louis Comfort Tiffany and a divorced single mother of four, who was also her partner in life. Dorothy put her children under Anna's care, and Anna encouraged Dorothy to enter analysis with her father. Yet in most ways, while her father was alive, Anna repressed her sexuality to protect his primacy in her life and hers in his.

For Freud's eightieth birthday, in 1936, Anna gave him a copy of the book she had just finished writing, *The Ego and the Mechanisms of Defense*, which built on his idea that people arranged their lives to protect themselves against old wounds. After her father's death, Anna would live with Dorothy Burlingham for the rest of her life, but she never acknowledged a romantic or sexual relationship.

*   *   *

When the Nazis crossed the border into Austria on March 13, 1938, Anna took charge of the Freud household. Troops immediately pillaged Freud's publishing house, called him out by name, and burned his books. One biographer has suggested that Hitler read Freud's work on group psychology and modeled his public performances on it, but no evidence for this exists apart from the performances themselves.[46] Virginia Woolf wrote that year in *Three Guineas* that fascism was an extension of the patriarchal family into politics and culture—an extension of an ongoing war on women.

In Nazi Germany, citizenship rested on biological concepts of identity. Yet at that time "biological identity" could not be established with certainty, because paternity could not be. When it came to the practical matter of determining and classifying individual identities within officially defined racial categories, Nazi paternity tests compensated for the impossibility of certainty with complexity. Their tests, based on a comprehensive evaluation of the alleged father's physical features, "may have been the most complex paternity tests ever performed," according to historian Nara Milanich. They often involved full-body inspections and minute measurements of ears and nostrils that were then compared to the alleged children's.[47]

Especially after the official beginning of mass expulsions and executions in 1938, women used the arcane complexity of Nazi testing procedures, which were also rife with bribery and corruption, to dispute the paternity of their Jewish husbands, "admitting" to adulteries they hadn't committed in the hope of protecting their children. As long as a paternity inquiry remained open, family members were spared from deportation and imprisonment. Fathers who had already been deported and imprisoned were even released from camps to give statements and undergo tests. Such cases of contested paternity did not necessarily disturb the self-identification of Jewish families, for according to Torah law, Jewish identity is passed from mother to child.[48]

"Wouldn't it be better if we all killed ourselves?" Anna Freud had asked her father in despair as the Nazis swept into Austria in the spring of 1938. "Why?" he answered. "Because they would like us to?"[49] On March 22, Anna was taken by the Gestapo for questioning and held for seven hours. Her father waited for her in their apartment, pacing and smoking one cigar after another. When Anna returned, he wept openly, which was entirely out of character, and insisted that they all leave Vienna.

Anna negotiated their flight from Vienna with the Gestapo, which required the Freuds to give up their family home and property and pay the equivalent of hundreds of thousands of dollars today. With the help of friends and colleagues, she arranged for her father, her mother, and herself to move to London. They departed Vienna in June, and later that summer they settled near Hempstead Heath in a brick house with enough room for both father and daughter to see patients. While Anna treated half a dozen patients each day, she continued to play the role of "chief nurse" to her father, on call around the clock.[50]

By then a large part of Freud's cancerous jaw and palate had been removed. Only his prosthetic plate separated his sinuses from his mouth to allow him to chew and speak. When the plate was properly and tightly installed, it rubbed the inside of his mouth raw. Freud called it "the monster." When he wanted to remove it, for cleaning or relief, Anna helped him. On one occasion she struggled with it for at least half an hour. Anna, as biographer Peter Gay put it, was her father's "ally against death."[51] Sometimes Freud called her "St. Anna." Other times she was "Antigone," after the daughter who remained fiercely loyal to Oedipus even after the truth of his identity was out.[52]

Even so, there was a limit to what Anna could do for her father, and by the start of 1939 they had reached it. Freud tried a course of radiation therapy, but this resulted in dizziness and more suffering. He stopped seeing patients, but refused pain medicine so he could think. Gangrene ate a hole in his cheek, and netting was hung around his bed to keep flies away. His beloved dog began to avoid him, so powerful was the odor of his rotting jaw. Yet Anna still sat with him and took dictation. When the war started in September 1939, Freud's bed was moved to the center of the house, away from bombs and explosions outside.[53] At the end of September, he took an injection of morphine, closed his eyes, and did not wake up.

During the war, Anna Freud and Dorothy Burlingham worked together in London opening shelters and schools for displaced, abandoned, and orphaned children. The emphasis, unusual for the time, was on keeping contact between the children and their birth families.[54] This approach was based on the belief, derived from Freud's work, that children grew up, advancing through developmental stages, only in relationship to their parents, both father and mother. To maintain connections between parents and children, Anna and her staff regularly wrote letters to fathers fighting far away and women working in factories. In cases when parents were missing or out of reach, children were assigned to staff members who became substitute mothers. With male staff in short supply, substitute fathers were drawn from the neighborhoods surrounding the school, including men in charge of sounding air-raid sirens and fighting fires caused by bombs, who "were encouraged to visit as much as possible."[55] In theory, children didn't need their own fathers, but perhaps they did need someone they could grow up to resist, unseat, and honor.

From a child's perspective, Sigmund Freud's theories made it natural, even healthy, to despise your father. From a father's perspective, Freud made it normal, even good, to be hated, for that meant your children were growing up and coming into their own. The first view empowers youthful rebellion, while the second justifies patriarchal control, framing conflict as the regular course of family business. Most often, this conflict between parents and children takes place on unequal ground, where parents hold virtually all of the advantages except time.

In one sense, Freud's models and theories did not precisely fit his daughter's life. To ease his fears of losing her and her own fears of losing him, Anna shaped her reality to his expectations, avoiding romance, marriage, and children of her own. Yet in the end, she had the last word.

After the war was over, and for the rest of her life, Anna lived in the London house with Dorothy Burlingham even as she spent more and more time in the United States, where she served as a de facto ambassador, helping to bring psychoanalysis into the medical mainstream. When Anna died in 1982, she left instructions for turning the house where she and Dorothy had lived for nearly four decades into a museum dedicated to her father. To this day, Freud's treatment room and famous consulting couch remain in the very place where Anna delivered her father to safety, helped him fight the painful monster inside him, presided over his death, and made his story hers forever.

CHAPTER EIGHT

HOME: Bob Dylan

I n the fall of 1955, fourteen-year-old Bobby Zimmerman went
to see *Rebel without a Cause* at the Lybba Theater in Hibbing,
Minnesota, and then he went back to see it again, and again, and
again. He got in for free because the theater had been built by his
great-grandfather, named for his great-grandmother, and was
owned by his uncle. Bobby bought a red jacket like the one James
Dean wore in the film and hung posters on the walls of the basement
rec room where he and his younger brother, David, played.[1] Dean
had died in a car accident in the California desert in September,
and his image as a teenage outlaw became immortal.

The movie was based on the 1944 book *Rebel without a Cause:
The Story of a Criminal Psychopath*. The author was Robert Linder,
a psychologist who dug into the case history of a young man who
had been in trouble since age twelve. In the boy's past Linder found
a Polish immigrant father with limited resources, prospects, and
patience but plenty of "curses and unkind words" for his son,
plus regular beatings. "There seems to be little doubt," Linder

concluded, "that psychopathic behavior derives from a profound hatred of the father . . . [and] the inadequate resolution of the Oedipus conflict."[2] This became the plot of the film.

Father trouble unites the characters. James Dean's Jim is disgusted with his father for wearing a frilly yellow apron around the house. Natalie Wood's Judy is sobbing in the police station because her father called her a "dirty tramp" when she just wanted his attention. And Sal Mineo's Plato is an ambiguously gay teen of divorced parents with no father at home, lost, alone, and terrified that the end of the world is coming in a flash of light. It only appeared that the rebel had no cause. In fact, the cause was the father.

One night Bobby Zimmerman came home late from the movies and got in a fight with his parents. "We've given you a good home," his father, Abe, scolded him. "We buy you the best of everything. What more do you want?"[3] The question wasn't as simple as it once had been, but when Bobby Zimmerman became Bob Dylan, he answered it for millions.

For some American families after World War II—for more families than ever in the history of families—money wasn't the problem.

The U.S. government was giving it away, through the GI Bill, in the form of tuition and loans for veterans. There was money not only for building and buying houses but also for everything that went into them, kitchens and living rooms, new appliances and furniture, which is exactly what Abe Zimmerman and his brothers sold at their store, Zimmerman Furniture and Appliance, in downtown Hibbing, an iron-mining town in northern Minnesota. These postwar subsidies disproportionately benefited families like

the Zimmermans, lifting generations of stigmatized "new immi-
grants" from Eastern and Southern Europe into the heart of the
white American suburban middle class. In the process, the GI Bill
underwrote white male authority, at home and more broadly. Segregation in education, housing, and jobs made it extremely difficult
for Black men to benefit from federal loans. Sixty-seven thousand
GI mortgages were given out in the suburbs around New York
City, but fewer than one hundred of them went to Black veterans.[4]

There were also gender inequities. Vastly more veterans were
men, but even those women who had served found it harder to
access the benefits. In a lot of states, married women needed their
husband's permission to take out a loan. In some states, women
couldn't borrow money at all.[5] Men's names were on loans, mortgages, and deeds.

The idea of the "baby boom"—the explosion in births following the end of the war—framed family life as a masculine proving
ground of money and power, a battlefield, a stock market, a construction site, a factory. "I'd like six kids," one prospective father
said in 1955. "It just seems like a minimum production goal."[6]
All the children were proof that the future was American. Home
and family were identified as crucial fronts in the early Cold War.
Having a nice house and raising nice children meant fighting on
the right side of this new global conflict, potentially even more
devastating than the one that had just ended. In 1950, more than
half of Americans believed their homes would be bombed in a war
with the Soviet Union.[7]

But money alone wasn't enough to achieve these goals. Freud
had shown that parents were responsible for more than the basic
survival of their children—there was also their psychological health
and their personal development to think about. What happened

inside the person was related to what happened inside the home, within the family. With the right care at home, you could make a successful doctor or lawyer, and there were parenting manuals that explained how to do it.[8] But without the right care at home you could make a "juvenile delinquent" who threatened to undermine the whole system.

"Not even the Communist conspiracy," said Senator Robert C. Hendrickson in 1954, "could devise a more effective way to demoralize, disrupt, confuse, and destroy our future citizens than apathy on the part of adult Americans to the scourge known as juvenile delinquency." "Let's Face It," the cover of *Newsweek* announced in 1956, "Our Teenagers are Out of Control." *Rebel without a Cause* was only one of the teenage movies that symbolized and sought to capitalize on the fear that, across the country, gangs of out-of-control kids were more powerful than their parents.[9]

In the context of the Cold War, parents had important work to do, and the stakes could not have been higher. "The domestic version of containment," writes historian Elaine Tyler May about the U.S. policy to fight international Communism, "was the home. Within its walls, potentially dangerous social forces of the new age might be tamed."[10] Yet there was also new uncertainty and anxiety about who was supposed to do what and how.

After the war, government campaigns urged women to go back to homemaking so returning male veterans would feel needed, strong, and victorious.[11] But more than a decade of depression and war had unsettled the domestic balance of power, symbolically if not always in fact. Wonder Woman first appeared in 1941, stronger than Superman in some ways, but vulnerable to being tied down—literally, in the comic books, by men with ropes. Norman Rockwell's 1943 image of Rosie the Riveter had arms like body builder Charles Atlas. Three-quarters of women wanted to keep working, yet "working mother" was often taken to be synonymous with "delinquent children."[12] At the same time, too much mothering, according to the 1942 bestseller *Generation of Vipers*, was "Momism," which rhymes with "communism," and was said to breed weak, passive, homosexual, un-American kids who made the country susceptible to invasion and conquest.[13]

Fathers were supposed to be the strong ones again, but not exactly in the same old way. Now overbearing fathers were accused of raising fascist, un-American kids—Adolf Hitler's father was cited as a prime example.[14] More up-to-date was *Father Knows Best*, debuting on radio in 1949 and television in 1954 and remembered as one of the earliest sitcoms, though its title was a reminder, not a joke.

In the culture of the Cold War baby boom, the Freudian figure of the stern, resented, resisted, but ultimately respected patriarch was replaced by an ideal of a playmate and pal: the "dad," a name that was often enclosed in quotation marks in the first years after World War II. The name came from baby talk: a child's idea of a man.[15] The job of the dad was to prove Freud's theories of generational conflict wrong by acting as friend rather than foe: to raise happy, normal children by being happy and normal himself. This was a fundamental shift in the idea of fatherhood, though the world of work, money, and politics outside the home had not itself become more friendly. Sociologist William H. Whyte observed that postwar America wasn't a patriarchy but a "filiarchy."[16] Everything was for the children.

By 1955, an average American teen spent more than $500 a year.[17] Young people bought 100 million comic books per month. Record sales nearly tripled between 1954 and 1960.[18] The stuff kids had, the records, the toys, the clothes, the hobbies, reflected on their fathers. If your children had what the Zimmerman kids had, that was a sign that the family had a good, manly dad.[19]

Abe Zimmerman wanted to be a good dad. He had two rules at home: "One, don't come and ask me for anything useless you are prepared for me to say no, and two, do things for us because you like us, not because you are afraid of us."[20] The rules were easy to follow because Abe rarely said no to Bobby and his younger brother, David, and their big, boxy stucco house on a corner lot on 7th Avenue had more new stuff in it than most other houses in Hibbing.

The boys shared an upstairs bedroom with cowboy wallpaper, bongo drums, a radio, a record player, and a library of albums. The living room had a piano where Bobby practiced most days and, after 1952, a television, a big deal in Hibbing. The rec room in the basement was packed with toys and sports equipment.

All the new stuff symbolized how far they had come. Abe Zimmerman was from an Odessa Jewish family who had fled pogroms in 1905. In Duluth, Minnesota, an iron town with a busy port on Lake Superior, they found a place that felt like home. Abe's father had peddled textiles from farm to farm, and once he learned to speak English he worked as a shoe salesman in a department store, then as an insurance salesman at Prudential.[21] Abe got his first job when he was seven. All his friends shined shoes, sold papers and fruit, and spoke Yiddish at home. In high school, Abe was a star athlete in handball.

He met his wife, Beatty, in Duluth. She was from a family of Lithuanian Jews who had a clothing store in the small town of Hibbing, and she was always stylishly dressed. They got married at her house in Hibbing when Abe was twenty-two and Beatty was eighteen. Soon Abe was working for Standard Oil and they were "living high" on his salary of $100 a month. Their oldest son was born in May 1941. They chose his name from the top of a list: Robert was the most popular boy's name in the United States. Every day they dressed him in elaborate outfits, sometimes all white. His mother said he was so beautiful he should have been a girl: "Even when he was dirty, he was clean," Beatty remembered.[22]

In 1946, Abe got polio and spent weeks in the hospital. When he came home, he had to drag himself up the stairs "like an ape."[23] He lost his job at Standard Oil and walked with a limp for the rest of his life. The Zimmermans moved northwest from Duluth to Hibbing, where Abe's brothers also had a store, to be closer to Beatty's family, so they could help with the boys.

In Hibbing, Abe joined two of his brothers selling appliances and furniture into the early stages of the Cold War baby boom. Their store was downtown, a ten-minute walk from the house. Initially they called the store Micka Electric Co., but after the war the brothers changed the name to something more family-friendly, Zimmerman Furniture and Appliance. They started selling on credit and expanded the showroom.

When Bobby was old enough to go to school, he refused to go unless his father took him, so Abe left work and came home to do it, feeling like the only man who showed up to enroll a child at the kindergarten.[24] At school, everyone thought Bobby was "average, unassuming," respectful, and unfailingly polite, which was exactly what most parents then wanted for their kids.[25] At eleven, Bobby wrote a poem about how much he loved his dad, "the best in the world," and how he tried to be good and quiet so Abe wouldn't get angry.

Bobby's first guitar was a starter model his father bought him; then he moved up to a twenty-two-dollar electric Sears Silvertone, and then to a sixty-dollar electric, a black Supro Ozark with a hot gold sunburst. As a teenager, Bobby stayed up late listening to a radio station out of Shreveport, Louisiana, at the other end of the Mississippi, that played "race music," rhythm and blues and doo-wop, and came in especially clear on summer nights. He started calling everyone "man" because he heard it on the radio—what Black men in the South called one another in defiance of the white men who called them "boy."[26]

More and more, everything was about music. After school, Bobby and his friend John Bucklen sat in Melrad's Diner and talked music. They hung out at Hautala's Music Store and ogled new guitars. They went to Feldman's Department Store and bought turquoise hats like Gene Vincent's band wore. Bobby and John practiced in Bobby's upstairs bedroom, holding their electric guitars against the window, using the glass as a homemade amplifier. They played records and danced and lip-synced to "Long Tall Sally," "Be-Bop-a-Lula," and "Tutti Frutti"—until one afternoon Abe Zimmerman walked in on them in the middle of a performance. "Oh my god," he said, disgusted, and turned around and walked out, shaking his head.[27]

Early rock and roll was so profane it was childish. The hits were primarily written by men in an infantile language that did as much to highlight sex as disguise it. Dave Bartholemew's "My Ding-a-Ling," which would eventually be Chuck Berry's first and only number-one single. Lloyd Price's "Lawdy Miss Clawdy," which sold more than a million copies in 1952, four years before it was recorded by Elvis Presley. Big Maybelle's 1955 "Whole Lotta Shakin' Goin' On," a number-one hit for Jerry Lee Lewis and Sun

Records two years later. According to music critic Ann Powers, the first rock and roll songs sounded like "nonsense" to many adults.[28]

But if some of the words didn't mean anything, the sound of them was unmistakable. Even after Little Richard took the original references to "good booty" and anal sex out of "Tutti Frutti" ("all fruits"), first recorded in 1955, the message was still clear. Ann Powers writes: "This was the sound of young black men being amorous, openly and innocently. In a way, it was a form of protest."[29] Little Richard had been kicked out of his house at thirteen by his father, for being gay. Abe Zimmerman didn't have to understand the lyrics to get the point. It was easy for Abe to see his son, his miniature Little Richard, as a "shiftless bum." Abe's community life in Hibbing revolved around the Rotary Club. His idea of a man was a businessman.[30] Abe made Bobby sweep up the showroom downtown at Zimmerman Appliance, and began to send him out to repossess furniture from customers who couldn't make their payments, knowing he would hate it.

By the same token, Bobby started seeing his father as a "miserly tyrant," even though Abe never stopped buying him things. First Bobby got the exact car he wanted, a '50 Ford convertible lowered in back. Then he got the exact motorcycle he wanted, too, a Harley 45, and started playing chicken in the driveway with his younger brother, David, like James Dean had done in *Rebel without a Cause*.[31] Abe ripped Bobby's James Dean posters off the walls and tore them up.[32]

Rock and roll may have been a "corrupting impulse," as J. Edgar Hoover and parents everywhere feared, but arguably one of the worst things children of the baby boom could do to their anxious suburban parents was embrace folk music, which came from a labor tradition—a socialist tradition. When he went to college in Minneapolis, Bobby Zimmerman traded Little Richard for Woody Guthrie. "Hearing his voice," Bob Dylan later said, "I could tell he was very lonesome, very alone, and very lost out in his time."[33] For Bob, being lost now seemed like a good thing. He cast off the last name Zimmerman.[34] He chose Dylan, perhaps as a tribute to the Welsh poet Dylan Thomas who had died in 1953, or perhaps as a variation on "Dean." When people found out Bob's real name anyway, he told them he had left home because he couldn't stand his father.[35]

Dylan got to New York when he was nineteen and looked sixteen, with dirty fingernails, ill-fitting clothes, and an orchestra of nervous tics. He was obviously from out of town, but he had an uncanny talent for getting exactly what he wanted—a record deal with Columbia within a year. The label promoted him as a "rebel with a cause." Dylan reported his success to his family back in Hibbing and assured them that he was keeping clean and brushing his teeth.[36]

When it began to matter professionally where he had come from, the only true thing that Dylan said was the first thing: that he had been born in Duluth. Then the story wandered. He had been roaming the country since he was at the breast; he was raised in New Mexico; he ran away at ten; he lived in Iowa, South Dakota, North Dakota, Kansas, performed with carnivals, learned the blues in Chicago, saw Woody Guthrie in California, wrote hillbilly songs for Carl Perkins. "He was living with these enormous lies," one friend said. "He was a nervous wreck."[37] In the liner notes to his first album, released in 1962 and called *Bob Dylan*, Dylan said that if he had a lot of money he "would buy a couple motorcycles, a few air-conditioners, and four or five couches."[38] It was meant to be absurd. He didn't mention his father's store.

Bob Dylan's made-up biography took classic tales from blues and folk songs and turned them around backward. For Blind Willie Johnson, who had a hit with "Mother's Children" in 1927—later remade by Eric Clapton and countless others as "Motherless Child"—the problem was that his parents were gone. "Baby's got a heart like a piece of railroad steel / If I leave here this morning, never say 'Daddy how do you feel?'" sang Charley Patton on his 1930 record "Rattlesnake Blues," sad to go. When Woody Guthrie lamented, "I ain't got no home in this world anymore," he wanted one. Tom Joad was trying to find his family, not running from them. Johnny B. Goode had a very supportive mother.

Bob Dylan told the opposite story. He has often been credited with bringing poetry to popular music. What he brought was the emotional turmoil of the postwar white family. "Blowin' in the Wind" sounded a lot like "No More Auction Block," a Civil War–era protest song about how enslaved people were always vulnerable to being sold away from family, home, beloveds, and community. But Dylan sang about being on your own, away from the safety and comfort of home and family, as if that were the true, ecstatic meaning of life, and he told mothers and fathers to get out of the way.

"The ironic thing," *Newsweek* reported in November 1963, not long after Dylan had written "The Times They Are A-Changin'," "is that Bob Dylan, too, grew up in a conventional home, and went to conventional schools. He shrouds his past in contradictions, but he is the eldest son of a Hibbing, Minnesota, appliance dealer named Abe Zimmerman, and, as Bobby Zimmerman, he attended Hibbing

High School." When Abe himself was asked about Bob's lies, he translated them into a businessman's terms: "My son is a corporation and his public image is strictly an act."[39] Dylan sat down with the *Newsweek* reporter and denied it, showing him a draft card that said "Bob Dylan." "I don't know my parents," Dylan said, and "they don't know me. I've lost contact with them for years. . . . My past is so complicated you wouldn't believe it, man." In fact, Abe had been the legal witness when his son changed his name to Bob Dylan. And even as Dylan talked to the reporter, Abe and Beatty were staying a few blocks away in New York City, where they had traveled to see Bob perform at Carnegie Hall.[40]

In 1965, psychologist Kenneth Keniston published *The Uncommitted*, exploring why so "many bright, affluent young people despised their society." His answer was that young people thought "adulthood . . . involves materialism, boring work, being controlled by the demands of others." This was the "generation gap": music was arguably its "defining symbol," and Dylan was its voice and icon.[41]

His songs became the soundtrack to an unprecedented coalition that challenged patriarchy on multiple fronts. The Civil Rights Movement. The women's movement. The antiwar movement. The student movement. All were against "the man"—the name soldiers in World War I had given to their superior officers, repurposed by those who refused to fight their fathers' wars.[42] For the protest movements of the 1960s, achieving peace, justice, and equality meant confronting patriarchy around the world and at home.

The eagerness of reporters to discover the truth about where Bob Dylan had come from missed the point. His stories didn't have to be factual, because they told a deeper truth. "Maybe I was happy when I was little or I was unhappy," he said in an interview in 1962, the year his first album was released, "a million other kids were the same way."[43] Dylan understood, arguably before anyone else, one of the defining emotional truths of rock and roll: a perfectly nice home can sometimes be the worst kind of all. His songs made a lot of kids at home feel like they needed to get out on their own to be free.

In 1963, Sara Lownds was a twenty-four-year-old single mother in New York City. Four years earlier, at twenty, she had been a Playboy Bunny named Vicky. Before that, she had been Shirley Noznisky from Wilmington, Delaware, where her father, who never learned to read or write in English, ran a scrap-metal salvage yard. Not long after Shirley graduated from high school, her father was shot and killed in a fight.[44]

Shirley moved to New York to model and ended up at the Play-boy Club. She signed with Ford Models, got her pictures published in *Harper's Bazaar*, and married a photographer who was twenty-five years older, Hans Lownds—originally Heinz Lowenstein. At Hans's insistence, Shirley changed her name to Sara. Their daughter, Maria, was born in October 1961.

The next year Sara and Maria left Hans and moved to Greenwich Village and then to the Chelsea Hotel. She started working in the office of Time-Life Films and hung out with future members of the Velvet Underground and Albert Grossman, Bob Dylan's manager. The first time she met Bob Dylan, she was expecting Bobby Darin, the star behind hits "Splish Splash" and "Dream Lover."[45]

In 1964, Dylan moved into Room 211 at the Chelsea Hotel to be near Sara and Maria.[46] Hans Lownds didn't want the man he called Zimmerman to raise his daughter, Maria, and threatened to sue for full custody. Instead, Lownds disappeared and never saw Maria again.[47] Living with Sara and Maria at the hotel, Dylan wrote songs for electric guitar like he had done as a kid and put them out on the album he called *Bringing It All Back Home.*

For years Dylan and Joan Baez had been the "king and queen" of folk music, and their on-again, off-again romance added to the mystique around them. In March of 1965, they did a tour of East Coast colleges. After the last show, in Pittsburgh, they split up for good. "Hey, man," Dylan said to Baez, "I heard those kids.... I can't be responsible for those kids' lives." "You rat," Baez replied, "You mean you're gonna leave them all with me?" Dylan answered: "Take them if you want them. But man, I can't be responsible."[48] Baez was committed to the role of music in the politics of the sixties, but Dylan didn't want a kingdom of loyal subjects. He wanted a family of his own.

At the same time he was rejecting the generation that saw him as a leader, Dylan took on new responsibilities as a father. After his 1965 tour ended, he bought a house in Woodstock, New York, and moved there with Sara and Maria. Soon Sara was pregnant, and before the year was over, they got married. Dylan's tour manager at the time, Victor Maymudes, was surprised. "I asked him, 'Why Sara?!'" Maymudes later recalled. "'Why not Joan Baez?' Dylan answered: 'Because Sara will be there when I want her to be home, she'll be there when I want her to be there, she'll do it when I want to do it. Joan won't be there when I want her. She won't do it when I want to do it.'"[49] Dylan had given voice to the antipatriarchal politics of a rising generation, but his own values had not been revolutionized. At home, he still wanted to be the man.

That year Dylan wrote "Subterranean Homesick Blues," the song from which the radical activist group the Weather

Underground later took their name. Like many others in the sixties and since, the core members of the Weather Underground
rejected monogamy and conventional domesticity as a part of their
opposition to patriarchy, war, and capitalism. But Dylan himself,
at arguably the height of his renown as a political songwriter, and
beneath his public image, was homesick for a conventional idea
of fatherhood and family.

That was exactly what the U.S. government was hoping for—exactly
how policymakers imagined the end of the social upheaval of the
1960s: stronger men at the head of stronger nuclear families.
Especially after the passage of the Civil Rights Act in July 1964,
Black fathers became a special focus of concern and policy. Many
of the landmark bill's leading champions, including Martin Luther
King Jr., argued that new laws alone weren't enough to address
centuries of racism and inequality. That summer Black Americans
clashed with police in Harlem, Rochester, Chicago, and Philadelphia. In Washington, the Johnson administration worried that
continuing discontent would gather into outright rebellion. To
achieve meaningful equality and avert a "new crisis in race relations," something more than rights was needed, and in the fall of
1964 the answer came to Daniel Patrick Moynihan in his sleep.[50]

One night in November, Moynihan, then an ambitious assis-
tant secretary in the Department of Labor, woke up at 4:00 a.m.
certain that the key to resolving America's racial and social crisis
was to help Black fathers stay with their families.[51] Moynihan
spent much of the next year working on a study, published in
the spring of 1965 under the title *The Negro Family: The Case
for National Action*. Initially confidential and anonymous, the

241

document quickly became indelibly identified with its author and known as the Moynihan Report.

In the six decades since its publication, the Moynihan Report has often been read as evidence of the depth of systemic racism in American culture and politics, illustrating how distorted and harmful assumptions of racial difference have skewed even ostensibly liberal programs aiming for social equality. Fair as these charges are, Moynihan's initial idea was as much about sex, gender, and psychology as it was about race, and it was shaped by his own experiences with fatherhood.

Moynihan had grown up in New York City during the Depression, the eldest child of a struggling Irish-American family. In 1937, when Pat was around ten, his alcoholic father abandoned them to move to California. Pat, his siblings, and his mother were left to scramble for food, work, and shelter. Sometimes they stayed in an apartment for only a month before moving on.

They had few other options and no help. Around the turn of the twentieth century, in response to fears that packs of immigrant children were overwhelming American cities with thieving and begging, many local and state governments passed laws requiring paternal child support. Yet enforcement was all but impossible, for there was no way to track down absent and delinquent fathers, especially those who moved all the way across the country, as Moynihan's father had. Public welfare programs were largely reserved for the families of veterans. For everyone else, there was only private charity, which in practice went almost exclusively to widows, for even mission-driven do-gooders were loath to let absent fathers off the hook by helping their children.[52]

While he shined shoes and sold papers to help his mother and siblings, Pat Moynihan graduated from his East Harlem high school at sixteen. The navy sent him to college in 1944, and after that he started graduate work on the international labor movement, which led to a Fulbright fellowship at the London School of Economics. For Moynihan, succeeding in England meant finding "a wife and a job—simple enough."[53] To help, he started psychoanalysis.

Quickly Moynihan's Freudian analyst concluded that his loyalties had been split by his father's desertion—Moynihan wanted to love his father despite his abandonment; he was grateful to his mother but feared her anger. Female authority had become entangled with the pain of his father's absence. In sessions, Moynihan dug up old memories of his father, all of them good. Between appointments he was "literally overwhelmed by simple tender childish emotions" when he saw fathers and children together. When Moynihan had a month left in London, he dreamed that he woke up sobbing because he wanted his father to come back. His analyst said this was the breakthrough. Moynihan had faced his father and was finally ready to honor him.[54]

Soon after Moynihan got back to the United States in 1954, he married and had three kids. The youngest was named John, after Moynihan's still absent and estranged father. Through friendly connections, Moynihan got a post in Kennedy's Labor Department and moved his family to Washington in July 1961.

In Washington, Moynihan made himself into something of an expert on and advocate for men. He saw a link between the dual problems of poverty and juvenile delinquency: failing men. Reports from the military said that young men were struggling to meet the physical and mental standards required for enlistment. Moynihan got Kennedy to put him in charge of a Task Force on Manpower Conservation. Three months later Moynihan's task force had determined that many of the struggling young men had come from single-parent households like the one he had grown up in, and were heading for "a lifetime of recurrent unemployment" and poverty that they would pass on to their own children in turn—unless the government intervened.

Moynihan came up with a training program aimed especially at Black men, who were then proportionately underrepresented in the military. "Above all things," Moynihan's proposal concluded, "the down-and-out Negro boy needs to be inducted into the male American society." He believed enrollment and employment in the military would positively connect Black men to the nation and help put them on more solid financial ground, just as it had for him.[55]

Two years later, in the fall of 1964, Lyndon Johnson gave Moynihan the go-ahead to look into new ways to help Black fathers and families. Moynihan reached out to Kenneth Clark, a distinguished Black psychologist and professor.[56] Clark had been influenced by Alfred Adler's concept of the "inferiority complex." In 1950, Clark conducted an experiment that gave Black children a choice of different-colored dolls to play with. Again and again the children chose white, and some also defaced the Black dolls. Clark interpreted the results as evidence of a learned and internalized sense of inferiority, and his conclusions informed the Supreme Court's 1954 repudiation of segregation in *Brown v. Board of Education*. Through Clark, Moynihan began to see, as his now-infamous phrase put it, a "tangle of pathology" ensnaring Black families—a complex set of social disadvantages that perpetuated racial inequality.

Moynihan borrowed "tangle of pathology" directly from Kenneth Clark, but pathology was the standard language of postwar psychology. In January of 1965, just as Moynihan was getting his study underway, Anna Freud published *Normality and Pathology in Childhood*, arguing that a normal, healthy childhood required two parental figures, male and female—not necessarily mother and father, or married, or even together, but present. That was Moynihan's belief, too, derived from his own childhood experience, from the guidance of his Freudian analyst in London, from his research on Black life, and from his reading of the statistics on marriage and family in the United States.

Moynihan saw in nationwide statistics that divorce and illegitimacy were becoming more common across the country, but not equally everywhere. "Fatherless nonwhite families" appeared to be increasing, while fatherlessness was down among white families. Most Black children lived at some point with only one parent at home. Most also received federal welfare, which was only available if one parent was absent or incapacitated. Nearly two-thirds of the families on welfare were eligible because there was no man living in the household. Merging these statistics together, Moynihan concluded that a disproportionate number of Black fathers were not living at home with their children.

Why were some Black men not living with their children? Moynihan's answer had two parts. First was the history of slavery. "It was by destroying the Negro family under slavery that white America broke the will of the Negro people," he wrote. "Although that will has reasserted itself in our time, it is a resurgence doomed to frustration unless the viability of the Negro family is restored."

245

This was a conclusion drawn in part from leading scholars of slavery. Historian Stanley Elkins, comparing American slavery to the concentration camps of Nazi Germany, argued that enslavement had forced Black men into "infantile regression," because they were treated as "boys" and denied the "honorific attributes of fatherhood."[57]

The second, compounding problem, according to Moynihan, was the welfare system. Because it had started out as a program to aid families of dead and injured veterans, the eligibility requirements of welfare programs unintentionally encouraged men to leave. Families who needed help could get it most readily if fathers weren't at home. Moynihan concluded that the result of these conjoined histories was a Black culture of matriarchy that, he thought, had negative consequences for the children who grew up in it, especially given the "dominant" culture of patriarchy.

Moynihan believed that all men needed something to be proud of, a way to feel good about themselves, and Black men especially. "The very essence of the male animal," Moynihan wrote, "from the bantam rooster to the four-star general, is to strut." Black men in America, he believed, had been denied this opportunity twice over—first by white men who treated them as "boys," and then by women who, given the structure of existing welfare programs, had come to rule over Black households. "We must not rest until every able-bodied Negro male is working," Moynihan told President Johnson. "Even if we have to displace some females."[58]

In June 1965, Johnson incorporated Moynihan's ideas into a major speech at Howard University that was lauded by civil rights leaders. Triumphant, Moynihan had already started planning his own run for the New York City Council.[59] But before Moynihan's campaign could take off, the political ground shifted. Johnson committed more money and troops to Vietnam, limiting the resources available for domestic programs. Then Moynihan's full report, still anonymous, was leaked to the press. On August 9, *Newsweek* identified him as the author. Two days later, the violent arrest of a Black driver by a white police officer developed into a widespread protest centered in Watts, a Black neighborhood of Los Angeles.

Moynihan was alternately hailed as a prophet who had foretold the summer's violence and condemned as a racist and misogynist who was only "blaming the victim," especially Black women. As scholar Angela Davis pointed out, the Black single mothers of America did not constitute a matriarchy in any sense that implied a real hold on social power.[60]

Moynihan's defense was a simplified version of his own family story, which he told in the press in a tone that suggested others might follow his upward path. "I grew up in Hell's Kitchen," he told the *New York Times* in December 1965. "I know what this life is like."[61] Among other blind spots, he seemed not to have considered that his college scholarship, fellowship in England, and friendly connections within the Kennedy administration might be opportunities that would have been near impossible for a person of color to receive. In 1966, feeling like an exile from Washington, Moynihan took a position at Harvard, where he would lead a center for urban studies.

That June, the Johnson administration finally did something for fathers in the hope of strengthening their bonds with their families as Moynihan had proposed. "In the homes of our Nation, we look to the fathers to provide the strength and stability which characterize the successful family," President Johnson announced,

Moynihan's phrases still echoing. In the preceding years, Johnson had used his legislative savvy to shepherd civil rights and voting rights into law. Now Congress had given official recognition to a tradition that had long been an informal holiday, a distant second to the widely observed Mother's Day. By special resolution, Father's Day would be officially celebrated on the third Sunday in June.

In 1969, Pat Moynihan took a leave from Harvard and went back to work on family policy and welfare reform in the Nixon administration. He succeeded in convincing Nixon that a guaranteed basic income would help encourage fathers to remain with their families. Nixon was in favor, but the proposal was cut down in Congress as an undeserved handout. With Moynihan's most ambitious proposals to support men and families scuttled again, Nixon, too, was left only with symbolic gestures and formalities. In 1972, he went one step further than Johnson and declared Father's Day a permanent national holiday. As we know it, Father's Day is an unintended and unrecognized consequence of the fractious American politics of race, gender, and class.

Even as Bob Dylan was forming a family of his own, he hardly kept in touch with his parents. "I don't dislike them or anything," Dylan said in a November 1965 interview. "I just don't have any contact with them."[62] He didn't tell his parents about his marriage to Sara in November 1965. He didn't tell them about the birth of his first son, Jesse, two months later. And he didn't tell them that he crashed his motorcycle on July 29, 1966.

Instead, Abe and Beatty got updates about their son from the news, just like everyone else. When they heard that Bob had been injured in an accident, they didn't even have his telephone number, so they called journalist Robert Shelton to find out what happened.[63]

Almost every story about the life of Bob Dylan turns on his motorcycle accident. Usually it's told as a mystery—no one knows the truth except Dylan himself; no one else was there to witness what happened that morning on the back roads of Woodstock. But everyone agrees on what happened next: Dylan disappeared. Once he had been a political force, writing scathing antiwar lyrics, a biting critic of mass culture, an activist onstage with Martin Luther King Jr. at the March on Washington. But now, at a crucial moment for the Vietnam War protest movement, he went quiet, stayed at home, and sang country songs in a soft, round voice.

The only other version of the story is Dylan's own. "I have more responsibilities now," Dylan explained to a journalist who asked why he was spending so much time at home in the woods of upstate New York.[64] He was "vulnerable with a family to protect," as he put it in his 2004 memoir, *Chronicles*. "Having children changed my life and segregated me from just about everybody and everything that was going on," Dylan wrote. "Outside of my family nothing held any real interest for me and I was seeing everything through different glasses. . . . I had a wife and children whom I loved more than anything else in the world. I was trying to provide for them, keep out of trouble."[65] In 1967, he and Sara had a daughter, Anna. In 1968, another son, Samuel Isaac. In 1969, Jakob.

Mornings in Woodstock, Dylan would walk Sara's daughter Maria to the bus stop down the hill from their mountainside house with one of the other parents, an artist named Bruce Dorfman. Talking about their kids at drop-offs, they became close. When Dylan wanted to legally adopt Maria, he asked Dorfman for a reference. Dorfman was happy to give it, because he had seen how seriously Dylan took fatherhood. That was Dylan's true ideal, Dorfman said: "the closeness and comfort of family."[66]

Dylan wanted to be a good dad, which is what all his kids called him.[67] He took the kids to Little League games, birthday parties, camping trips, boating, rafting, canoeing, fishing. He bought cheap clothes for himself at Sears but spent piles of money on toys and sports equipment and cars, just like his father had. He set up a pool table in his garage and a basketball hoop in the yard.[68] He researched Sara's genealogy and found out her family had come from Odessa too.[69] When he was recording the Basement Tapes with the Band in nearby Saugerties, he left the sessions in time to get home for dinner.

On the afternoon of June 5, 1968, Bob got a call at his house. He hung up, asked his driver to pull the Cadillac around, packed a suitcase and a guitar, and went to the airport in New York without saying a word about why. Abe was dead of a heart attack. At the funeral in Minnesota, some attendees were surprised to see Bob upset. After the service, Dylan slept in his father's bedroom.[70] When he got home to Woodstock, his mother, Beatty, came and stayed with him and his family for a long time.[71]

The next summer, 1969, the Woodstock Festival in upstate New York drew crowds to his town and drove Dylan away. "I couldn't get any space for myself and my family," he said.[72] They went back to New York City, but outside their house in Greenwich Village people picked through their garbage and peeked in their windows. "They've got furniture inside!" one snooper announced.[73]

Dylan and Sara and their five kids moved to Malibu and built a big fantasy house in the dunes, filled with painstakingly chosen things. Each of the kids designed tiles for their own bathroom. Dylan had a copper dome made to put on top of the house, like the domes of Odessa, where his family and Sara's had come from. It was all wrong for California, but Bob said that when he saw the dome he knew he was home. He traveled to Minnesota, bought back the first car he owned, and told the architect he wanted to hang it from the ceiling in Malibu.[74]

In 1973, after trying to hide his family life for more than a decade, Dylan wrote "Forever Young," a father's wish for his children and, by association, for himself. He said the song had been in his head for five years, since Jakob was born. In the studio, he recorded five versions of the track, as if there were one for each of his kids.[75]

"Forever Young" is a kind of psalm, a sung prayer of intercession. Its lyrics pray for a child to stay "forever young" by growing up to be all things good always: righteous, steady, joyful, strong, kind, blessed. Every parent has at some point wanted that very same thing, though none has ever got it. The song is a father's chanted incantation against time and reality, a spell to put off growing up forever, so that all things might always be possible, and all such wishes may yet come true. The power of the best music that Bob Dylan created is that it expands the boundaries of the possible, even for a few minutes at a time. Once he wrote as a rebellious son calling for generational social change. Now he wrote as a protective father praying for everything to stay the same. Dylan put two versions of "Forever Young" on the album *Planet Waves*, one rocker and one ballad, and it was his first album ever to go to Number One.

In the strained and anxious decades after World War II, the role of the dad was to make his kids happy, to demonstrate by joining his children in fun, games, and make-believe that everything was and would be okay. The dad looked different from the man, one a friend, the other foe, but they worked together to keep order amid the social discontent and disillusionment that threatened to break into a larger revolution. Both were essentially conservative figures, charged with weighty political duties in reaction to the spirit of rebellion and openness that took popular new forms in the second half of the twentieth century, and gained arguably its widest expression in music. In different ways, the dad and the man both worked to domesticate that spirit, to keep it at home.

In these same years, especially after Betty Friedan's 1963 bestseller, *The Feminine Mystique*, growing numbers of women articulated in bold terms the limits of being defined primarily by your children, family, and home. Apart from rock and roll, men never developed, individually or collectively among themselves, the same sorts of language or conversations, though perhaps they remained more likely to act on such feelings.

For eight years, from 1966 to 1973, Bob Dylan had mostly stayed at home with Sara and their children. But that summer came the first reports that Dylan's marriage had broken up. Now he went back to Minnesota to live by himself for the summer and wrote *Blood on the Tracks*, his "divorce album."[76] For his birthday Dylan went to France alone. He went on tour in the winter of 1974 and at the end of it he told Joan Baez that he wanted to stay on the road forever.[77]

Instead, he went unhappily home to Malibu. Dylan burst into Sara's room uninvited, glowered at her aggressively, and ordered her out of the house: "I was in such fear of him that I locked doors to protect myself from his violent outbursts and temper tantrums," Sara claimed in her divorce petition. One morning she came down to breakfast to find another woman sitting in her place with Bob and their kids—when Sara objected, Dylan told her to get out and, Sara alleged, hit her in the face.[78]

The record executive David Geffen, who had put out *Planet Waves* and "Forever Young," referred Sara to Marvin Mitchelson, a celebrity divorce lawyer.[79] Between 1950 and 1980, divorce rates tripled in the United States.[80] In 1968, California had passed the nation's first no-fault divorce law, though Sara Dylan did not pursue that option. She "loved Bob Dylan," the filings said, "but he chose to spend his time elsewhere."[81] Among other things, Sara claimed Bob had missed the births of their first three children, once for a chess game. She asked for full custody, child support, and a division of assets, including music rights.

Dylan countered that he wanted permanent custody, because he was worried that Sara would take the children to live in Hawaii. He retained a psychiatrist to testify that his home was safe for his children, and the expert agreed with Dylan that he was the best candidate for custody. Dylan's lawyers advised him to wear a suit to the custody hearings, and he borrowed one from a Hollywood studio set.[82] When Sara won, she and their kids moved to Beverly Hills. They saw their father on holidays, in Malibu or in Minnesota, where he was spending more time.

"I could be happy pounding metal all day," Dylan said in 1978, the year his divorce went through, "going home to a big fat wife and eating a meal, and you know, going to bed." It was a fantasy of how men in Hibbing and other Iron Range towns had lived. "You give me a woman who can cook and sew, and I'll take that over passion any day of the week."[83] But it wasn't true this time, either.

After his divorce, Bob started dating his backup singers, including Carolyn Dennis, hired that May. When Carolyn got the call about going on tour with Bob, she didn't know who he was.[84] Bob also hired Carolyn's mother, who had sung with Ray Charles, as another backup singer. They were part of a quartet of Black women Dylan called "The Queens of Rhythm" and sometimes introduced onstage as "My ex-wife, my next wife, my girlfriend, and my fiancée."[85] For years Bob and Carolyn toured together and kept up an on and off relationship.

In January 1986, Carolyn Dennis and Bob Dylan had a daughter, Desiree. Her birth was "one of the most closely guarded secrets" of Dylan's secretive life. Three days later, he went on tour in the Pacific. When he got back in June, he and Dennis were married. That was a secret too—from the press and from the other women Dylan was then dating.[86] Two years later, in the summer of 1988, he moved Carolyn and Desiree into a house he bought in suburban Los Angeles, near the Ventura Freeway, and took off to start a tour designed to go on forever. Carolyn filed for divorce in 1990. Desiree stayed with her, and Dylan stayed on the road, living for long stretches in his tour bus.

MEN AFTER FATHERHOOD

During the Bicentennial American summer of 1976, the Founding Fathers were everywhere—on stamps, the new two-dollar bill, Pez dispensers, ads for McDonald's, Coke, and used cars—but poet Adrienne Rich was finishing a book called *Of Woman Born: Motherhood as Experience and Institution.* "For the first time in history," Rich wrote, marking a different occasion, "a pervasive recognition is developing that the patriarchal system cannot answer for itself; that it is not inevitable; that it is transitory; and that the cross-cultural global domination of women by men can no longer be either denied or defended."[1] Lining up clauses as if they were already self-evident truths, she echoed Thomas Jefferson's style in the Declaration of Independence.

Like Jefferson, Rich was building on decades of philosophy and protest. The social revolutions of the sixties had especially drawn attention to "the problem of men," as Simone de Beauvoir had described patriarchy in *The Second Sex*, her 1949 history of womanhood. The book had sparked a new generation of feminist writers to challenge the constraints of what Beauvoir called "man-made" motherhood. Betty Friedan dedicated *The Feminine Mystique* to Beauvoir, and Rich thanked Beauvoir in her acknowledgments, singling her out as one of the women "who created pioneering feminist insights to which I shall always stand in debt."

But Rich saw more to be done. Simone de Beauvoir had never married or had children. Rich, on the other hand, had gotten married, given birth, and raised a family. She wanted to know how women experienced the "man-made" institution of motherhood, how they remade it and reshaped it to fit their own lives, and what that revealed about what motherhood had been and could be.

Rich's own experience of motherhood was complicated in part by her experiences with fatherhood, both as a daughter and as a wife. She was keenly sensitive to the dynamics between men and women, and this tension was at the heart of her book. By the mid-seventies, fathers had largely disappeared from Rich's life, and in the space where they had been, Rich could see a question but not yet an answer: "For the first time," she wrote, "we are in a position to look around us at the Kingdom of the Fathers and take its measure."

When Rich was born in 1929, her parents, Arnold and Helen, had been expecting a boy, whom they planned to name Arnold also. Arnold Rich was a renowned pathologist at Johns Hopkins in Baltimore. Helen was an accomplished pianist and composer, and Arnold had courted her with florid love poems and proclamations. But Arnold's tone changed after they married in 1925. He wrote out a numbered list of his expectations and insisted that Helen wear a long-sleeve black dress of his design: her "uniform."

Arnold Rich took a similar approach to fatherhood. He taught Adrienne and her younger sister, Cynthia, at home until they were eleven and seven, respectively, and the City of Baltimore intervened. When Adrienne was five, her father assigned her to copy out lines from the English Romantic poets and graded her work. When she was six, he printed up her first book of poems. Arnold's presence loomed so large over Adrienne's life that "she could hardly distinguish between his directive and her desire to fulfill it."[2] Even when she was married and expecting a child of her own, Adrienne hoped for a son, so she could do what her mother had not done and deliver the boy her father had wished her to be. Rich's oldest son was born on her father's birthday.

When Arnold died in 1968, Rich's grief was mixed with relief. By 1970, she had embraced feminism and separated from her husband, Alfred Conrad, a professor of economics. That summer, she got her own apartment in New York City, left her three sons, ages eleven to fifteen, with Conrad on Central Park West, and started a book of poems she called *The Will to Change, 1968–1970*. In October, Alfred Conrad drove from New York to Vermont, where the family had a vacation home, and killed himself.

For a few months, Rich couldn't write. Then in early 1971 she began to work on the poems in her 1973 book, *Diving into the Wreck*. The wreck was not her life. It was her life under patriarchy—"the power of the fathers," as she would define it. Rich wanted to see this wreck for what it was, instead of repeating the myths and stories about it. The poems she wrote were born of "feelings of rage at being a woman in a patriarchal society," mixed with the sense that she was finally free to become herself.[3]

For Rich, more and more, being free meant living in a world apart from men. When she got a job offer at Brandeis University near Boston, she insisted on negotiating the terms with a woman instead of the male chair of the English Department. When *Diving into the Wreck* won the National Book Award for Poetry, Rich donated her prize money to the Sisterhood of Black Single Mothers of New York. When she did a reading at Haverford College, she refused to take questions from men in the audience. Rich told poet Hayden Carruth, one of her most trusted friends and readers, that she was tempted to give up on men altogether.[4]

Yet she also had three boys lined up at the border of manhood. Rich often felt that caring for them was "eating away" at her life, but she was not going to give up on her sons. She remembered the summers they had spent in Vermont, just the four of them, while Conrad was working abroad. They had "lived half-naked, stayed up to watch bats and fireflies, read and told stories, slept late," their "little-boys' bodies" growing tan, "like castaways on some island of mothers and children." On their own in the country, they were "outlaws from the institution of motherhood."[5] But when the usual routines resumed in the fall, Rich and her sons got caught up in their old roles again.

Raising her boys during the Vietnam War, Rich worried that the Western tradition was to train men to kill, and to train women to heal men's wounds so they could go back out and kill again. She did not want her sons to kill or be killed. She did not want to nurse them. She wanted them "to remain . . . sons of the mother, yet also to grow into themselves, to discover new ways of being men even as we are discovering new ways of being women."[6] Men could have a feminism of their own.

In one sense, Rich's idea for "new ways of being men" borrowed from the Founding Fathers. She thought it might be possible to replace the traditional role of the individual father with a group of fathers who would collectively guide her boys toward "a manhood of nourishment and solace." But she feared she couldn't find enough men who could do it. New fathers were needed, but Rich didn't know who they would be, or where they would come from. "We have to recognize," she concluded, "at this moment of history, as through centuries past, that most of our sons are—in the most profound sense—virtually fatherless."[7] By the time *Of Woman Born* was published in the fall of 1976, Rich had begun a relationship with its copy editor, the Jamaican-American writer Michelle Cliff, that would last for the rest of her life.

Since the 1970s, the dominant theme in the history of fatherhood has been extinction. For some, social conservatives especially, the perceived decline and fall of "traditional" breadwinning father figures and patriarchal nuclear families is a catastrophe that must be reversed. For others, including those building on the insights of Simone de Beauvoir and Adrienne Rich, this is cause for hope, and they see an opening for more flexible identities and configurations of family.

Yet the widely discussed contemporary crisis of fatherhood and masculinity more generally is not especially contemporary. Instead, it is only the latest recurrence of the kind of identity crisis that has always defined their history.

The current crisis coincides with two new realities for men: precise paternity testing and an expanded role in caregiving.

For the first time in human history, it has become possible to establish paternity with certainty. Blood-typing tests pioneered in the 1920s were able to rule out paternity, but not to confirm it. In the 1960s, early gene-based testing provided positive identifications with roughly 80 percent accuracy. Then in the 1980s, British investigators working on immigration and rape cases developed the first methods of genetic profiling by comparing small sections of DNA sequences. These techniques, now further refined and more precise still, yield virtually indisputable results even from the minute traces of fetal DNA that begin to circulate in a mother's blood mere weeks after conception.

At the same time, fathers have taken on new roles in the everyday care of their children, especially newborns and infants. "For more than 200 million years," writes anthropologist Sarah Baffler Hrdy, "the nurture of mammalian young has been the nearly exclusive preserve of mothers."[8] But no longer. Men now spend more time taking care of their children than their fathers did—in fact, Hrdy says, more time than fathers have ever spent on child-care.[9] This change is partly a result of the successes of feminism, as increasing numbers of women seek fulfillment beyond the home. Even so, in the United States especially, the politics of family life are still not equitable or well supported, and women continue to spend more time caring for children than men do. Yet in some concrete ways, fatherhood has become more like motherhood.

It may seem paradoxical or ironic that the experience of fatherhood has been clarified and enlarged at the same time as the institution of fatherhood is said to be in crisis. More likely, this is cause and effect. The reality of fatherhood now—anchored in biologically indisputable paternity and the everyday work of caring for children—has undercut inherited ideas about fatherhood that were built on myths, wishes, and impossible promises.

Now the old stories about men and fathers seem to be missing their grandest parts—the miraculous, inexplicable, just-so, made-up parts that worked to elevate fathers above everyone else. Efforts to restore these old images and models of fatherhood to their former condition can seem absurd to the point of parody, fantasies of continuity born from a fear of changes that have already taken place. Yet at a deeper level, this is exactly the source of their power, and the widespread and sometimes justifiable claims that men and fathers are in crisis reveal that we are once again in search of a new idea of what men and fathers could and should be. If we were to recognize these questions as ancient ones—consequences of the recurrent collapse of one story about men, love, and power, and the fraught and contested search for another—we might yet understand ourselves in a new way.

That, anyway, has been my experience.

On July 4, 1979, the night before I was born, my parents went to see a Woody Allen movie, hoping some laughs would speed things along. Most Thursday evenings when I was growing up, my father would take a small black-and-white television out of the closet where he kept the suits he wore to work every day. He would set it on the cedar trunk at the foot of the bed he shared with my mother, extend the antenna toward the window, and my brother and I would climb up onto their bed and wait for the cast of *The Cosby Show* to start their family dance. The only other show we had official permission to watch was *The Wonder Years*, and usually my father sat on the edge of the bed and watched with us.

The father on *The Wonder Years* had fought in Korea and worked for a defense contractor. My grandfather, my father's father, fought in World War II, went to college on the GI Bill, bought two houses with GI loans, worked at a defense firm, and then quit to start his own business, which made and sold precision machines of his own invention. By the time I knew him, he had a garage full of antique cars in various states of disassembly and repair, as well as, for some reason that remains a mystery to me, a couple of rusty earthmoving machines whose spidery levers he helped us operate. I once asked him why he had bought two houses after the war, instead of the usual one, and he said to me, "You know your grandpa always does it big." One of his inventions had become a small but crucial component of what the Department of Defense has described as "the most powerful missiles in the world."

My father's father was always thinking of some problem or solution that he was working on, and when he was in the thick of it he had no patience for anything else. My father and his three siblings went on summer vacations in the car with their mother while their father, my grandfather, stayed home in his workshop, wearing grease-smeared work pants held up by a length of wire. He had no time for or interest in a belt or family vacations.

My parents met in law school. The year I was born, my father started the job he would have for the rest of his career. He represented people who had been hurt at work, especially by machines, and he always said that he specialized in cases involving complex engineering problems. My father would figure out what was dangerous about or wrong with the machine or tool or product that had injured his client, and he would sue the company that built and sold it. Every morning he went to work in a suit and tie and heavy leather wingtip shoes that we helped him shine, and when he came back in the evening, never very late, we knew he was home because we heard his footsteps on the wood floors. On Friday afternoons we would call him at the office and ask for him by his full name. When the receptionist put us through, we would first pretend to be lawyers, too, and then we would ask him to bring home pizza. He played us Bob Dylan tapes in the car on the way to ski lessons, he took us to get donuts and to the hardware store on weekend mornings, he took us to the mall in the evenings to buy shin guards and notebooks, he took us on family vacations, and he took it perfectly in stride when I scratched his face out of the picture of my baseball team, which he had helped to coach.

About ten years ago, in the middle of a January night in Maine, my father started hitting my mother while she was asleep next to him in their bed. She woke up and said his name in the dark, but he didn't answer. She tried again, louder, and again, and then she was panicking, thinking that he was having a heart attack, which is how her father had died.

The bleeding in my father's brain had probably started a few days earlier. Maybe he had headaches and dizziness, but nothing that had kept him home from work. That night it worsened, and by midnight, around the time he woke my mother, he could no longer move the right side of his body or form words.

When she drove him home from the rehab hospital a month later, he could talk again, but not as fluently, and he could walk again, but not as steadily. He retired from lawyering, so he was home every day for the first time in my life, and around the dinner table we all watched him anxiously while he chewed.

My father had always been a forthright and solid presence. Now he was slightly indefinite and reluctant, quicker to laugh and embarrass, yet also remote somehow. The qualities I had known to be his, to be him, had been repainted in a new shade.

Abruptly, and against the wishes of my own wife, I moved home to help care for him. Most afternoons for the rest of that winter and into the spring, we did some exercises together and tossed a tennis ball for few minutes. I cooked dinner, which had always been my mother's role in our family, then my father did the dishes, as he always had, and everyone went to bed early.

After my father's birthday in May, I decided just as abruptly that this wasn't what he wanted, his grown son living at home. Yet my life had become too heavy and awkward to simply pick up and carry forward from where I had set it down months earlier. When I thought about my wife, I thought about how easy it had been to find something that made us laugh so hard we cried. And I thought that I would really miss that. If only I hadn't changed so irrevocably.

Still I was trailed by a hope—a dim mix of history, literature, and delusion—that I might restore order by becoming a father myself. Yet when I imagined taking care of my child, the pictures in my head didn't fit the models of fatherhood I had known. In my imagination, I was always on my own, a single father inside a walled fantasy of safety, vulnerable to the smallest possible number of alarms and surprises.

Bill Cosby's mistrial was on every television in the hospital when my son was born at the beginning of the summer of 2017. In August, thousands of young men dressed up like "suburban dads," as style magazines put it, to march for hate in Charlottesville. That fall, I settled into an afternoon routine of buckling my son's skinny body into the secondhand maroon baby carrier, faded and lightly vomit stained, that I wore over my shoulders like a backpack in reverse. Outside I would get a coffee and we would roam our neighborhood at half speed.

At the time, my son was still so small that once I got used to the straps of the carrier, and even when I was holding his invertebrate feet in my hands, I often forgot that he was attached to me. Then I would catch a flicker of us in a storefront window, or a meaningful look from a passerby, and in those moments I was always brought up short by surprise. I thought I would try to establish a language we could use to call each other across a distance, should that become necessary, so periodically I would bow my head toward his and howl softly, and every so often he would make a sound that I was able to interpret as a reply.

But mostly I waited for his eyes to close, and as soon as they did I would take out my phone and read the latest news of sexual misconduct, all the accusations, admissions, resignations, and prosecutions, more every day during that fall of Me Too. The carrier held him high on my chest, just under my chin, so his cheek rested on my breastbone and his head rose and fell with my breath. Occasionally he would stir and shift around to look up at me or turn his face to the other side, and once he settled in again I would pass my phone to the other hand and keep reading.

Walking with my son that fall, I understood for the first time that the fathers I had grown up with, the men and families I had known as a boy, no longer existed as I remembered them. Yet I had no idea who or what was left. Instinctively I doubted that I would be able to make my son feel as safe and taken care of as my father had made me feel, but I had no sense of what I might teach my son about being a boy or a man, or whether such a thing should be taught, whether it should even be. I had no vision of what I might add to his life as his father that could overcome my fears, playing out every day on my screen, playing out everywhere around us, about what having a father and being my son might cost him. But I wanted one.

Almost as soon as he started going to school every day, my son began to ask what I had done at home while he was gone. Before

I answered, and with every paternal instinct flashing red, I would think back over the day's unnarratable antiheroics—rounding up fugitive pieces of cereal after breakfast, teaching the Gilded Age to a hundred blank faces, the almost-imperceptible wasting of a promising afternoon—and then I would lie.

I told him that I had eaten an entire box of Popsicles while watching episode after episode of *Wild Kratts*, then his favorite TV show. Or that I had been all around the city shopping for toys with Jeppy, his beloved stuffed monkey. Entirely aware of and exasperated by these fabrications, my son was also indignant at having missed out, so I assured him that not having to go to school was merely one of the benefits of having finished school. Admittedly I would have said almost anything to deliver us out of my middle-aged world and back into his—where, as he told me one morning in the predawn darkness of my bedroom, while I was trying to go back to sleep, car alarms sound like music.

Then one evening in the late fall we were eating dinner in our usual sidelong places at our small round table. Already at 5:30 the street below our apartment was as dark and still as the surface of the moon, and our reflections were vivid in the windows opposite our seats. When, spoon in fist, my son looked up from his soup and asked what I had done all day, some new authority in his manner suggested that he really wanted to know, even had a few opinions on the subject, a suggestion or two. I could no longer pretend that I too was a child, and there was nothing to do but tell him the truth. I said that I was writing a book about fatherhood.

My son eyed me doubtfully. "What's fatherhood?" he asked, as if this was just another invention.

*　　*　　*

CONCLUSION: MEN AFTER FATHERHOOD

Let's make the question smaller, like it was before someone tried to make it into the biggest thing in the world. Do you remember that evening in the early spring when we were walking to have dinner with your mother, and I asked you what you thought a father should be? I had been thinking back over all the fathers in this book—how their stories had in some ways shaped our own, but didn't have to define it. Without a moment's hesitation, while we were crossing the street, you told me that a father should be funny and good at hugging. My first thought was that you were talking about your mother, and only later, only recently, when I was working on this story, did I see that there is another possibility, which is simply that I had never learned to think of myself as funny and good at hugging—to think in those terms about my own capacity to care for you.

Acknowledgments

I'm so happy to be able to finish this book by thanking the people who helped me start it, especially Sarah Stillman, Simon Winder, and Eve Crandall, along with Adam Eaglin, Beniamino Ambrosi, and everyone at the Cheney Agency.

Vital support and encouragement came from friends and colleagues when it was most needed: Ben August, Mitch Bach, Ken Baron, Stephanie Bastek, Christopher Benfey, Sven Beckert, Jenna Bimbi, Kate Bolick, Bill Crandall, Tom Derose at the Freud Museum London, Reed Gochberg and the staff of the Concord Museum, Bob and Ann Gross, Bridget Kearney, Corey Kingston, Bob Miller, Michelle Neely, Doug Shanks, David Singerman, Nan Wolverton and the staff of the American Antiquarian Society, in-house biologist Tim Whitesel, and the CPF AMP apostrophe D crew.

This is a book about the most joyful and painful things I know. Luckily, I had Chris Richards to help me make sense of them. I'm so grateful for his sparking insights and steadying wisdom, and for the fun we had working together again. Joie Asuquo, Georgia

ACKNOWLEDGMENTS

Brainard, Mark Galarrita, Mark LaFlaur, Madison Thân, and the team at Scribner made essential contributions, as did Andrea Henry and the team at Picador UK. I hope they're proud of the book we made together.

Like writing a book, being a parent means asking for help. All my gratitude to Zaii Santos and Doug Sellers, Upali and Suneetha Seneviratne, my brothers Michael and Christopher Sedgewick, my sister-in-law Jenn Marsidi, my nieces Eleanor and Emmeline Marsidi-Sedgewick, and especially Samantha Seneviratne.

This book is dedicated to my parents, John Sedgewick and Deborah Keefe, and to my son, Arthur, who are the reason it exists, and who have given me everything, most of all an idea of what it means to be loved.

Notes

1 Homer, *The Odyssey*, trans. Emily Wilson (New York: W. W. Norton, 2018), 375.

INTRODUCTION MEN BEFORE FATHERHOOD

1 Marshall Berman, "The Man Who Invented Himself," *New York Times*, March 30, 1975, https://archive.nytimes.com/www.nytimes.com/books/99 /08/22/specials/erikson-history.html?scp=3&sq=Mayday!%20Lost%20 at%20Sea&st=Search.

2 Based on Lawrence J. Friedman, *Identity's Architect: A Biography of Erik H. Erikson* (Scribner, 1999).

3 In Deborah Solomon, *American Mirror: The Life and Art of Norman Rockwell* (Farrar, Straus and Giroux, 2013), 19, 272–73.

4 Solomon, *American Mirror*, 313–14, italics in original.

5 Solomon, *American Mirror*, 315.

6 Solomon, *American Mirror*, 20.

7 Quoted in Solomon, *American Mirror*, 339.

8 Clifford Geertz, "Deep Play: Notes on the Balinese Cockfight," in *The Interpretation of Cultures* (Basic Books, 1973), 448.

9 Andrew Kahn and Rebecca Onion, "Is History Written about Men, by Men?," *Slate*, January 6, 2016 (www.slate.com/articles/news_and_politics

/history/2016/01/popular_history_why_are_so_many_history_books_about
_men_by_men.html).

10 See John Demos, "The Changing Faces of Fatherhood," collected in
    Stanley H. Cath, Alan R. Gurwitt, and John Munder Ross, eds., *Father and
    Child: Developmental and Clinical Perspectives* (Routledge, 1994); and Anna
    Machin, "The Marvel of the Human Dad," *Aeon*, January 17, 2019, www.aeon
    .co/essays/the-devotion-of-the-human-dad-separates-us-from-other-apes/.

11 Ingela Alger et al., "Paternal Provisioning Resulting from Ecological
    Change," *Proceedings of the National Academy of Sciences* 117:20 (May 19,
    2020): 10746–54.

12 Sarah Baffler Hrdy, *Father Time: A Natural History of Men and Babies* (Prince-
    ton University Press, 2024), 311–319.

13 Adrienne Rich, *Of Woman Born: Motherhood as Experience and Institution*
    (W. W. Norton, 1976), 112.

14 Rich, *Of Woman Born*, 121.

15 Hrdy, *Father Time*, 232.

16 Leonard Shlain, *Sex, Time, and Power: How Women's Sexuality Shaped
    Human Evolution* (Viking, 2003).

17 Shlain, *Sex, Time, and Power*, 5.

18 Hrdy, *Father Time*, 175–205.

19 For example, Kristen Hawkes, "The Centrality of Ancestral Grandmothering
    in Human Evolution," *Integrative and Comparative Biology* 60:3 (September
    2020): 765–81.

20 Karen R. Rosenberg, "The Evolution of Human Infancy: Why It Helps to
    Be Helpless," *Annual Review of Anthropology* 50 (2021): 423–40.

21 Alain Dainelou, *The Phallus: Sacred Symbol of Male Creative Power* (Inner
    Traditions, 1995).

22 Discussed in Rich, *Of Woman Born*, 161–62.

23 Quotations from *The Instructions of Shuruppag*, The Electronic Text Corpus
    of Sumerian Literature, Faculty of Oriental Studies, Oxford University,
    https://etcsl.orinst.ox.ac.uk/section5/tr561.htm.

24 See Pamela Barmash, *The Laws of Hammurabi: At the Confluence of Royal
    and Scribal Traditions* (Oxford University Press, 2020).

25 Quotations from "The Code of Hammurabi," translated by L. W. King, Avalon
    Project, Yale Law School, https://avalon.law.yale.edu/ancient/hamframe.asp/.

26 Rich, *Of Woman Born*, 55.

27 Gerda Lerner, *The Creation of Patriarchy* (Oxford University Press, 1986), 76.

28 See Stephanie Lynn Budin, "Phallic Fertility in the Ancient Near East and
    Egypt," in Nick Hopwood, Rebecca Flemming, and Lauren Kassell, eds.,

Reproduction: Antiquity to the Present Day (Cambridge University Press, 2020), 25–38.

29 Elizabeth Fisher, *Woman's Creation* (McGraw-Hill, 1975).

30 Ian Hodder, "Çatalhöyük: The Leopard Changes Its Spots," *Anatolian Studies* 64 (2014): 1–22.

31 Quoted in Angela Saini, *The Patriarchs: The Origins of Inequality* (Beacon, 2023), 92.

32 Fisher, *Woman's Creation*, 192–93.

CHAPTER ONE NATURE: Plato and Aristotle

1 Sarah Pomeroy, *Goddesses, Whores, Wives, and Slaves: Women in Classical Antiquity* (1975; Schocken, 2011), 5.

2 David D. Leitao, *The Pregnant Male as Myth and Metaphor in Classical Greek Literature* (Cambridge University Press, 2012), 227–70.

3 Paul Allen Miller and Charles Platter, *Plato's Apology of Socrates: A Commentary* (University of Oklahoma Press, 2012), 4.

4 Xenophon, *Apology of Socrates*, Perseus Digital Library, Tufts University, http://www.perseus.tufts.edu/hopper/text?doc=Perseus:text:1999.01.0212.

5 Plato, *Apology of Socrates*, trans. Benjamin Jowett, Center for Hellenistic Studies, Harvard University, www.chs.harvard.edu/primary-source/plato-the-apology-of-socrates-sb/.

6 See especially Nancy Demand, *Birth, Death, and Motherhood in Classical Greece* (Johns Hopkins University Press, 1994).

7 Robert Garland, *The Greek Way of Life: From Conception to Old Age* (Cornell University Press, 1990).

8 Demand, *Birth, Death, and Motherhood*, 128–32.

9 Quoted in Cynthia Patterson, "'Not Worth the Rearing': The Causes of Infant Exposure in Ancient Greece," *Transactions of the American Philological Association* 115 (1985): 103–123.

10 Quotations from Plato, *The Republic*, trans. Desmond Lee (1955; Penguin, 2003).

11 Werner Jaeger, *Aristotle: Fundamentals of the History of His Development* (Clarendon Press, 1948), 14.

12 Leitao, *The Pregnant Male*, 227–70.

13 Diogenes Laërtius, *Lives of Eminent Philosophers*, ed. R. D. Hicks, Perseus Digital Library, Tufts University, www.perseus.tufts.edu/hopper/text?doc=Perseus%3Atext%3A1999.01.0258%3Abook%3D5%3Achapter%3D1.

14 Jaeger, *Aristotle*, 110–111.

15 G. E. R. Lloyd, *Aristotle: The Growth and Structure of His Thought* (Cambridge University Press, 1968), 68.

16 Carlo Natali, *Aristotle: His Life and School* (Princeton University Press, 2012), 14.

17 Armand Marie Leroi, *The Lagoon: How Aristotle Invented Science* (Viking, 2014), 32.

18 Leroi, *The Lagoon*, 182.

19 Leroi, *The Lagoon*, 185.

20 Quotations from Aristotle, *Die Generatione Animalium*, trans. Arthur Platt (Clarendon Press, 1910).

21 Leroi, *The Lagoon*, 216.

22 Aristotle, *Parts of Animals*, book 1, ch. 1.

23 Bertrand Russell, *A History of Western Philosophy* (1946; Routledge, 2009), 83.

24 Adrian Goldsworthy, *Philip and Alexander: Kings and Conquerors* (Basic Books, 2020), 134.

25 Robin Lane Fox, *The Classical World: An Epic History from Homer to Hadrian* (Basic Books, 2006), 203.

26 Quotations from Aristotle, *The Nicomachean Ethics*, trans. David Ross (1980; Oxford University Press, 2009).

27 Quotations from Aristotle, *The Politics and the Constitution of Athens*, ed. Stephen Everson (Cambridge University Press, 1996).

28 Mariska Leunissen, *From Natural Character to Moral Virtue in Aristotle* (Oxford University Press, 2017), 158–59, 176.

29 David Brion Davis, *The Problem of Slavery in Western Culture* (Oxford University Press, 1966), 69.

30 Leunissen, *Natural Character to Moral Virtue*, 84–90.

31 Peter Green, *Alexander of Macedon, 356–32 B.C.: A Historical Biography* (University of California Press, 1991), 452.

CHAPTER TWO GOD: Augustine of Hippo

1 Peter Brown, *Augustine of Hippo: A Biography* (University of California Press, 1967), 130.

2 Brown, *Augustine of Hippo*, 131.

3 Robin Lane Fox, *Augustine: Conversions to Confessions* (Basic Books, 2015), 419.

4 Fox, *Augustine*, 419–20.

5 Catherine Johns, *Sex or Symbol: Erotic Images of Greece and Rome* (University of Texas Press, 1982).

NOTES

6 Brown, *Augustine of Hippo*, 192.

7 Brown, *Augustine of Hippo*, 188–92.

8 Michael Peppard, *The Son of God in the Roman World: Divine Sonship in Its Social and Political Context* (Oxford University Press, 2011), ix.

9 Richard P. Saller, *Patriarchy, Property and Death in the Roman Family* (Cambridge University Press, 1994), 43.

10 Richard I. Frank, "Augustus's Legislation on Marriage and Children," *California Studies in Classical Antiquity* 8 (1975): 41–52.

11 Peppard, *Son of God*, 36.

12 Beth Severy, *Augustus and the Family at the Birth of the Roman Emperor* (Routledge, 2004).

13 Tim Parkin, "The Ancient Family and the Law," in Nick Hopwood, Rebecca Flemming, and Lauren Kassell, eds., *Reproduction: Antiquity to the Present Day* (Cambridge University Press, 2020), 83–84.

14 Saller, *Patriarchy*, 93.

15 Saller, *Patriarchy*, 143–44.

16 Severy, *Augustus and the Family*, 13.

17 Severy, *Augustus and the Family*, 34.

18 Quoted in Frank, "Augustus's Legislation on Marriage and Children," 43.

19 Frank, "Augustus's Legislation on Marriage and Children," 47.

20 Saller, *Patriarchy*, 120.

21 Robin Lane Fox, *The Classical World: An Epic History from Homer to Hadrian* (Basic Books, 2006), 430.

22 Severy, *Augustus and the Family*.

23 Fox, *The Classical World*, 433.

24 Quoted in Fox, *The Classical World*, 435.

25 Severy, *Augustus and the Family*.

26 Sarah T. Cohen, "Augustus, Julia, and the Development of Exile Ad Insulam," *Classical Quarterly* 58:1 (May 2008): 209.

27 Nara Milanich, *Paternity: The Elusive Quest for the Father* (Harvard University Press, 2019), 12.

28 See Parkin, "The Ancient Family and the Law," 86–87.

29 Adela Yarbro Collins, "The Origin of the Designation of Jesus as 'Son of Man,'" *Harvard Theological Review* 80:4 (October 1987): 391–407.

30 John Behr, "Calling upon God as Father: Augustine and the Legacy of Nicaea," in *Orthodox Readings of Augustine*, George E. Demacopoulos and Aristotle Papanikolaou, eds. (St. Vladimir's Seminary Press, 2008), 162.

31 Bart Ehrman, *How Jesus Became God: The Exaltation of a Jewish Preacher from Galilee* (Harper, 2014), 211–246.

32 Elaine Pagels, *The Gnostic Gospels* (Random House, 1979), 28.

33 Ehrman, *Jesus*, 289.

34 Pagels, *Gospels*, xxxvv, 48–69.

35 Ehrman, *Jesus*, 339–340.

36 Karen Armstrong, *A History of God* (Gramercy, 2004), 117.

37 Armstrong, *God*, 117.

38 Pagels, *Gospels*, 60–61.

39 Quotations from Vergil, *The Aeneid*, trans. Shardi Bartsch (Modern Library, 2021).

40 Quotations from Augustine, *Against the Academicians and The Teacher*, trans. Peter King (Hackett, 1995).

41 Saller, *Patriarchy*, 105.

42 Quotations from Augustine, *Confessions*, trans. Sarah Ruden (Modern Library, 2017).

43 Quotations from Saint Augustine, *The City of God*, trans. Marcus Dods (Modern Library, 1993).

44 Paul D. Miller, *Just War and Ordered Liberty* (Cambridge University Press, 2021), 27.

45 Saint Augustine, *On the Baptism of Infants*, trans. Peter Holmes, http://www.logoslibrary.org/augustine/merits/index.html, book 3, ch. 22.

46 Brown, *Augustine of Hippo*, 219.

CHAPTER THREE KING: Henry VIII

1 Steven Ozment, *When Fathers Ruled: Family Life in Reformation Europe* (Harvard University Press, 1985), 9–10; Beverley A. Murphy, *Bastard Prince: Henry VIII's Lost Son* (Sutton, 2001), 49.

2 Ozment, *When Fathers Ruled*, 144.

3 Based on Murphy, *Bastard Prince*, 36–39.

4 Allison Weir, *Henry VIII: The King and His Court* (Ballantine, 2001), 250.

5 Robert Bartlett, *Blood Royal: Dynastic Politics in Medieval Europe* (Cambridge University Press, 2020), 162–163; Murphy, *Bastard Prince*, 12–13.

6 Quoted in Weir, *Henry VIII*, 172.

7 G. R. Elton, *Reform and Reformation: England, 1509–1588* (Harvard University Press, 1977), 103.

8 Peter Hunter Blair, *An Introduction to Anglo-Saxon England*, 2nd ed. (1956; New York: Cambridge University Press, 1977), 195–196.

9 *Oxford English Dictionary*, www.oed.com/dictionary/sire_v?tab=meaning _and_use, s.v. "sire."

10 Murphy, *Bastard Prince*, 40–41.

11 J. Duncan and M. Derrett, "Henry FitzRoy and Henry VIII's 'Scruple of Conscience,'" *Renaissance News* 16:1 (Spring 1963), 2.

12 Valerie Shrimplin and Channa N. Jayasena, "Was Henry VIII Infertile? Miscarriages and Male Infertility in Tudor England," *Journal of Interdisciplinary History* 52:2 (2021): 155–76.

13 Lauren Kassell, "Fruitful Bodies and Astrological Medicine," in Nick Hopwood, Rebecca Flemming, and Lauren Kassell, eds., *Reproduction: Antiquity to the Present Day* (Cambridge University Press, 2020), 237.

14 Murphy, *Bastard Prince*, 26–27.

15 Blair, *Anglo-Saxon England*, 198.

16 Tim McInerney, "The Better Sort: Ideas of Race and Nobility in Eighteenth-Century Great Britain and Ireland" (Ph.D. thesis, Université Sorbonne, 2014), 34.

17 Beatrice Gottlieb, *The Family in the Western World: From the Black Death to the Industrial Age* (Oxford University Press, 1993), 221.

18 Chris Given-Wilson and Alice Curteis, *The Royal Bastards of Medieval England* (Routledge, 1984), 4.

19 "1431 Henry Fitzroy," in *Letters and Papers, Foreign and Domestic, of the Reign of Henry VIII: Preserved in the Public Record Office, the British Museum, and Elsewhere in England*, vol. 6 (Longman, Green, Longman, & Roberts, 1870), 638.

20 Peter Ackroyd, *The Life of Thomas More* (Nan A. Talese/Doubleday, 1998).

21 Quotations from Thomas More, *Utopia: A Norton Critical Edition*, trans. Robert M. Adams (W. W. Norton, 2010).

22 Quoted in Ackroyd, *The Life of Thomas More*.

23 Michelle DeRusha, *Katharina and Martin Luther: The Radical Marriage of a Runaway Nun and a Renegade Monk* (Baker, 2017), 35.

24 Quoted in Ozment, *When Fathers Ruled*, 119; DeRusha, *Katharina and Martin Luther*, 65–66.

25 DeRusha, *Katharina and Martin Luther*, 137–38.

26 Ozment, *When Fathers Ruled*, 8.

27 Hans H. Hillerbrand, ed., *The Annotated Luther*, vol. 5: *Christian Life in the World* (Fortress, 2017), 75.

28 Lawrence Stone, *Family, Sex and Marriage in England, 1500–1800* (Harper, 1979), 111.

29 Stone, *Family, Sex and Marriage*, 111.

30 DeRusha, *Katharina and Martin Luther*, 151.

31 Martin J. Lohrmann, "A Table Talk of Terror," *Currents in Theology and Mission* 50:2 (April 2023): 26–30.

32 Murphy, *Bastard Prince*, 64.

33   John Guy, *A Daughter's Love: Thomas More and His Dearest Meg* (Houghton Mifflin Harcourt, 2009), 155–56.

34   Quoted in Murphy, *Bastard Prince*, 66.

35   Murphy, *Bastard Prince*, 83.

36   Murphy, *Bastard Prince*, 85.

37   Murphy, *Bastard Prince*, 106; Peter Gardella, *Innocent Ecstasy: How Christianity Gave America an Ethic of Sexual Pleasure* (New York: Oxford University Press, 1985), 13.

38   Guy, *A Daughter's Love*, 227–28.

39   Murphy, *Bastard Prince*, 153.

40   Murphy, *Bastard Prince*, 163–164.

41   Quoted in Murphy, *Bastard Prince*, 163.

42   Murphy, *Bastard Prince*, 173.

43   Weir, *Henry VIII*, 386–87.

44   Stone, *Family, Sex and Marriage*, 109–10.

CHAPTER FOUR   NATION: Thomas Jefferson

1   Fawn Brodie, *Thomas Jefferson: An Intimate History* (1974; W. W. Norton, 1998), 3–14.

2   To Thomas Adams, February 20, 1771, Founders Online, https://founders.archives.gov/documents/Jefferson/01-01-02-0040/.

3   Russell Martin, "Welsh Ancestry," *Thomas Jefferson Encyclopedia*, www.monticello.org/research-education/thomas-jefferson-encyclopedia/welsh-ancestry/.

4   Lucia C. Stanton, "Coat of Arms," *Thomas Jefferson Encyclopedia*, www.monticello.org/research-education/thomas-jefferson-encyclopedia/coat-arms/.

5   Jay Fliegelman, *Prodigals and Pilgrims: The American Revolution against Patriarchy* (Cambridge University Press, 1982), 197.

6   Steven Mintz, *Huck's Raft: A History of American Childhood* (Belknap Press, 2004), 10.

7   Mintz, *Huck's Raft*, 9, 17.

8   Annette Gordon-Reed, *The Hemingses of Monticello: An American Family* (W. W. Norton, 2009), 40.

9   "Women in Colonial Virginia," *Encyclopedia of Virginia*, https://encyclopediavirginia.org/entries/women-in-colonial-virginia/.

10   Mary Ann Mason, *From Father's Property to Children's Rights: The History of Child Custody in the United States* (Columbia University Press, 2014), 5.

11   Mintz, *Huck's Raft*, 37.

12 Mason, *Father's Property*, 7.

13 Edmund Morgan, *American Slavery, American Freedom: The Ordeal of Colonial Virginia* (Alfred A. Knopf, 1975), 168.

14 *Oxford English Dictionary*, www.oed.com/dictionary/father_n?tab=meaning_and_use#4492009, s.v. "father," n. 10.

15 Hugh Cunningham, *Children and Childhood in Western Society since 1500*, 3rd ed. (Routledge, 2020), 60.

16 Patrick Romanell, "Locke's Aphorisms on Education and Health," *Journal of the History of Ideas* 22:4 (1961): 549–54.

17 Michael P. Rogin, *Fathers and Children: Andrew Jackson and the Subjugation of the American Indian* (Alfred A. Knopf, 1975), 21.

18 To Thomas Jefferson Randolph Washington, November 24, 1808, Gilder-Lehrman Institute of American History, www.gilderlehrman.org/collection/glc00496178/.

19 To James Maury, June 16, 1815, Founders Online, https://founders.archives.gov/documents/Jefferson/03-08-02-0439/.

20 Quoted in Gordon Wood, *The Radicalism of the American Revolution* (Alfred A. Knopf, 1992), 27, 65.

21 Wood, *Radicalism*, 181.

22 Joseph J. Ellis, *American Sphinx: the Character of Thomas Jefferson* (Alfred A. Knopf, 1997), 257.

23 Quoted in Wood, *Radicalism*, 184–85.

24 Winthrop D. Jordan, "Familial Politics: Thomas Paine and the Killing of the King, 1776," *Journal of American History* 60:2 (September 1973): 294–308.

25 Lee Alan Dugatkin, *Mr. Jefferson and the Giant Moose: Natural History in Early America* (University of Chicago Press, 2009), 15–16.

26 Count de Buffon, *Natural History of Quadrupeds*, vol. 2 (Thomas Nelson and Peter Brown, 1830), 39.

27 Gordon-Reed, *Hemingses*, 138–46.

28 Dugatkin, *Mr. Jefferson*, 69–74.

29 Mason, *Father's Property*, 69.

30 Quotations from *Notes on the State of Virginia* in Thomas Jefferson, *Writings* (Library of America, 1984).

31 Elspeth Martini, "'Visiting Indians,' Nursing Fathers, and Anglo-American Empires in the Post–War of 1812 Western Great Lakes," *William and Mary Quarterly* 78:3 (July 2021): 459.

32 Richard White, "The Fictions of Patriarchy," in Frederick S. Hoxie, Ronald Hoffman, and Peter J. Albert, eds., *Native Americans and the Early Republic* (Charlottesville: University Press of Virginia, 1999), 81–83.

33 White, "Fictions," 75.

34 Jefferson to a Delegation of Indian Chiefs, January 4, 1806, Library of Congress Online, https://loc.gov/exhibits/lewisandclark/transcript45.html/.

35 Reginald Horsman, "The Indian Policy of an 'Empire for Liberty,'" in Hoxie, Hoffman, and Albert, eds., *Native Americans*, 48–52.

36 Alan Taylor, *American Republics: A Continental History of the United States* (W. W. Norton, 2021), 4.

37 Gordon-Reed, *Hemingses*, 632.

38 Quoted in Gordon-Reed, *Hemingses*, 585.

39 Gordon-Reed, *Hemingses*, 326–52.

40 Gordon-Reed, *Hemingses*, 45.

41 Jennifer Morgan, "Partus Sequitur Ventrum: Law, Race, and Reproduction in Colonial Slavery," *Small Axe* 22:1 (March 2018): 4.

42 Kathleen M. Brown, *Good Wives, Nasty Wenches, and Anxious Patriarchs: Gender, Race, and Power in Colonial Virginia* (University of North Carolina Press, 1996), 135.

43 Quoted in Thomas D. Morris, *Southern Slavery and the Law* (University of North Carolina Press, 1996), 17.

44 Morris, *Southern Slavery*, 44.

45 Figures from Michael E. Rouane, "Virginia Is the Birthplace of American Slavery and Segregation—and It Still Can't Escape That Legacy," *Washington Post*, February 6, 2019, https://www.washingtonpost.com/history/2019/02/06/virginia-is-birthplace-american-slavery-segregation-it-still-cant-escape-that-legacy/#.

46 *Online Etymological Dictionary*, https://www.etymonline.com/word/raise, s.v. "raise, v."

47 Peter S. Onuf and Annette Gordon-Reed, *"Most Blessed of the Patriarchs": Thomas Jefferson and the Empire of the Imagination* (W. W. Norton, 2016).

48 Quoted in Gordon-Reed, *Hemingses*, 550.

49 Gordon-Reed, *Hemingses*, 542–43.

50 Gordon-Reed, *Hemingses*, 594.

51 Gordon-Reed, *Hemingses*, 530.

52 Alan Pell Crawford, *Twilight at Monticello: The Final Years of Thomas Jefferson* (Random House, 2008), 60.

53 Gordon-Reed, *Hemingses*, 614.

54 Quotations from Jefferson to Francis C. Gray, March 4, 1815, Founders Online, https://founders.archives.gov/documents/Jefferson/03-08-02-0245/.

55 Gordon-Reed, *Hemingses*, 603.

56 Gordon-Reed, *Hemingses*, 595–96.

57 Jefferson, *Notes on the State of Virginia*, ch. 15.

58 Gordon-Reed, *Hemingses*, 598–600.

59 Brown, *Good Wives*, 183.

60 Edward Baptist quoted in Libra R. Hilde, *Slavery, Fatherhood, and Paternal Duty in African American Communities over the Long Nineteenth Century* (University of North Carolina Press, 2020), 1.

61 Hilde, *Slavery, Fatherhood, and Paternal Duty*, 92–148.

62 Gordon-Reed, *Hemingses*, 341.

63 Annette Gordon-Reed, *Thomas Jefferson and Sally Hemings: An American Controversy* (University of Virginia Press, 1997), 150; Gordon-Reed, *Hemingses*, 598.

64 Gordon-Reed, *Hemingses*, 611.

65 Gordon-Reed, *Hemingses*, 618.

66 Gordon-Reed, *Hemingses*, 637.

67 Gordon-Reed, *Thomas Jefferson and Sally Hemings*, 189.

68 Quoted in Gordon-Reed, *Thomas Jefferson and Sally Hemings*, 27–28; Gordon-Reed, *Hemingses*, 599.

69 Gordon-Reed, *Hemingses*, 595–96.

70 Gordon-Reed, *Hemingses*, 597.

CHAPTER FIVE MONEY: Emerson and Thoreau

1 Gay Wilson Allen, *Waldo Emerson: A Biography* (Viking, 1981), 285.

2 Allen, *Waldo Emerson*, 336.

3 Robert D. Richardson Jr., *Emerson: The Mind on Fire* (University of California Press, 1995), 194.

4 Richardson, *Emerson*, 254.

5 Quotations from Ralph Waldo Emerson, "Self-Reliance," in *Essays: First and Second Series* (Library of America, 1983).

6 Thomas L. Dublin, *Women at Work: The Transformation of Work and Community in Lowell, Massachusetts, 1826–1860* (Columbia University Press, 1981), 3.

7 Steven Mintz and Susan Kellogg, *Domestic Revolutions: A Social History of American Family Life* (Free Press, 1989) , 49.

8 Robert L. Griswold, *Fatherhood in America: A History* (Basic Books, 1993), 15.

9 Quotations from *Nature*, in *Emerson: Essays & Lectures* (Library of America, 1983), 5–49.

10　Robert A. Gross, *The Transcendentalist and Their World* (Farrar, Straus and Giroux, 2021), xv.

11　Phyllis Cole, "A Legacy of Revolt, 1803–1821," in Jean McClure Mudge, *Mr. Emerson's Revolution* (Open Book, 2015), 3–9.

12　Peter S. Field, *Ralph Waldo Emerson: The Making of a Democratic Intellectual* (Rowman & Littlefield, 2003), 38–40.

13　Allen, *Waldo Emerson*, 10.

14　To William Emerson, December 24, 1828, *Letters of Ralph W. Emerson*, Vol. 1, ed. Ralph L. Rusk (Columbia University Press, 1941), 256.

15　Allen, *Waldo Emerson*, 165–66.

16　Richardson, *Emerson*, 1.

17　Caleb Crain, "Did Emerson Believe in Vampires?" *Steamboats are Ruining Everything*, https://steamthing.com/2005/08/did_emerson_bel.html.

18　Robert D. Richardson, *Three Roads Back: How Emerson, Thoreau and William James Responded to the Greatest Losses of Their Lives* (Princeton University Press, 2023), 12.

19　Richardson, *Three Roads*, 14.

20　Quoted in Gross, *Transcendentalists*, 306.

21　George E. Horr, "How Emerson Gained an Income," *Watchman*, May 14, 1903, 10–11.

22　Richardson, *Emerson*, 84.

23　Richardson, *Emerson*, 167.

24　Quoted in Paula S. Fass, *The End of American Childhood: A History of Parenting from Life on the Frontier to the Managed Child* (Princeton University Press, 2016), 14.

25　Richardson, *Emerson*, 260.

26　For the advent of "dead broke," see Scott A. Sandage, *Born Losers: A History of Failure in America* (Harvard University Press, 2005), 25.

27　Quoted in Andrew Kopec, "Emerson's Market Forces," in Christopher Hanlon, ed., *The Oxford Handbook of Ralph Waldo Emerson* (Oxford University Press, 2024), 279–95.

28　James Marcus, *Glad to the Brink of Fear: A Portrait of Ralph Waldo Emerson* (Princeton University Press, 2024), 179.

29　*Oxford English Dictionary*, www.oed.com/dictionary/breadwinner_n?tab=meaning_and_use#14519962, s.v. "breadwinner," n. 2; Sandage, *Born Losers*.

30　Mintz and Kellogg, *Domestic Revolutions*, 62.

31　Mintz and Kellogg, *Domestic Revolutions*, 54.

32　Dublin, *Women at Work*, 179.

33 Quoted in Dublin, *Women at Work*, 55.

34 Jean-Jacques Rousseau, *Confessions* (Reeves and Turner, 1861), 343.

35 Leo Damrosch, *Jean-Jacques Rousseau: Restless Genius* (Houghton Mifflin, 2007), 189–90.

36 Damrosch, *Rousseau*, 191.

37 Damrosch, *Rousseau*, 333.

38 Damrosch, *Rousseau*, 338.

39 Jean-Jacques Rousseau, *Émile, or, On Education*, trans. and ed. Christopher Kelly and Allan Bloom (Dartmouth College Press, 2010), 175.

40 Quotations from "Self-Reliance," in *Emerson: Essays and Lectures* (Library of America, 1983), 259–82.

41 Richardson, *Emerson*, 256.

42 Richardson, *Emerson*, 356.

43 Richardson, *Emerson*, 358–59.

44 Richardson, *Three Roads Back*, 33.

45 Laura Dassow Walls, *Henry David Thoreau: A Life* (University of Chicago Press, 2017), 190.

46 Henry David Thoreau, *Walden; or Life in the Woods*, ed. Stephen Fender (Oxford University Press, 1997), 83.

47 Quoted in Morton Berkowitz, "Thoreau, Rice, and Vose on the Commercial Spirit," *Thoreau Society Bulletin* (Fall 1977): 1–5.

48 Transcript of the unpublished autobiography of William Munroe, primarily 1837, Concord Museum, Concord, MA.

49 Gross, *Transcendentalists*, 522.

50 Walls, *Thoreau*, 253.

51 Gross, *Transcendentalists*, 532.

52 Walls, *Thoreau*, 319.

53 Robert A. Gross, "Quiet War with the State: Henry David Thoreau and Civil Disobedience," *Yale Review*, July 2005, 1–17.

54 Quoted in Gross, *Transcendentalists*, xv.

55 See Robert A. Gross's comments in Lawrence A. Rosenwald, "The Theory, Practice, and Influence of Thoreau's Civil Disobedience," in William E. Cain, ed., *A Historical Guide to Henry David Thoreau* (New York: Oxford University Press, 2000), 153–79, n. 4.

56 Quotations from "Civil Disobedience," in Henry D. Thoreau, *The Essays of Henry D. Thoreau*, ed. Lewis Hyde (North Point Press, 2002).

57 Walls, *Thoreau*, 348–49.

58 "A Plea for Captain John Brown," in Henry David Thoreau, *Collected Writings of Henry David Thoreau*, vol. 4 (Houghton Mifflin, 1906), 409–40.

59 "Experience," in Ralph Waldo Emerson, *Emerson: Essays and Lectures* (Library of America, 1983), 469–92.

CHAPTER SIX FAMILY: Charles Darwin

* 1 Quotations from Charles Darwin, *Autobiographies* (Penguin, 2002).
 2 Adrian Desmond and James Moore, *Darwin* (W. W. Norton, 1991), 27.
 3 From Gavin de Beer, ed., "Darwin's Notebooks on Transmutation of Species, Part IV," in *Bulletin of the British Museum* 2:5 (1960): 151–83.
 4 Desmond and Moore, *Darwin*, 240–41.
 5 Janet Browne, *Charles Darwin: The Power of Place* (Princeton University Press, 2003), 7.
 6 To J. D. Hooker, January 11, 1844, Darwin Correspondence Project, University of Cambridge, https://www.darwinproject.ac.uk/letter/?docId=letters /DCP-LETT-729.xml/.
 7 Quoted in Desmond and Moore, *Darwin*, 245.
 8 Quoted in Desmond and Moore, *Darwin*, 246.
 9 For a discussion of the ambiguities of the document, see Peter W. Graham, *Jane Austen & Charles Darwin: Naturalists and Novelists* (Routledge, 2016), 91–98.
 10 See Graham, *Jane Austen & Charles Darwin*, for a consideration of Darwin's tone; for a transcription of the document itself, see Janet Browne, ed., *The Quotable Darwin* (Princeton University Press, 2018), 60–61.
 11 From Emma Wedgwood, January 23, 1839, Darwin Correspondence Project, University of Cambridge, https://www.darwinproject.ac.uk/letter /?docId=letters/DCP-LETT-492.xml/.
 12 See especially Adrian Desmond and James Moore, *Darwin's Sacred Cause: How a Hatred of Slavery Shaped Darwin's Views on Human Evolution* (Houghton Mifflin Harcourt, 2009).
 13 Quoted in Desmond and Moore, *Darwin*, 287.
 14 Marjorie Lorch and Paula Hellal, "Darwin's 'Natural Science of Babies,'" *Journal of the History of the Neurosciences* 19 (2010): 144.
 15 James T. Costa, "On the Face of It: Darwin and the Expression of Emotion," Undark (November 3, 2017), https://undark.org/2017/11/03/wilo-darwin -evolution/.
 16 Quoted in Browne, *Charles Darwin*, 234.
 17 Randal Keynes, *Darwin, His Daughters, and Human Evolution* (Riverhead, 2002), 196.

18 "Darwin Notes for His Physician, 1865," Darwin Correspondence Project, University of Cambridge, https://www.darwinproject.ac.uk/tags/darwin /darwin-on-his-health/.

19 Quoted in Keynes, *Darwin*, 13.

20 Keynes, *Darwin*, 102.

21 Keynes, *Darwin*, 103.

22 Steven Mintz and Susan Kellogg, *Domestic Revolutions: A Social History of American Family Life*, 44–45.

23 Vivianna Zelizer, *Pricing the Priceless Child* (Basic Books, 1985).

24 To Emma Darwin, [July 1, 1841], Darwin Correspondence Project, University of Cambridge, https://www.darwinproject.ac.uk/letter/?docId=letters /DCP-LETT-600.xml&query=Darwin%2C%20W.%20E.

25 Tim Berra, *Darwin and His Children: His Other Legacy* (Oxford University Press, 2013), 38.

26 Quoted in Keynes, *Darwin* , 181.

27 Quoted in Browne, *Charles Darwin*, 280.

28 Quoted in Keynes, *Darwin*, 180.

29 Quoted in Keynes, *Darwin*, 197.

30 Quoted in Keynes, *Darwin*, 215.

31 "Charles Darwin's Memorial of Anne Elizabeth Darwin," Darwin Correspondence Project, University of Cambridge, https://www.darwinproject .ac.uk/people/about-darwin/family-life/death-anne-elizabeth-darwin/.

32 Browne, *Charles Darwin*, 277.

33 To W. D. Fox, October 24, 1852, Darwin Correspondence Project, University of Cambridge, https://www.darwinproject.ac.uk/letter/?docId=letters /DCP-LETT-1489.xml&query=Darwin%2C%20Emma%20Darwin%2C%20 Emma/.

34 Quoted in Browne, *Charles Darwin*, 235.

35 Desmond and Moore, *Darwin*, 399–400.

36 Browne, *Charles Darwin*, 235.

37 Quoted in Keynes, *Darwin*, 257.

38 To W. D. Fox, October 24, 1852, Darwin Correspondence Project.

39 Keynes, *Darwin*, 272.

40 For instance, Graham, *Jane Austen & Charles Darwin*, 130, n. 13.

41 Quotations from Charles Darwin, *On the Origin of Species*, ed. Gillian Beer (1859; Oxford University Press, 1996).

42 See Jenkin's review, published anonymously in the *North British Review* 46 (June 1867):277–318, reprinted at https://darwin-online.org.uk/content

/frameset?pageseq=1&itemID=A24&viewtype=text/ and discussed in Browne, *Charles Darwin*, 283.

43 From Charles Darwin, *The Descent of Man and Selection in Relation to Sex* (1871; D. Appleton, 1896).

44 Quoted in Keynes, *Darwin*, 267.

45 Browne, *Charles Darwin*, 276.

46 To H. W. Bates, February 22, 1868, Darwin Correspondence Project, University of Cambridge, https://www.darwinproject.ac.uk/letter/?docId=letters /DCP-LETT-5914.xml&query=animals/.

47 In Browne, *Charles Darwin*, 288–90.

48 In Browne, *Charles Darwin*, 328.

49 From Francis Galton, May 12, 1870, Darwin Correspondence Project, University of Cambridge, https://www.darwinproject.ac.uk/letter /?docId=letters/DCP-LETT-7185.xml&query=%22Good%20Rabbit%20 news%21%22/.

50 Browne, *Charles Darwin*, 291–92.

51 Quotations from Darwin, *The Descent of Man*.

52 Desmond and Moore, *Darwin*, 454.

53 Browne, *Charles Darwin*, 345–46.

54 Browne, *Charles Darwin*, 435.

55 Quoted in Browne, *Charles Darwin*, 435–36.

56 Quoted in Browne, *Charles Darwin*, 349–50.

57 Keith Thomson, "Darwin's Enigmatic Health," *American Scientist* 97:3 (May–June 2009), https://www.americanscientist.org/article/darwins-enigmatic -health/.

58 Quoted in Berra, *Darwin and His Children*, 75.

CHAPTER SEVEN WAR: Sigmund Freud

1 To Wilhelm Fliess, September 29, 1896, in Jeffrey M. Masson, ed., *The Complete Letters of Sigmund Freud to Wilhelm Fliess, 1887–1904* (Harvard University Press, 1985), 200.

2 Quoted in Peter Gay, *Freud: A Life for Our Time* (W. W. Norton, 1988), 24.

3 Gay, *Freud*, 449.

4 Marianne Krull, *Freud and His Father* (W. W. Norton, 1986), 140–47.

5 Quoted in Gay, *Freud*, 11–12.

6 Élisabeth Roudinesco, *Freud: In His Time and Ours*, trans. Catherine Porter (Harvard University Press, 2016), 26–27; Gay, *Freud*, 26.

7 To Wilhelm Fliess, February 8, 1893, in Masson, ed., *Letters*, 40.

8   See especially Carol Smith-Rosenberg, "The Hysterical Woman: Sex Roles and Role Conflict in Nineteenth-Century America," in *Disorderly Conduct: Visions of Gender in Victorian America* (Alfred A. Knopf, 1985).

9   To Wilhelm Fliess, February 8, 1893, in Masson, ed., *Letters*, 42.

10 Gay, *Freud*, 91.

11 Gay, *Freud*, 93–94.

12 Quoted in Gay, *Freud*, 88.

13 Quoted in Gay, *Freud*, 88.

14 Quoted in Gay, *Freud*, 97.

15 Gay, *Freud*, 94.

16 Quoted in Gay, *Freud*, 95.

17 Quoted in Gay, *Freud*, 104.

18 Quoted in Roudinesco, *Freud*, 79.

19 Quotations from Sigmund Freud, *The Interpretation of Dreams*, trans. and ed. James Strachey (1955; Basic Books, 2010).

20 Sigmund Freud, *Dora: An Analysis of a Case of Hysteria*, intro. Philip Rieff (Simon & Schuster, 1997), 49.

21 Sigmund Freud, *Three Case Histories*, ed. Philip Rieff (1963; Simon & Schuster, 1996), 13, italics in original.

22 Gay, *Freud*, 264–65.

23 Quoted and discussed in Peter L. Rudnytsky, *Freud and Oedipus* (Columbia University Press, 1987), 18.

24 Quoted in Gay, *Freud*, 332.

25 Damon Freeman, "Reconsidering Kenneth B. Clark and the Idea of Black Psychological Damage, 1931–1945," *Du Bois Review* 8:1 (Spring 2011): 271–83.

26 Frank McLynn, *Carl Gustav Jung* (Thomas Dunne, 1996), 210–11.

27 Quoted in Gay, *Freud*, 324.

28 Quotations from Sigmund Freud, *Totem and Taboo*, trans A. A. Brill (1913; Alfred A. Knopf, 1960).

29 Gay, *Freud*, 331.

30 Quoted in Gay, *Freud*, 327.

31 Martin Freud Letters, trans. Laura Langeder in "Sigmund Freud's War," based on MF1-MF65, Freud Museum London, www.freud.org.uk/2019/07/15/sigmund-freuds-war/.

32 Quoted in Roudinesco, *Freud*, 174.

33 Elisabeth Young-Bruehl, *Anna Freud: A Biography* (Yale University Press, 2008), 70.

34 Roudinesco, *Freud*, 175.

35 Roudinesco, *Freud*, 243.

36 Patrizia Cupelloni, "Anna and Her Father," *European Journal of Psychoanalysis* (Winter-Fall 2000), https://www.journal-psychoanalysis.eu/articles/anna-and-her-father/.

37 Quoted in Gay, *Freud*, 438–39.

38 Young-Bruehl, *Anna Freud*, 104.

39 Quoted in Young-Bruehl, *Anna Freud*, 109.

40 Quoted in Gay, *Freud*, 429.

41 Lucy Freeman and Herbert S. Strean, *Freud and Women* (Ungar, 1981), 7.

42 Young-Bruehl, *Anna Freud*, 176.

43 Young-Bruehl, *Anna Freud*, 186.

44 Young-Bruehl, *Anna Freud*, 189–90.

45 Quoted in Young-Bruehl, *Anna Freud*, 178–79.

46 Mark Edmundson, *The Death of Sigmund Freud: The Legacy of His Last Days* (Bloomsbury, 2007).

47 Nara Milanich, *Paternity: The Elusive Quest for the Father* (Harvard University Press, 2019), 162–63.

48 Milanich, *Paternity*, 164–66.

49 Quoted in Young-Bruehl, *Anna Freud*, 227.

50 Young-Bruehl, *Anna Freud*, 234.

51 Gay, *Freud*, 443.

52 Young-Bruehl, *Anna Freud*, 15.

53 Young-Bruehl, *Anna Freud*, 237.

54 Young-Bruehl, *Anna Freud*, 249.

55 Young-Bruehl, *Anna Freud*, 252.

CHAPTER EIGHT HOME: Bob Dylan

1 David Hadju, *Positively 4th Street* (Picador, 2001), 67.

2 Robert M. Linder, *Rebel without a Cause: The Story of a Criminal Psychopath* (1971; Other Press, 2003), 25, 7.

3 Robert Shelton, *No Direction Home: The Life and Music of Bob Dylan* (1986; Backbeat, 2011), 28.

4 Ira Katznelson, *When Affirmative Action Was White: An Untold History of Racial Inequality in America* (W. W. Norton, 2005), 140.

5 Kathleen J. Frydl, *The GI Bill* (Cambridge University Press, 2009), 274.

6 Quoted in Elaine Tyler May, *Homeward Bound: American Families in the Cold War Era* (1988; Basic Books, 2008), 152.

7 May, *Homeward Bound*, 25.

NOTES

8 John Broadus Watson, *Psychological Care of Infant and Child* (W. W. Norton, 1928).

9 Quotations from Steven Mintz, *Huck's Raft: A History of American Childhood* (Harvard University Press/Belknap Press, 2004), 291–94.

10 May, *Homeward Bound*, 16.

11 May, *Homeward Bound*, 74.

12 Quoted in May, *Homeward Bound*, 201.

13 Discussed in May, *Homeward Bound*, 73.

14 Robert L. Griswold, *Fatherhood in America: A History* (Basic Books, 1993), 208–209.

15 Steven Mintz and Susan Kellogg, *Domestic Revolutions: A Social History of American Family Life*, 196.

16 Quoted in Mintz and Kellogg, *Domestic Revolutions*, 185.

17 Mintz and Kellogg, *Domestic Revolutions*, 200.

18 Griswold, *Fatherhood*, 197.

19 Griswold, *Fatherhood*, 199.

20 Robert Shelton, "Interview with Abe and Beatty Zimmerman," in *Isis: A Bob Dylan Anthology*, ed. Derek Barker (Helter Skelter, 2001), 12–25.

21 Michael Gray, *The Bob Dylan Encyclopedia* (Continuum, 2006), 729.

22 Shelton, "Interview with Abe and Beatty Zimmerman."

23 Shelton, "Interview with Abe and Beatty Zimmerman."

24 Shelton, "Interview with Abe and Beatty Zimmerman."

25 Bob Spitz, *Dylan: A Biography* (W. W. Norton, 1991), 51; Howard Sounes, *Down the Highway: The Life of Bob Dylan* (Grove, 2011), 21; Mintz, *Huck's Raft*, 281.

26 *Oxford English Dictionary*, s.v. "man," n. 18.e.

27 Spitz, *Dylan*, 45.

28 Ann Powers, *Good Booty: Love and Sex, Black and White, Body and Soul in American Music* (Dey Street, 2017), 96–97.

29 Powers, *Good Booty*, 97.

30 Shelton, *No Direction Home*, 49.

31 Spitz, *Dylan*, 61–62; Shelton, *No Direction Home*, 45.

32 Shelton, *No Direction Home*, 23–24.

33 Hadju, *Positively*, 71.

34 Clinton Heylin, *Bob Dylan: A Life in Stolen Moments, Day by Day* (Schirmer, 1996), 8.

35 Anthony Scaduto, *Bob Dylan: An Intimate Biography* (Signet, 1973), 17.

36 Shelton, "Interview with Abe and Beatty Zimmerman."

37 Quoted in Hadju, *Positively*, 75.

38 In Jeff Burger, ed., *Dylan on Dylan: Interviews and Encounters* (Chicago Review, 1998), 11.

39 Quoted in Shelton, *No Direction Home*, 49.

40 Shelton, *No Direction Home*, 49.

41 Quoted in Mintz, *Huck's Raft*, 316.

42 *Oxford English Dictionary*, https://www.oed.com/dictionary/man _nl?tl=true#110484070/, s.v. "man," n. V.18.b.

43 Quoted in Burger, ed., *Dylan on Dylan*.

44 Sounes, *Down the Highway*, 167.

45 Hadju, *Positively*, 249.

46 Barney Hoskyns, *Small Town Talk* (DaCapo, 2016), 53.

47 Sounes, *Down the Highway*, 169.

48 Hadju, *Positively*, 240.

49 Quoted in Victor Maymudes and Jacob Maymudes, *Another Side of Bob Dylan: A Personal History on the Road and off the Tracks* (St. Martin's, 2014), 131.

50 Quotations from *The Negro Family: The Case for National Action*, Office of Policy Planing and Research, U.S. Department of Labor, March 1965, https:// www.dol.gov/general/aboutdol/history/webid-moynihan/.

51 Timothy Crouse, "Ruling Class Hero," *Rolling Stone*, August 12, 1976, www .rollingstone.com/politics/politics-news/daniel-patrick-moynihan-ruling -class-hero-228185./

52 Mary Ann Mason, *From Father's Property to Children's Rights: The History of Child Custody in the United States* (Columbia University Press, 1994), 95–96.

53 *London Journal*, 1950–1953, Daniel P. Moynihan Papers, 1:455:3, LOC.

54 *London Journal*, 1950–1953, Daniel P. Moynihan Papers, 1:455:3, LOC.

55 James T. Patterson, *Freedom Is Not Enough: The Moynihan Report and America's Struggle over Black Family Life* (Basic Books, 2010), 309, n. 10.

56 Patterson, *Freedom Is Not Enough*, 46.

57 Quoted in Patterson, *Freedom Is Not Enough*, 59.

58 Quoted in Daniel Geary, *Beyond Civil Rights: The Moynihan Report and Its Legacy* (University of Pennsylvania Press, 2015), 69.

59 Patterson, *Freedom Is Not Enough*, 43.

60 Angela Davis, "Reflections in Black Women's Roles in the Moynihan Report," *The Nation*, November 22, 1965, 380–84.

61 Quoted in John Herbers, "Moynihan Hopeful U.S. Will Adopt a Policy of Promoting Family Stability," *New York Times*, December 12, 1965, https://archive

.nytimes.com/www.nytimes.com/books/98/10/04/specials/moynihan
-stability.html.

62 Interview with Joseph Haas, November 27, 1965, collected in *Bob Dylan: The Essential Interviews*, ed. Jonathan Cott (Simon & Schuster, 2017), 59–64.

63 Hadju, *Positively*, 291–92.

64 Quoted in Shelton, *No Direction Home*, 259.

65 Bob Dylan, *Chronicles: Volume 1* (Simon & Schuster, 2005), 123–24.

66 Quoted in Hoskyns, *Small Town Talk*, 77.

67 Sounes, *Down the Highway*, 313.

68 Sounes, *Down the Highway*, 234.

69 Shelton, "Interview with Abe and Beatty Zimmerman."

70 Shelton, *No Direction Home*, 52.

71 Sounes, *Down the Highway*, 235.

72 Quoted in Sounes, *Down the Highway*, 252.

73 Quoted in Sounes, *Down the Highway*, 264.

74 Sounes, *Down the Highway*, 279.

75 Spitz, *Dylan*, 411.

76 Sounes, *Down the Highway*, 286.

77 Sounes, *Down the Highway*, 304.

78 Sara Dylan's divorce petition quoted and described in Sounes, *Down the Highway*, 308.

79 Sounes, Down the Highway, 308.

80 Mintz and Kellogg, *Domestic Revolutions*, 216.

81 Quoted in Sounes, *Down the Highway*, 308.

82 Sounes, *Down the Highway*, 312.

83 Quoted in Spitz, *Dylan*, 525.

84 Sounes, *Down the Highway*, 318.

85 David Yaffe, *Bob Dylan: Like a Complete Unknown* (Yale University Press, 2011), 82.

86 Sounes, *Down the Highway*, 371–72.

CONCLUSION MEN AFTER FATHERHOOD

1 Quotations from Adrienne Rich, *Of Woman Born: Motherhood as Experience and Institution* (W. W. Norton, 1976).

2 Hillary Halladay, *The Power of Adrienne Rich: A Biography* (Nan A. Talese, 2020), 4.

3 Halladay, *Power of Adrienne Rich*, 293–94.

NOTES

4 Halladay, *Power of Adrienne Rich*, 309.
5 Rich, *Of Woman Born*, 276–77.
6 Rich, *Of Woman Born*, 296.
7 Rich, *Of Woman Born*, 297.
8 Sarah Baffler Hrdy, *Father Time: A Natural History of Men and Babies* (Princeton University Press, 2024), 304–5.
9 Hrdy, *Father Time*, 31–32.

Index